MW01141383

The Hollyhock Dolls

A Memoir

Growing Up in Michigan

DIANE G. WROBLESKI

ISBN: 978-1-4834-6744-3 (sc)
ISBN: 978-1-4834-6743-6 (e)

Library of Congress Control Number: 2017904646

Lulu Publishing Services rev. date: 04/27/2017

Contents

In Memoriam

This book is dedicated to the memory of my husband Jim who swept me off my feet when we first met at Cass Tech high school in 1957. Jim had the best sense of humor. He had a real thirst for knowledge, and also a fantastic memory for facts and figures, He was my best friend. He instilled good moral values in our children, Jim was a good. decent, and honorable man, who treated everyone with respect. He placed his family above all else, I pride myself on the fact that I chose the very best to be the father of my children.

This book is also dedicated to the memory of my daughter Julie who left us way too soon. We will remember her loving nature and wonderful sense of humor. She was always willing to forgive, and forget. You couldn't ask for a more loving and fun mother, daughter, and sister. When you were around her, you were laughing. Matt loved her. Her children adored her. She will forever be in our hearts.

Acknowledgements

The inspiration for this book came from Gayle Thomasson, a retired English teacher. I joined her Creative Memoir Writing class at Tellico Village in 2011. She inspired me to write my life's journey. She also helped in the editing of this memoir.

I want to thank my nephew John Gormley whose help was integral in the technical aspects of this work. John spent many hours after work assisting me in this endeavor.

Thank you also to Gail Washo who assisted me in numerous ways with the manuscript.

I could not have completed this work without their help. Thank you all so much.

Introduction

I believe a family's most valuable inheritance is its history. If you don't know where you're from, it makes it harder to know where you're going. Genealogy forces you to realize what it took for your ancestors to survive. Think how courageous they were to come across the ocean not knowing what to expect. Hard work, and love of God and family, is seen in every generation of ours. There is good and bad in all families and many lessons to be learned from these people who made us who we are.

A psychologist at Emory University, was studying myth and ritual in American families. After asking the children in his study several questions about their families, and giving them a battery of psychological tests, he came to the conclusion that the more children knew about their families' histories, the stronger their sense of control over their lives, the higher their self-esteem, and the more successfully they believed their families functioned. These children were more resilient.

The sole purpose of this memoir is to enable my grandchildren, Seth and Nathan Petrill and Carly Wrobleski to have a better understanding of their family and the individuals therein.

1

The Dolly Girls

My sisters and I decided to take a trip into Detroit to visit the neighborhood where we grew up. We drove down Fenkell, turned onto Pinehurst, passed Keeler, and just before Midland there it was, just as my husband, Jim told me, an empty lot where our childhood home once stood.

I couldn't figure out how a two-story brick colonial could completely disappear. What happened?

I was fighting back tears when Joanie remarked from the back seat, "Look, there's a car parked in our kitchen." That got us laughing and brought me out of my melancholia. Sadly, as in most cases, when we reminisce, we find that nothing remains the same. The trees, those magnificent elm trees, were gone. The neighborhood had seen better days.

Diane, Joanie, and Marguerite

In front of our childhood home there was a beautiful, tall elm tree. The driveway leading to the backyard was lined with hostas and lily of the valley.

In May, which is the month of Mary, my sisters and I would make bouquets of lily of the valley to place before the statue of the Blessed Mother at school. I remember we would then sing songs to Mary like:

> O Mary we crown thee with blossoms today,
> Queen of the angels, queen of the May.

Towards the back of the yard, next to our one-car garage, was a large cherry tree that we loved to climb and play in. They are the best trees for climbing, because their crotch is low to the ground. We loved to hang upside down from a branch part way up the trunk that was parallel to the ground. When the cherries were ripe we'd sit on it and eat cherries until we were "blue in the face," as Mama would say.

Dad cultivated the soil under the cherry tree with scraps from our dinner table, coffee grounds, and such. It made the soil rich with nutrients and very black in color. Whenever Dad grew his delicious tomatoes, he used that wonderful rich soil. I think backyard composting was just becoming popular at that time, the 1940's. We also had a pear and a peach tree.

Mama chose the area between the cherry tree and the back fence to grow her hollyhocks. She lined them along the back fence to give the yard privacy from the alley. These beautiful flowers can get quite tall, so they were the perfect choice to grow along the back fence.

Their tall, upright stalks were covered from top to bottom with endless blossoms in stunning shades of red, yellow, peach, pink, purple, blue and white- every color in the rainbow, it seemed, and then some. In late spring we'd eagerly await the appearance of the first blossoms. Hollyhocks attract birds, butterflies and especially bumble bees. We always had to be on the look-out for them.

Making hollyhock dolls is an old fashioned craft that many children have been doing for generations. Hollyhocks grow everywhere, but are usually grown along the back fences and were nicknamed "Alley Orchids."

I have great memories of my sisters, Marguerite (who was three years older than me) and Joanie (who was one year older), and me, making wedding dolls from the hollyhocks that grew along our back fence in the late 1940's. Their beautiful blossoms were perfect for our wedding dolls, as they were large and showy. The fuller the blossoms the more beautiful the dresses. We couldn't wait to pick out our favorite colors for our bridesmaid's dresses. But what we were really on the lookout for, were those white blossoms that we needed for our brides.

Making hollyhock dolls is simple. You pluck the blossom from the hollyhock, turn the blossom upside down to make the dress, and then put the bud on top, for the head.

We never had anything with which to make the groom. But, that didn't bother us. We had a ledge on either side of the front steps where we'd line up our wedding parties. We could play with those hollyhock dolls all afternoon. If we couldn't find three white blossoms, we would just make one large wedding party.

My childhood - and in fact my whole life - has been wrapped around my sisters. They have always been at the major events in my life. We're intertwined with one another, like a braid. I can't imagine life without them. They have always been there for me.

Joanie, Diane, boy, and Marguerite

One Fourth of July, Dad bought us each an American flag. We had a large canvas awning on our front porch. It had rained the night before, so it was sagging a little in the middle from the rainwater.

I think I was four years old, so we were quite young at the time. One of us discovered that when we poked a hole in the canvas with the pointed top of the stick that held our flags, not only did some of the water leak out, but it also made the neatest sound. So we just poked away and laughed until we couldn't laugh anymore. Then Dad came home… I think the swearing went on for, oh I don't know, the rest of the day, perhaps. We must have put fifty holes in that awning. Dad was furious. Of course, all the blame fell on Marguerite's shoulders. "You're the oldest," he said. "You should have known better." I think that's when I realized that my position as the youngest in the family could really work to my advantage. Dad patched all the holes up with duct tape, and every day until the end of summer, those patches reminded us of our little Fourth of July caper. As time went by, we were all able to laugh about it, even Dad.

When Marguerite was in third grade and Joanie in first grade, they would go off to school leaving me home, waving good-bye.

Their school, St. Francis de Sales, was just down the block. I would watch out the window for them, waiting for them to come home for lunch. I remember to this day how sad I was.

Mama would have me sit on the floor between her legs, and she would brush my hair. In the background, she would have J.L. Hudson Hour or Don McNeill's Breakfast Club on the radio. It was an all music station, mostly classical music. Don McNeill played music and then he'd say, "Let's all march around the breakfast table." All the while Mama was brushing my hair. I loved the attention.

All three of us had really long hair. Mama would try different hairdos on me: braids on top of my head, or over my ears, or around the nape of my neck. My sisters had beautiful, long, naturally curly hair, but mine was straight as a ruler. I was the only one who wore braids.

The year I entered first grade, Marguerite and Joanie contracted measles a couple of weeks before school started. I waited on them hand and foot until they got better. Then when school started, I contracted measles, and my sisters were nowhere to be found. They both told me years later that they felt guilty about not paying more attention to me when I had the measles, which, by the way, I had caught from them.

Mama worked hard to get me caught up in school. She worked with me each day and taught me how to read, to add, and to subtract. I was always comfortable at school because the nuns knew me as Marguerite and Joanie's little sister. That was good for the most part, but I remember one year when I kept getting cited for talking in class, which didn't seem to surprise my family. But, the nun told me she had a hard time believing I was Joanie's sister since she was so quiet in school.

One of the things we girls loved to do was skip rope. Everyone took turns twirling the ends of the rope. When we'd jump in, we'd all sing songs like:

> Five little monkeys jumping on a bed,
> One fell off and bumped his head.
> Mama called the doctor and the doctor said,
> "No more monkeys jumping on the bed."
> Another:
> It ain't gonna rain no more no more,
> It ain't gonna rain no more,
> How in the heck am I gonna wash my neck
> If it ain't gonna rain no more.
> Another:
> Engine, engine number nine
> Running on the Chicago line.
> If the train should jump the track,
> Do you want your money back?

My sisters and I would sing the *Policeman Song* for Dad. He loved it:

> The big policeman on the corner is a friend of mine.
> He beckons me to cross the street while traffic waits in line,
> And then he say 'Good morning,' I hope you're feeling fine.
> I love the big policeman, he's a special friend of mine.

I grew up on a beautiful tree lined street in Northwest Detroit. There were lots of kids on our street, because we were less than two blocks from St. Francis de Sales Catholic School. We had lots of kids to play with; Joel, Judith and Paulette Bussell, Richard Baker, Pat and Johnny Lesner, Maureen and Kathleen Clifford, Jimmy and Suzie Devereaux and Mary Lou and Patsy Vanderveldt. We played all kinds of games that involved only girls, like dolls, doll houses, or just plain house, and with regular toys that all little girls loved. We also played tag, hide-and-seek, and baseball with the boys in the neighborhood.

We were all musicians. Mama loved it when the family gathered in the dining room to play music together. Dad on flute, Joanie on piano, Marguerite on violin and I on cello. Dad had taught himself to play the flute. Mama played the piano, and was a professional singer. Marguerite played piano in the beginning, and then switched to violin. She played violin throughout high school. Joanie played piano and still plays at home.

I started out playing piano in second grade, but switched to cello in third grade. I loved the cello, I was only a block and a half from school, but in third, fourth and fifth grade it sure was a long way to carry a cello. I don't know how many pounds it weighed, but it was a lot for a little kid to handle. It seemed like miles. I would have kept on playing the cello but Sr. Cecelia, the nun who taught me, was transferred to another school. That ended my cello career.

We all sang in the children's choir at church. At the Ursuline Academy we continued in music under the auspices of the Ontario Conservatory of Music, and the Toronto Conservatory of Music. Marguerite continued playing the violin throughout high school and also sang in the glee club. Joanie continued with her piano lessons and sang in the glee club and I took singing lessons and also sang in the glee club.

We loved to have tea parties. We had several little tea sets that were brought out on the front porch, and we'd pour Kool-Aid from our tea pots. Mama would give us crackers to eat with it. We also loved to play with our doll houses. We had two beautiful doll houses. One of them was given to us by a wealthy family friend, Mr. Rhodemeier. The doll house had miniature Duncan Phyfe furniture and a little sterling silver tea set. It had miniature bone china dishes, a beautiful chandelier in the dining room, and tiny, expensive rugs in each of the rooms. We weren't allowed to take that doll house outside. Years later Mama donated the doll house to The Ursuline Academy. The nuns were having a garden party and auction, and I assume Mama didn't know how she would be able to eventually split that doll house amongst us, so this was quite a charitable thing to do, and of course, the nuns were happy to have it at the Garden Party.

We went to the Ursuline Academy, a boarding school in Canada. We came home once a month on the train, and waited for Dad and Mama to pick us up at the depot. I would have been frightened if I had been by myself.

Your relationship with your sisters shapes your personality and your life.

Marguerite, the oldest, is independent and tends to be bossy. I remember when we were kids she liked to play school and she was always the teacher. One of her students, while we were playing school, left our house in tears. As she passed by Dad, he could see she was crying. This girl was the same age as Marguerite, mind you. Dad wanted to know what happened, she said. through her tears, "Marguerite's making me do homework." I suppose that was a punishment for something, but that's the kind of influence Marguerite could wield.

Teaching must have been in her blood. Years later she became a Special Ed teacher in Waterford, Michigan

One afternoon, after roller skating, we were late getting to the Five Points bus. We were too far from home to walk. There were three of us girls, and we didn't know what to do, so we decided to hitchhike, We were desperate. It was around five o'clock, and we were pretty nervous about the whole situation. Finally, a man pulled up and offered us a ride. We no sooner got into the car, when this man started to read us the riot act. His lecture continued all the way home. To this day I think the man was an off-duty policeman. He told us how dangerous it was, and that he had to go out of his way to make sure we got home safely. I thought it couldn't have been worse if Dad had caught us. I was sure this man was going to talk to Mama about it, but he didn't, though he made us promise we wouldn't do anything that foolish again.

We were almost in tears because he kept preaching to us, That night when I said my prayers, I thanked God for sending that man to see us home safely.

Marguerite met Jim Kirby at the Northland Roller Rink that we used to skate at. It was located at 8 Mile and Telegraph road. They married August 31, 1957 at St. Francis de Sales Church.

Jim was in the Air Force stationed at MacDill Air Force Base. In the 50's and 60's it was a Strategic Air Command Base for B-47 and later B-52 bombers. Jim was stationed there for two years. He passed away July 17, 1998 the result of an aneurism brought on by peripheral arterial disease. Its direct cause was smoking.

Marguerite had three sons, Michael Clayton, Mark Thomas and William James (Billy). Her youngest child, Billy, was born with severe Down Syndrome. Jim and Marguerite were told by doctors to put him in an institution. They refused. Billy would just languish there, and it would probably shorten his life. As it turned out, Billy died of a massive stroke at age 44. I remember telling my Jim, that I'd seen lots of Down children in my life but never one as severely disabled as Billy. "That's because most of them are in institutions," he said.

Billy didn't walk until he was eight. He never learned to talk, and never learned to chew food. He wore diapers all his life and died one month after Marguerite retired.

Marguerite worked for the Waterford, School District as a Special Ed teacher for 35 years. Billy had lived a very comfortable life surrounded by a family who loved him and cared deeply for him. It was because of him that Marguerite became a Special Ed teacher. I have always admired her.

Marguerite has three children, seven grandchildren, and three great-grandchildren. A great-grandson will join the family in March.

Michael Clayton and wife Tammy (Ohl) Kirby have four children, and three grandchildren, and a little grandson expected in March (2017).

1. Cassandra Diane (Cassie) and husband Daniel Hack have a daughter: Mila Ann and a son Lincoln James.
2. Genevieve Rose (Jenna) and Luke McKenna have a daughter: Madelina Bella McKenna and a son Liam due in spring.
3. Nicolas Michael (Nick) Kirby
4. Griffin Michael Kirby

Second Child: Mark Thomas and Liz (Miller) Kirby have a son Bryan Thomas. He and his wife Krisanne (Garrett) Kirby have a daughter, Aurora (no middle name) Kirby

Mark's second marriage to Linda (Cleaver) have two children: Thomas Mark and Jennifer Kirby

Third Child: William James Kirby (Billy)

Bryan Thomas was in the Marines with two tours of duty in Iraq and one tour of duty in Afghanistan, and achieved the rank of Staff Sergeant (E6) with a total of 9 ribbons: Iraq Campaign Medal, Sea Service Deployment ribbon, Marine Corps Good Conduct medal. Nato Medal-ISAF Afghanistan, Global War on Terrorism Service medal, Navy Unit Commendation, Navy and Marine Corps Achievement medal, Afghanistan Campaign medal, Meritorious Mast, National Defense Service medal.

Bryan's half-siblings are: Mark Thomas Kirby, Jennifer Kirby, and John Gormley.

Joanie, is not the typical middle sister, unlike Marguerite and me, Joanie enjoys being alone. I always wondered what it would be like to be a middle, the younger to one and the older to another. Maybe that would explain why Joanie is an introvert. Joanie's quiet, and can be quite funny at times with hilarious comments at just the right moment. For instance, when we were in Vancouver B.C. on a tour bus, some years ago, we heard lots of sirens coming our way, police cars, and ambulances, I don't know what all. The bus pulled over right in front of a large bank. The cavalcade stopped, and all these uniformed men darted up the steps of the bank, there was a lot of commotion going on. Joanie turned to me and said, "I think someone just found out the rate of exchange." The people on the bus started laughing. Joanie was embarrassed.

Joanie became a nurse and worked the night shift in the Geriatric Ward at Botsford Hospital in Redford. It was the perfect spot for her. In the mornings, she would get Quinto off to work, Tony, Theresa and Tina off to school, then she would sleep until time to pick the kids up, fix dinner, and go to work. It worked very well for Joanie and her family.

She spent many nights holding the hands of dying patients who just wanted to talk, and there is no better listener than Joanie. People like to confide in her because they know she never passes on a confidence. Joanie is my rock. Jim commented once, "You've got to feel sorry for Joanie. She's like a quiet book stuck between two noisy book-ends. No wonder she doesn't talk much, she can't get a word in edgewise."

My Jim taught Joanie how to drive, and then she and Jim taught me. I was 22 and pregnant with Steve when I took my driver's test, in 1962. In the 50's and 60's we didn't take Drivers Ed in school, we learned to drive and then took the driving test with a policeman in the car.

After Joanie got her driver's license, she took her cousin Josianne, who was eleven years her junior, to shows and different places. Joanie bought her first brand new car, 1960 Ford Falcon and took André, Josianne's older brother, Josianne and Mama, around the shoreline of lower Michigan. They started north toward Lake Huron, went to the bridge and then down along Lake Michigan until somewhere around Muskegan or St. Joseph and then cut across to Detroit. They all had a great time.

In 1958, Joanie met Quinto Serra at a party across the street, given by our neighbors the Gaviglios. They were married on November 23, 1963, at St. Francis de Sales Church, the day after President Kennedy was assassinated. My great-grandparents, Henry and Samantha Schindehette were married in Howell, the day after Abraham Lincoln was assassinated. Quinto died April 14, 2012 from the debilitating effects of Parkinson's Disease.

Joanie has three children and four grandchildren:

1. Anthony Martin and Sarah (Schut) their little girl has such a beautiful name: Sofia Bellaluna.
2. Theresa Ann and Joe Czarnecky's have two girls: Celia (pronounced like the cel in celery) Alysia and Angelina Celeste, named after Quinto's father, Celestino.

3. Valentina Mary, who was named after Quinto's younger sister who died in Italy during WWII. Tina and Nasser Algalham have a son Zane Nasser, known to all as "The Little Prince." Tina refers to him as the "Benevolent Dictator." Tina explained to me that it's a common practice in Yemen to take the father's name as a middle name, even the females.

Jim and I have three children: Steven James, David Michael and Julie Marie;

1. Steve helped his wife Bonnie (Adams) raise her four Sorrel children: Earl (Bucky); Amanda, Walter (Rusty) and Brittney. Steve's second wife Tammy (Martin) has a son Josh Bednarik .He has three sons: Logan, Andrew and Cameron. Tammy's daughter is Jessica Bednarik.
2. David is helping his wife Lisa (Hamilton) raise her daughter Courtney Pethers and also their daughter Carly Diane Wrobleski.
3. Julie and Matt Petrill have two sons: Seth Mathew and Nathan James.

Marguerite use to say that Dad spoiled me and now Jim spoils me. I tell her, "I'm not complaining." She knows I live up to the reputation of the youngest in most families...But my sisters have always been there for me. Most recently (2000), when my daughter was killed. They were with me through the whole terrible ordeal. Joanie and her husband had many memorial masses dedicated to Julie, and Marguerite listened for hours on the phone as I cried my way through that awful nightmare.

Joanie, Diane, and Marguerite

When we were teenagers we double and triple dated, though not very often. After we married, we had readymade baby-sitters for each other, and since we all lived near each other, our children are close also.

When I'm in Michigan in the summer, we have several "Sister Days" where we go to lunch. Our favorite place is Frankenmuth. It's a lovely town about an hour north of Detroit. It's a Bavarian town known far and wide for it's chicken dinners. It also has the largest Christmas store in the world, Bronners. Their ornaments and decorations come from all over the world.

I feel sorry for anyone who doesn't have sisters. Sisters are guaranteed best friends for life. My mother had four older sisters, and I have two older sisters, and I thank God everyday for them.

2

Grandma

My Grandma, what can you say about her, except that she was a character. I always had ambivalent feelings toward Grandma. Sometimes I would be upset with her, but I kept it to myself. Sometimes I felt sorry for her, but I always loved her, and so did everyone who knew her. In time I came to admire her as well.

I was ten when Grandma came to live with us. It was 1950, right after her husband, Edward Stuhlfaut, died from throat cancer. He was a big smoker and so was Grandma. She is my paternal grandmother. Her name was Elisabeth Martha Stuhlfaut. She was born in Bay City, Michigan, July 31, 1879, to Heinrich Schindehette and Samantha Diamon. She was the second youngest of eight children. The Schindehettes were Evangelical Lutherans. Grandma was baptized at Bethel Evangelical Lutheran Church in Bay City in 1880. In adulthood, her sister Anna became a Methodist, and Clara, the youngest in the family, who was a deaf mute due to a bout with measles at an early age, converted to Catholicism.

Grandma and Dad

Grandma, on the other hand, was not what you would call a religious person. However, there were two hymns that Grandma loved, "The Old Rugged Cross" and "The Battle Hymn of the Republic," made famous during the Civil War. Her father fought and was wounded at the Battle of Gettysburg. He was in the famous Michigan 24th, the Iron Brigade, also known as the Black Hat Brigade. Upon the death of President Lincoln, his family requested the Iron Brigade of which the Michigan 24th was a part, to accompany his caisson to the cemetery in Springfield, Illinois. The family of Lincoln knew how much he admired the Iron Brigade.

It was Grandma's stories about her dad being in the Civil War that got me interested in history and which in turn led to my interest in genealogy. It's been a passion of mine ever since.

On February 6, 1898, Grandma married a farm laborer, Henry Johann Sautter, from Sebewaing, a town about 30 miles from Bay City, in the thumb area. He was hired to work on her dad's farm.

Grandma was 19 years old when Dad was born in Bay City, Michigan, May 28, 1898. In doing the genealogy of Grandma's family, I found that she divorced Henry Sautter, my dad's father in 1900 when Dad was two years old. The divorce papers stated that he was abusive to her. Dad never saw his father again. I admired Grandma because she divorced my Grandpa knowing that she had no job and no prospects of a job, and really no place to go, but she was not going put up with an abusive man. Grandma moved to Wisconsin, probably Pewaukee, to live with her mother's family, and Dad stayed in Bay City with his grandma and grandpa. Years later, when she married Edward Stuhlfaut, she had my Dad come and live with them in Milwaukee. Dad would probably have been in the seventh or eighth grade at that time.

This is just conjecture on my part, but I think Grandma's father, Heinrich Schindehette, was very upset with her getting a divorce. He was well known and respected in town. Bay City had a large German population, and he and his brothers were proprietors of the National and the Republic hotels, the Johnson Bottling Works, plus several biergartens. He was also a large land owner and a member of the Evangelical Lutheran Church in Bay City. I think Grandma's untimely marriage and her divorce two years later, embarrassed him since he was well respected in the community.

Around 1915 or 1916, Grandma had moved with Pap and my Dad to Erie Pennsylvania, at 2695 Peach Street. We referred to Grandpa Stuhlfaut as Pap. He was my Dad's step-father. Pap loved the Detroit Tigers, and he and Grandma would visit us in the summer for a few weeks. That enabled Pap to see the Tiger games while Grandma visited with her sister Clara who lived practically next door to Briggs Stadium, formerly known as Navin Field and later known as Tiger Stadium. The new stadium in downtown Detroit is called Comerica Park. Grandma's other sister Anna lived in Howell, about fifty miles from Detroit, so her son Fred would bring her to visit Grandma. Aunt Del (Mary Adele), Grandma's oldest sister, lived north of Howell, but she never visited us.

We always looked forward to these visits from Grandma and

Pap. They would bring us "clacks," wooden beach shoes with a cloth strap that went over our feet to keep them on. We referred to them as clacks because of the noise they made when we walked on the sidewalk in them. That didn't last too long because the shoes weren't that comfortable, plus Mom and especially Dad got sick of the noise.

When Grandma wasn't able to visit us, we wrote to her, and when she wrote back, she always enclosed a stick of gum and a shiny dime. In the 1940s we could buy a lot with a dime: coloring books, cutout books, little toys, even an ice cream cone, all kinds of things like that, at the Kresge Five and Dime Store near us. That dime seemed like a lot of money to us..

When Grandma moved in with us we had to switch our sleeping arrangements.

We had two bedrooms downstairs and two bedrooms upstairs. Grandma was given one of the downstairs bedrooms, right across the hall from the bathroom. Dad and Mama had the other bedroom. Joanie and I shared the upstairs, front bedroom, and Marguerite had the back bedroom. Since there was only one bathroom in the house, and it was downstairs toward the back, going to the bathroom in the night was a real odyssey. If we got up in the night to go to the bathroom, we had to walk through the upstairs hall, go down the stairs through the front hallway, through the living room, through the dining room, and through the hall to the bathroom. By that time we were really wide awake. Then, of course, we reversed everything to go back upstairs.

One of the things that Grandma did that really irritated me, and probably everyone else in the family, was when we were all in the living room watching a TV program, she would come into the room and change the channel saying, "You weren't watching that were you?" Mama gave us her look, so we knew not to say anything. Grandma never seemed to do that when Dad was home...

Grandma loved Bingo, and she went every Tuesday night to St. Frances de Sales, money in hand, ready to win. I'd help her fill in the Bingo cards. One night she won something like $100, and she gave me $5.00 for helping her. That was quite a bit of money.

Grandma tended to be a hypochondriac. We just all figured she needed attention. Dad came home from work one day, and Mama told him his mother had been under the weather all day. Dad asked Mama what day it was. She said, "Tuesday."

Dad said, "She'll be okay, it's Bingo night at church." Sure enough, when 7:00 o'clock came around, Grandma was dressed and ready to play Bingo.

Grandma was taller than I am. She was 5'8" and thin. She was a good looking woman with nice white hair, and unlike most of the elderly of her day, she very seldom wore black. I remember her bright red coat. It looked very attractive with that white hair of hers.

Grandma once told me, "The best years of my life were my school years." She also said, she loved to ice skate, especially backwards, because she could pick up more speed. Grandma grew up near Saginaw Bay, so I assume that's where she skated. You could skate way out into the bay backwards without fear of skating into anything. The bay was frozen solid all winter. It's part of Lake Huron.

Grandma was hard of hearing but never felt the need for a hearing aid. One day we heard a terrible screeching from the kitchen. It was Grandma trying to close the refrigerator door but couldn't because the cat's tail was in the way. She kept slamming the door, and the cat kept screeching. When we got to the kitchen to see what all the commotion was about, Grandma said, "This door is getting harder and harder to close." From that day on, our beautiful, white, Persian Angora cat had a kink in her tail, a constant reminder of Grandma and her encounter with our Snowball.

Though Grandma couldn't hear well, she had a low voice that carried extremely well. Her nephew Bob Hellers, her sister Clara's son, had been married to Helen for more than 25 years when he decided to divorce her and marry Ruth. The wedding took place at the prestigious Kirk in the Hills Presbyterian Church in Bloomfield Hills. This church is so beautiful. It looks like a small cathedral, with gorgeous stained glass windows. As the lovely strains of Wagner's Lohengrin wafted from the pipe organ, the wedding procession proceeded down the aisle. As Ruth passed by Grandma's pew,

Grandma turned to one of the relatives, and in what she thought was a whisper, said, "I think Bob was better off with Helen." The wedding guests around her almost laughed out loud.

If you believe in the old axiom that all babies are cute, you might not want to read the following: Some family friends, the proud parents of a new baby boy, came over to visit, and Mama and Marguerite took the baby to Grandma's bedroom at the back of the house. As I was talking to the proud parents in the living room, we heard Grandma's low, gravelly voice saying, "My Lord, he looks just like Pinocchio." I was so embarrassed, all I could do was laugh a little, and tell them that Grandma had a great sense of humor. I don't know, to this day, if they bought that explanation or not. Years later Marguerite ran into the now, adult Pinocchio, and she said he was a Marine and was tall and handsome. You couldn't prove it by Grandma.

My dad loved his Uncle Will, Grandma's brother. Dad told me he became a police officer because of his Uncle Will. Will was a special officer for the Pére Marquette Railroad. The following articles appeared in *The Detroit Free Press*. The first one on July 6, 1922, the second, a few days later.

FRIENDS WOUNDED IN A ONE GUN-DUEL
Railway Men Quarrel, Shoot Each Other, Say Police

What started as a playful prank in the saloon of Frank Prowruzek, 3549 Hammond Avenue, early in the evening of Independence Day, resulted in a possible fatal shooting affray between two friends, at 4:30 o'clock Wednesday morning, when both men were much under the influence of liquor, police declare.

Frank Heppner, 33. of 5924 Kulick street, a switchman, and William Schindehette, 44, of 332 East Larned street, a special officer of the Pere Marquette railroad, were the principals in the one-gun "duel" which sent both to the hospital with bullet wounds to the abdomen.

Prowruzek, proprietor of the saloon and two of those present at the time of the shooting, Adam Dunninski, of 26 Central avenue, and William Guraki, 3421 Hammond avenue, were held as witnesses.

Heppner, witnesses declare, took a pistol out of Schindehette''s pocket, early in the evening, and hid it.

As the night wore on, the "joke" angered Schindehette more and more, and he and Heppner finally became involved in a violent quarrel. Heppner suddenly pulled Schindehette's pistol from its hiding place, and shot his friend in the abdomen, say witnesses.

Schindehette rushed his assailant, took the weapon away from him and turned it on Heppner, sending a bullet into Heppner's abdomen, according to stories told to the prosecutor.

Both men staggered out of the saloon and were found more than a block away, where they had collapsed.

ONE-GUN DUEL' PARTICIPANT DIES
P.M. SPECIAL OFFICER, SHOT BY FRIEND,
SUCCUMBS; OTHER MAN MAY DIE

William Schindehette, special officer for the Pere Marquette railway, who was shot through the abdomen by Frank Heppner, his close friend, during a fight that terminated in a "one-gun duel" early in the morning of July 4 in a saloon at 3549 Hammond avenue, died Friday morning in Receiving Hospital.

Not far away lay Heppner, who also was shot through the abdomen. Schindehette having grabbed the pistol and shot him after being wounded. Heppner, who is a switchman, 33 years old, and lived at 5124 Kullick Avenue, will not recover, it is believed. Schindehette who was 37, lived at 322 Larned Street East.

The following article appeared in, I assume, *The Livingston County Press.*

ONE GUN DUEL PARTICIPANT DIES

Special Pere Marquette Officer Killed in a Detroit Saloon
The Detroit Free Press of last Saturday, has the following relative to the death of an old Cohoctah boy:
William Schindehette, special officer for the Pere Marquette

railway, who was shot through the abdomen by Frank Heppner, his close friend during a fight that terminated in a "one-gun duel" early in the morning of July 4 in a saloon at 3549 Hammond avenue died Friday in Receiving hospital.

Not far away lay Heppner, who also was shot through the abdomen. Schindehette having grabbed the pistol and shot after being wounded. Heppner who is a switchman. 33 years old and lived at 5124 Kulick Avenue, will not recover it is believed. Schindehette, who was 37, lived at 322 Larned Street, East.

The remains were brought to Howell last Saturday, and the funeral was held at Goodrich's undertaking rooms Sunday afternoon, Rev. Schleicher officiating. Burial in Lake View Cemetery. There was a very large attendance of relatives and friends of the dead officer, quite a number of whom live in the county.

Note:

332 Larned, where Uncle WIll lived, is near the present day Renaissance Center. 3549 Hammond, the location of the saloon, is near Michigan and Military. 5124 Kulick, the residence of Frank Heppner, is near Michigan and Junction.

My interpretation of this is that since Uncle Will's friend wasn't required to carry a gun on the job, he may not have known how to use it. When handing the gun to Will, he could have accidentally shot him. In Uncle Will's state of being inebriated, he just retaliated and shot back.

Uncle Will is buried in the family plot next to ours, in Lakeview Cemetery. Grandma's sister Anna and husband Conrad Steinacker are in that same family plot, and Grandma is right in back of them. Jim and Julie are in our family plot in front of Uncle Will and Aunt Anna. I will be interred next to Jim.

When Seth was seven or eight years old and we'd go to the cemetery to see his mom, Julie, I'd always bring a dozen roses, her favorite flower. Seth would very carefully help me arrange the flowers, and then he'd take one rose and place it on "Elisabeth's" grave, as he always referred to her, never Grandma, just Elisabeth. He loves that name. In my family plot, directly across from Uncle Will, is John and Emma Diamon. John was Great-grandma Samantha Schindehette's half-brother. John inherited the Diamon farm that was just north of Howell by Brewer and Bauer roads. A few years later the property was sold at auction at the old Howell Courthouse. His wife Emma was a piano teacher in Fowlerville.

In 1945 when Dad's Uncle Coon died (he was Grandma's brother-in-law) Dad called from work and asked Mama if she would call the sheriff in Howell to get the information concerning Uncle Coon. Mama called the sheriff and asked if he knew where Conrad Steinacker was going to be laid out. "Old Coon died?" the sheriff said. He then looked out the window and said, "The lights are on at the Schnackenburg funeral home; that's where he'll be."

Mama proceeded to call the florist and told the gal she would like to have flowers sent to a Conrad Steinacker. The florist asked, "How do you spell that?" Mama spelled the name. She then told the florist that he would be laid out at the Schnackenburg Funeral Home. The florist asked Mama, "How do you spell that?" Again, Mama spelled the name for her. Then the florist wanted to know who the flowers were from. When Mama told her, "Mr. and Mrs. Stuhlfaut and Elisabeth Schindehette," the florist burst out laughing.

One day at the dinner table, the conversation about Grandma's brother George came up. My dad loved all his relatives, except Uncle George. In fact no one seemed to like George. He had a twin sister Samantha who died at age four. Grandma remembers it as George having a twin who died shortly after birth; in fact, she didn't even know the little girl's name. Back to the dinner table and the conversation about George. Grandma said, "You know George was a twin? I like to say the twin died and the afterbirth lived." I looked across the table at Mama as she rolled her eyes toward heaven, yet again.

This happened all too often with Grandma's colorful stories. Of course this was at the dinner table which made it worse. Mama would always reprimand us if our stories weren't suitable for dinner conversation. But there was no stopping Grandma. She did have a good sense of humor; unfortunately it sometimes clashed with

Mama's. However, Mama never said anything to Grandma about it, and evidently neither did Dad. I would later overhear Mama asking Dad, "Can't you do something about your mother?"

"I don't know what to do." he'd say. Mama had always told us to respect our elders, and also never to repeat any of Grandma's stories. Of course, I couldn't wait to get outside and start talking. Many of her stories, I think, were off color, and even though I'd repeat them, I didn't know what half of them meant.

One really nice trait of Grandma's, I realized as I got older, was that she never got involved in any family disputes. She never took sides. She always seemed to be in a good mood. She was not a complainer. She was never crabby. She didn't swear, but she would use the word "hooey" every now and then, as in "that's a bunch of hooey."

I'd heard from several relatives that Grandma was an alcoholic, and she probably was, but I never saw her drink. We think Dad told her when she came to live with us that there would be no drinking. I always thought my Dad didn't drink because his mother did, and that was one of the reasons why she couldn't raise him.

Grandma was never a very demonstrative person. I never knew her to hug or kiss us, or Dad. We never sat on her lap when we were little, either. Mom and Dad, on the other hand, were very loving and affectionate.

In 1957, at my Dad's funeral, Grandma and I were sitting in the front row, next to each other. I was sixteen at the time. I wanted to hold her hand; she seemed so alone, but I didn't know what she would do. Finally, I reached over and took her hand in mine, and she never let it go through the whole funeral. That meant a lot to me.

Grandma's episodes with hypochondria increased after Dad died. Unfortunately, those episodes were taking a toll on Mama's pocketbook. It all came to a head when Mama went to Henry Ford Hospital to bring Grandma home. The hospital refused to release Grandma until Mama paid her "mother's bill." Mama politely informed them that she was not her mother, she was her mother-in-law, and they could keep her. Mama turned and proceeded to walk out. They quickly called her back and told her they'd work things out. Consequently, Grandma came home with us.

When Dad died, Joanie and I were still in high school and money was getting tight. It was decided that Grandma would live near her sister Anna in Howell. Marguerite found a nice retirement home for Grandma close to Aunt Anna's. I think Grandma was only there a couple weeks when the home called Marguerite and told her to come and get Grandma. Evidently they were throwing her out! Marguerite asked Grandma, "What's this all about"?

All Grandma said was, "Nobody's going to tell me when I can or can't read my newspaper."

Marguerite then took Grandma to Aunt Anna's, which was really a good idea because Aunt Anna had just had cataract surgery and had those glasses on with the coke bottle lens, as they used to be called. The plan was that Grandma would help out Aunt Anna because at that time Anna could barely see. Years ago it took a while to recover from cataract surgery. When we went a few weeks later to visit Grandma, Aunt Anna was waiting on her, serving her lunch. So much for that idea. . .

On June 29,1962, Grandma passed away. The cause of death, a coronary occlusion. She was 82. Jim and I went to the funeral at the Schnackenburg Funeral Home, in Howell. My Jim liked Grandma, and she liked him. They always enjoyed each other's company. I was pregnant with Steve at the time. Fred Steinacker, Aunt Anna's son, came over and shook hands with Jim. Just then the undertaker approached and asked Jim if he would be a pallbearer. Jim's face turned pale white. He looked at me, startled. Jim, then 22, had never been to a funeral before, let alone been a pallbearer, so he was quite nervous, but he did fine.

Grandma was laid to rest in beautiful Lakeview Cemetery on Thompson Lake in Howell.

3

Memories of Dad

A day has not gone by that I haven't thought about my Dad. I've asked myself many times why I didn't appreciate him more when he was alive. I loved my Dad, but really took for granted just how wonderful he really was until he got sick. I was sixteen years old when Mama told me Dad was dying of cancer. As I looked back I realized I had the best dad in the world, but it wasn't until after he died that it really hit me, and I have always regretted not telling Dad more just how much he meant to me and how much I loved him, and how proud I always was of him.

Dad was a self-made man. He was a large imposing man, very good looking with the greatest dimples in the world. He was six foot tall, a Detroit police officer, and a judo instructor for the Detroit Police Department. He was also a translator for the deaf in the department. He was a man's man, a police sergeant trying to raise three girls—never an easy task for a policeman. Dad was also a Shriner and a 32nd degree Mason. He loved to read and had many hobbies. I get those characteristics from my dad.

In his spare time, among other things, he lifted weights. He had great physical strength, and great strength of character. He was a wonderful husband and father.

When my sisters and I were little, Dad referred to us as his "Dolly Girls." He was always so proud of us, and we knew it.

In contrast to my Dad, Mama was less than five feet tall. Mama's family moved from St. Boniface, Manitoba to Detroit in the early 1920s and rented an apartment on Collingwood. Grandpa Brault died during Mass at Visitation Church just after receiving communion. He evidently went back to his pew, said a few prayers, sat down, and his head went back, and he died instantly. It was 1935 when Grandma

Rose bought the house on Pinehurst. As luck would have it, they moved right next door to Dad. Dad and Mama met and fell in love and married. Dad purchased Grandma Rose's house, the house we grew up in, in exchange for a lot my Dad owned on Birwood. They had a house built and that's where Aunt Mac and Anna lived with Edno. It was during the Great Depression, but Dad, being a police officer, had work. The city had laid off many police officers during the Great Depression but Dad was not one of them. Mom and Dad had both been married before, so when they married on my Dad's birthday, May 28, 1936, Dad was 38 and Mama was 36. My sister Marguerite was born June 10, 1937; Joan on February 8, 1939, and I was born, April 26, 1940. It must have been difficult for them raising a young family in their early forties, but nowadays that seems to be the norm.

Dad was a kind, decent, thoughtful man who had a lot of integrity He was an honorable man. He was the one you could always depend on. He never once disappointed me. He was very good to Mama and our whole family. He was a true gentleman. He taught the three of us that we could be whatever we wanted to be in life and to never take guff (not Dad's word) from anyone. Mama probably didn't want us to be too aggressive, so she would remind us that, "There is never an excuse for rudeness." Mama could tell people off in such a way that they didn't even realize they were being told off until it dawned on them a while later. She was a master of the subtle putdown. Near as I can figure, because my Dad was not as well educated as Mama, her influence on him over the years showed in his good manners and his command of the English language.

I have wonderful memories of the whole family riding in the car with Dad and Mama in the front seat. There were no seat belts in the forties and fifties. Dad would turn corners rather sharply just to have Mama slide into him. Mama always laughing and saying, "mon Dieu!"

Since Mama was under 5 feet, whenever she'd ask Dad to get something out of the cupboard, he'd grab her by the waist and start to lift her up. All the while Mama was exclaiming in French, "mon Dieu!" and laughing.

My Grandma was nineteen years old when Dad was born in Bay City, Michigan in 1898, and his parents divorced in 1900. I admired Grandma for leaving an alcoholic who was also an abuser. However, that made life very difficult for Grandma because in 1900 there weren't many jobs for women, and certainly even less opportunity for a woman trying to raise a child alone. Divorces were almost unheard of at that time.

There could be two reasons why Grandma went to Wisconsin: Either because her mother's family lived in Pewaukee, or perhaps she could find work in Milwaukee. She left my Dad with her parents in Bay City, probably until she could make it on her own.

Her parents were well-off financially and were better able to take care of him. Everything went well until her father Henry, died in 1906 from lock-jaw, also known as tetanus. The tetanus was caused from wounds received years before at the Battle of Gettysburg. A year later their house burned to the ground. The cause of the fire was never known.

His Grandmother had no place for herself or for Dad, who was then eight years old, to stay. There was no insurance in those days, but Samantha did receive a pension from the government for her husband's participation in the Civil War. It wasn't much, and so she took Dad to Detroit to live with one of her daughters, my Dad's Aunt Clara who was a deaf-mute as was her husband Uncle Peter.

Dad's whole family, even Mama knew sign language to enable them to communicate with Aunt Clara and Uncle Peter, who were very nice people. Aunt Clara's home was one of many places my dad was shuffled around to when he was growing up.

Dad had an uncertain childhood. I used to think he was insecure because he went through the Great Depression, but then I remembered that he always had a job, so I figured that kind of insecurity comes from not having a place of your own, no place to call home when you're growing up, not even a bedroom to call your own. He was always living with his grandma and one of his many aunts and uncles. Dad told me that until about age ten he thought his Grandmother was his mother. His own mother wasn't able to care for him until he was older, probably middle school age.

Dad lived in several different places in Milwaukee with his mother and step-father, Edward Stuhlfaut, who we always referred to as Pap. They finally settled in Erie, Pennsylvania. Dad was known as Archie D. Stuhlfaut for most of his life even though he didn't get his name legally changed until the early 1940s. His given name was Dewey Archibald Sautter. When doing genealogy, I always make reference to that fact.

I asked Grandma why she named him, Dewey Archibald. She said that at the time Dad was born, in May 1898, Admiral Dewey had just won a naval victory over the Spanish at the Battle of Manila Bay during the Spanish-American War. He was the hero of the day. As for the name Archibald, I don't remember what she told me.

Dad was in the Coast Guard from 1919 to 1921. He was stationed at #236 Erie, Pennsylvania, also referred to as Presque Isle, as a #2 surfman, and was assigned to the care, operation and repair, as well as fitting and keeping the following boat types: English Lifeboat, self bailing and self righting type, 36 foot, powered with a 45-75 HP Sterling motor and a McClelland surfboat, self-bailing type, 26 foot, powered by an Aristox motor. I've always been proud of the fact that Dad was in the Coast Guard. It is the most selective service out there. On average, 1 out of 100 applicants successfully make it into the Coast Guard. There's very little advertising for the Coast Guard because they don't require as many people as the other branches of service, so they can be very selective.

Dad

Dad must have moved to Detroit in 1922 because he was taking classes in Automotive Mechanics and Electricity at Cass Tech. I'm speculating, but he probably lived with his Aunt Clara and Uncle Peter. They lived next to Navin Field (Tiger Stadium). Cass Tech is where I met and later married Jim. Marguerite also went to Cass Tech.

From 1923 to 1927 Dad was back in Erie, Pennsylvania and was employed by the New York Central Railroad. He learned Rules and Regulations of both the Road and the Property Protection Department. I'm assuming he was a Railroad Policeman because that's what his mother's brother Will was in Detroit. Dad loved his Uncle Will and told me he became a policeman because that's what his Uncle Will was.

In 1926 while still in Erie, Dad became Scoutmaster to Boy Scout Troop 34.

Before joining the Detroit Police Department, Dad took the following University of Michigan Extension courses at the Police Headquarter's Building: criminology, evidence, public speaking, finger printing, and a twenty hour course in first aid (American Red Cross). He also received instructions in civil defense, air raid precaution, chemicals, hand bombs and incendiaries. In the summer of 1927, Dad joined the Detroit Police Department. His first beat was Palmer Park, and he was assigned a German Shepherd dog named Jim. He loved that dog. Sometime in the late 30s Dad was on assignment as a Wayne County Sheriff's Deputy. He also had 150 hours of instruction in Jiu-Jitsu.

Dad made sure that his kids would never have to feel insecure. We lived in a house that was paid for, and the times when we had a car, Dad paid cash for it. That's what people did in the fifties. It's funny how you take things for granted. I just knew it was my house and that it would always be there for me to come home to. I always felt loved and secure. I thought everybody did. It wasn't until I was much older that I realized just how lucky I was.

The reason why I mention Dad's insecurity, and that might not be the correct term, was because he was a pack rat, not a hoarder, a pack rat. Mama would only let him use the attic, the basement and the garage. He could not pile up his "stuff" in any other part of the house, and he adhered to Mama's rule. We never once had a car parked in our garage. Open the garage door and inside it was piled to the rafters with Dad's "stuff."

Dad would have taken umbrage at the word junk, so we always referred to it as his "stuff." These were his things, and as much as there was of it, he could find things that he needed right away. I don't know how he did it. If he had a system, I had no clue what that system was. In the attic, there were cases of Campbell's Tomato soup, and other cases of food that I don't remember, and reams and reams of paper, and cases of toilet paper, and much more. Dad was never one to pass up a good deal either. He also had real interesting things in the attic. I remember a metal, toy circus wagon and a beautiful, wooden Noah's Ark with little wooden animals. These were toys we played with when we were little. Dad also had collections. The attic contained book shelves loaded with his collection of books. He collected stamps, coins and encyclopedias. He had encyclopedias of architecture, of history, and of education. I could go on and on. He was an avid reader. When I was older, Dad and I would go to the Bella

Hubbard Library on McNichols and James Cousins Highway, now the John Lodge Freeway, and browse through the stacks.

Dad also would take us to Classes Used Book Store and Antiques. It was located in a section of Dad's precinct known as Corktown. He knew Mrs. Class and her daughter because he stopped there many times on his way home from work to pick up a beautiful vase for Mama or a hand-painted, china cup and saucer that he knew would please her.

In the basement we had a wine cellar. It held several wooden wine barrels. Yes, Dad also made wine, but what the neighborhood couldn't wait for was when he made his famous root beer. Everyone loved it.

Dad was also famous for his chili. He started with suet, the hard white fat you get from the kidneys and the lower ribs of beef, that he put in the pressure cooker. I don't remember anything else, except that our neighbors and friends always asked Dad when he was going to be making his famous chili.

We also had a fruit cellar in the basement, and Dad stocked it with canned cherries from the cherry tree in our yard, canned peaches, applesauce and tomatoes. He also canned pickles and made sauerkraut. Mama wasn't too happy about that because it literally stunk up the whole house. Pretty much the rest of the basement was just full of what I considered to be his junk, ahem, his "things."

During World War II, the government encouraged people to plant Victory Gardens. They wanted individuals to provide their own fruit and vegetables. We had a Victory Garden that Dad would take us to. It was on Southfield near Schoolcraft. Family friends, Fred and Kate Hehl lived nearby. We would go with Dad and help him plant seeds, go back to make sure everything was watered, and later in the summer, help Dad pick the vegetables. I barely remember this time in my life, but I do remember that Dad was very patriotic.

It was well known that Dad swore a lot, so my sisters and I bought him a Swear Box. Each time he swore he had to put money in it. I think it was either a nickel or a dime. Well, every time we caught him swearing he'd put the money in and swear under his breath while he was doing it. He filled up the box so quickly we could hardly keep up with him. Finally, we just gave up.

I remember him, one time, saying to Marguerite, "I'll quit you of that swearing, God damn it." The other thing he would say sometimes at the dinner table was, "Who in the hell says Grace around here?"

Dad did all the grocery shopping and took us with him. I have fond memories of Dad waking us up early on Saturday morning to take us to the Western Market, on Michigan Avenue at 18th street, near downtown, in Dad's police precinct. We couldn't wait. Marguerite remembers us also going to the Eastern Market, but I have no recollection of that.

Mama never went on any of these excursions. When I was older I figured out why. Dad would buy bushels of peaches to can, apples to make applesauce, and elderberries for wine. He'd put the bushels in the car, usually the back seat, so that on the way home we could eat some of the fruit. Also on the way home he'd stop to pick up items on Dexter Avenue in the Jewish section of town, or in Hamtramck, the Polish section of town. They each had wonderful delicacies, and Dad always wanted to surprise Mama with something.

We'd wait in the car for what seemed like hours for Dad to return. He usually was talking to someone. He was known for that. He was very friendly and would pick up conversations with just about anybody, as we waited. My sisters and I played games in the car, but eventually we got sick of them and each other. Sometimes he'd stop by his precinct where all the shopkeepers knew him. That's when it seemed like we'd never get home.

It was because of these excursions and waiting forever for Dad to return to the car that I picked up a habit I have to this day, books, I always have a book with me no matter where I go. There's nothing worse than waiting somewhere and having nothing to occupy your time.

In our backyard, besides our one car garage, and several small fruit trees, Dad decided to tear up a large patch of grass to enable him to grow tomatoes. He waited and waited for those tomatoes to ripen, but every time he checked they were always green. One day he finally put two and two together and solved the mystery. It seems that

I started to break out in hives all over my arms and legs. Evidently Dad didn't realize until then, just how much I loved tomatoes.

Remember our cat Snowball that Grandma slammed the refrigerator door on her tail? Well, she had kittens every six months, like clock work. One time they were born in our laundry chute. We had to move her and her kittens to another place in the house because we needed our laundry chute. Another time we couldn't find her but knew she was about to deliver. She had those kittens in the back of the furnace, but the one time that really got Dad upset was when he found her and her kittens in his duffle bag. "Son of a b——" he said in a whisper, along with a few other choice words. He, of course, did not disturb Snowball. When it was all over and the kittens weaned, he threw the duffle bag out.

Joanie had a blue parakeet she named Mickey. On one particular day, Mama clipped Mickey's wings while Dad was shaving. He came into the dining room to say something to Mama, and accidentally stepped on Mickey. "Son of a b——," he said, and picked Mickey up and gently held the bird in his hands. Mama got some whiskey to put in its little beak, but poor Mickey's head dropped, he was gone. You could hear Dad mumbling his familiar, "Son of a b——" under his breath, but we knew he felt bad, and we were all crying. I think I was seven or eight at the time. Dad reverently placed Mickey in a shoe box, and we all went out to the backyard for Mickey's funeral.

I can only remember one Father/Daughter outing that Dad and my sisters and I went to. It was a Friday night formal dinner at the Masonic Temple. We had brand new dresses to wear. We sat at a table with two other fathers and their daughters. When the main course came, Dad asked if any of the others at the table wanted extra chicken because his daughters were Catholic and couldn't eat meat on Friday. I think they gave us their desserts. In spite of that, we had a great time.

The Freedom Train made its stop in Detroit on August 20-22, 1948. It started touring the country in 1947 and ended in 1949. It was the temporary home to America's most precious documents, including the Declaration of Independence, the Bill of Rights, the U.S. Constitution, the Emancipation Proclamation, the Gettysburg Address, and even

England's Magna Carta. In all there were 127 documents and many other treasures to see, including the flag that flew at Iwo Jima. U.S. Marines were on the train to protect its precious cargo. It was very hot that day, and I remember there was a lot of whining from all three of us. I'm surprised to this day that Dad didn't just take us home and forget the whole thing, but I'm sure grateful that he stayed. We waited in line forever, and finally when we got on the train, I just marveled at all the history before my eyes.

Many years later I received my degree in history from Eastern Michigan University. I think my love of history started back there on that Freedom Train. Then when Grandma came to live with us three years later, her stories about her father fighting in the Civil War, in particular the Battle of Gettysburg, just kept piquing my interest.

Dad always tried to expose us to as many interesting things as possible when we were young. He had a wonderful sense of history. Jefferson Avenue ran along the Detroit River, and it had many beautiful, old stately mansions on the riverfront right up to Belle Isle. I must have been eight or nine at the time, and I remember Dad taking us through those beautiful homes because they were going to be demolished to make way for high rises along the river. Dad said with a tone of sadness, "Remember these beautiful homes because you'll never see the likes of them again."

It made me sad, too, to think about it. The homes had wonderful, long porches and beautiful chandeliers in their dining rooms. From the windows you could see the river and Belle Isle. I would close my eyes and imagine a family with little children and a dog living there. The one thing I didn't like about those houses were the basements. They were rather claustrophobic with their low ceilings and musty odor.

When Dad was promoted to sergeant he took us to visit his new precinct, #11, Davison Station. While there, we had our finger prints taken. Not too many people can say, or would admit they had their fingerprints taken at the age of eight.

Grandma came to live with us when her husband, Pap died. We had four bedrooms in the house and one bathroom. I'll leave the rest to your imagination. Poor Dad with all these women in the house!

Even the cat was female! As I think back, Grandma was welcomed into our house by Mom and Dad without hesitation, even though Dad seemed to know his aunts better than his own mother. Until he was a teenager, Grandma never really had taken care of Dad. I would never have expected anything different from Dad, or Mama for that matter.

When Grandma called from Erie, Pennsylvania, to tell Dad that Pap had died, she asked Dad what was going to happen to her. Dad of course conferred with Mama. Both concurred, and Dad told his mother to come and live with us. Joanie and I had to double up in one bedroom, but it was a large room. and we really enjoyed each others company, for the most part. Grandma was fun, or I should say funny, and she smoked like a chimney. Mama was a very refined woman, my dad's mother was not. . .

Among Dad's many hobbies was carving leather. He made all of us beautiful, carved purses with intricate triple lacing on them. One evening Mama and Dad went out to dinner to an upscale restaurant. Mama was carrying her beautiful, unborn calf skin purse that Dad had just made for her. A gentleman came over to their table and bought it right out from under Mama's arm. He said he had never seen anything like it, his wife was admiring it, and he wanted to buy it for her as it was so unusual.

Dad made another purse similar to that one for Mama. He also made all of us beautiful, hand carved, prayer book covers, wallets, and bookmarks. He was very talented. He also took up lapidary and polished stones for bracelets and necklaces, even rings for all of us. My sisters and I have these pieces of jewelry to this day.

I remember when Marguerite was dating. I think she was around fifteen or sixteen at the time. Dad, in full uniform, met her date at the door, and believe me, Dad was a large, imposing figure. I believe he also had his gun in its holster. To this day I don't remember if Dad was actually going to work, or if he had the day off. Whatever time it was that Dad told the fellow to bring Marguerite home, he brought her home early. I don't know if she ever went out with him again.

Another time, a fellow in Levis, kind of bedraggled, rang the doorbell asking for Marguerite. Dad was not one bit impressed with this guy. He told Marguerite that the guy was a loser or some such thing, and eventually she quit seeing him. A year later, the doorbell rang. Dad answered the door and a nice looking, clean cut, Marine wanted to see Marguerite. Dad looked at him, and the fellow said to Dad, "Don't you remember me? I just got out of basic training." It was the bedraggled date of Marguerite's from a couple months back. Well, Dad was real happy with this guy now. He invited him in. Marguerite dated him a couple times and then broke it off. After Dad was told about this, he said to Marguerite, "Sure, you liked him when he was a bum, but now that he's joined the human race you won't have anything to do with him."

Yet another time, Marguerite started dating Joe, a man a little older than she was. Dad did not like him at all. He forbade Marguerite to ever go out with him again. She ignored him. Dad was really bent out of shape over it. Dad came home from work one day and told Mama that he had looked up files to see if Joe had a record. He said to Mama, "The son-of-a-bitch is clean." He sure sounded disappointed.

Dad retired from the police force in 1952 when I was twelve years old. He then took classes at the University of Michigan, and at the time of his death five years later, he was employed by the Oakland County Board of Supervisors. He really loved being a policeman though, that was his life, but after he retired he also loved working for Oakland County

Dad was a joiner. That's who I get it from. He belonged to the Detroit Lodge No. 34 B.P.O. Elks and was on their Honor Roll for the Detroit Police Department. At the time of his death he was a member of Tuebor Lodge No. 578. He also belonged to the Metropolitan Square and Compass Club, the Lieutenants and Sergeants Association, and the Retired Police Officers Association. He was a 32nd degree Mason and a Shriner. He was a patrol veteran with the Shriners and marched in all their parades around the country during the Shriners' conventions. He also belonged to the Detroit Consistory, and the F&AM.

The Police Department had a monthly newsletter called the *Tuebor*, the motto on the shield of the great seal of Michigan that translates to, "I will defend." For several years Dad wrote a column for his precinct; in it, he teased his fellow officers. They loved it.

One time on our way to the Police Picnic, Dad got into a verbal battle with the driver of the car next to us. I guess nowadays you'd call it road rage. Mama kept telling Dad to calm down, but he had a good string of swear words going, and he wasn't going to let up. Finally we got to the park, and the fellow that Dad was yelling at, followed us into the park. He was also a policeman. Mama scolded Dad under her breath, telling him he should be ashamed of himself. He didn't say anything, but he did look a little sheepish.

Dad loved being a police officer so much so, that even though he had been retired five years when he died, Mama wanted him to have a police funeral. All the pallbearers were uniformed policemen. Chester Warhus, our next door neighbor was one of the pallbearers. Dad was instrumental in getting Chester a job on the force. There were two police motorcyclists ahead of the hearse, and the procession was so long it went through two traffic lights at once on the way to Grand Lawn Cemetery. Several police cars were at the end of the procession. The graveside burial rite was done by the Masons. It was beautiful and the only funeral conducted by the Masons that I've ever attended.

One of the things Dad used to say, and I have repeated it many times to my children and grandchildren, and others: "Never be ashamed of honest work." According to Dad, it didn't matter how humble your job was, as long as you did your best.

I miss Dad everyday.

4

The Shrine Circus

In winter in the 1940s, my sisters and I looked forward to the Shrine Circus coming to Detroit. The circus was held in the coliseum at the Michigan State Fair Grounds, and it stayed for two weeks. Dad was a Shriner and a police officer. Every year since I could remember, when the circus came to town Dad was assigned the circus detail. He probably requested that because he loved the circus, and circus performers. He was well acquainted with most of the performers. Sometimes, when off duty, Dad would pile as many neighbor kids as possible into our car so we could all see the circus. Smaller kids sat on bigger kids' laps. This was before the seat belt laws were enacted. We went to the circus three or four times each season, but most often just Mama, my sisters and I would go.

This was a three ring circus. Dad made sure we'd get there an hour ahead of time in order to get the front row seats directly over the large archway where the animals and performers came out. The archways were located at both ends of the coliseum, but we always sat over the one where the performers and animals came out.

The light dimmed, everyone quieted down, the ringmaster came out, and a spotlight shone on him as his voice echoed all over the coliseum, when he announced, "Ladies and gentlemen, children of all ages, welcome to the Shrine Circus." Then all the bright lights were turned on, and the calliope started playing. The ringmaster then introduced the parade of performers as they came through right beneath us. It was so exciting and so much fun. It was magical. We were also thrilled because the spotlight was on us, too, since we were sitting where the action was. Sometimes the parade of performers would get backed up a little. It was at this time that we could look down at the animals. I especially loved the elephants. When they stopped underneath the archway, we shouted and waved at their trainers perched high on their backs. The parade of performers, and animals circled once around the coliseum, and then the ring master began introducing the acts.

I remember dogs that performed amazing tricks, bears that could dance, acrobats performing stunts on beautiful horses as they rode by, aerial acrobats, crazy clowns, and of course those enormous elephants. The main attraction was always the Great Wallendas. They were a family of aerial acrobats who performed all over the world. When they did the human pyramid on the tight rope, without a net, high above the crowd, it was very scary to watch. The other highlights of the show were Clyde Beatty, a famous lion tamer, and Emmett Kelly, the world famous clown. He was known for taking a broom and sweeping the spotlight on the floor into a little, tiny light until it disappeared.

Dad bought me an autograph book. He got many of the circus performers to sign it. One of the clown's autograph included a quickly drawn caricature of himself. It was very good, and looked just like him. On the nights that we didn't have the neighbor kids with us, Dad would take us to the dressing rooms to meet the performers.

I remember that most of them had foreign accents. When Dad introduced me to Clyde Beatty, I saw long scars on his arms. Mr. Beatty told me they were from a lion attack. Then, off to where the animals were, and where the odor back there was almost overpowering, but the chance to see all those animals up close and talk to their trainers was well worth the unpleasantness of the odors around us.

We could pet some of the animals, and some animals we were even allowed to feed. I remember this wonderful time in my life fondly. I still have the autograph book that Dad gave me with all the autographs he was able to get.

The anticipation and excitement, the wonder and the magic that circus generated was almost too much for a little girl, but it paled in comparison to when Dad brought some of the performers home for dinner. One particular evening we had several clowns all in costume, a bear trainer, a lion tamer, and a beautiful, trapeze artist named

Muzetta. I remember one of the clowns juggling in the living room, and another pulled a bouquet of flowers out of his sleeve. One clown performed magic tricks and then a disappearing act. My sisters and I looked all over for him. In the closet, outside, and I don't remember when or where he reappeared. I think I was five or six at the time. With all the excitement and laughter at the dinner table, I could hardly eat.

Muzetta was a beautiful lady. She came in her circus costume with lots of sparkly makeup. I begged Mama for weeks to buy me makeup like Muzetta's. Her brightly colored clothes, along with her sequined tiara had quite an effect on me. I often dreamt about joining the circus.

Years later I ran into an old schoolmate, Mary Jean Guidobono. When we were kids she lived on the corner of Pinehurst and Keeler, just four houses from St. Francis de Sales where we went to school. We attended grade school together. She remembered piling into our car to go to the circus. She told me that if it hadn't been for my dad, she would never have been able to see the circus.

5

Remembering Mama

When Mama, Elissa Madeleine Brault was born, January 10, 1900, the century itself was just beginning. She was born of French Canadian parents from Quebec who settled in Manitoba in the 1880s and had seven children. Two boys died in infancy, and four of their five daughters lived to old age. Mama was born in St. Boniface, Manitoba, a French enclave just across the Red River from Winnipeg, amid French Canadian family traditions firmly set in the 19th century.

Memories of her childhood are full of the Catholic tradition. Mama was the youngest of five daughters.

Mama

Mama was the tallest at 4'11." The family was bilingual. They were all sophisticated, well educated, accomplished women. My Grandfather was a successful business man, having owned rental property, a liquor store, a grocery store, and an insurance business. I never knew Mama's parents. They both died before I was born. My Grandfather, Philias Michael, died on March 3, 1935, just after receiving Holy Communion at Visitation Church in Detroit. My Grandmother, Rose Velina died of cancer in 1938 at home at 15494 Pinehurst, my childhood home.

St. Boniface was known as the Cathedral City. The beautiful St. Boniface Cathedral was just a few blocks from Mama's house. Her maternal grandparents lived down the street from her. Her Grandpa Desiré Fisét was one of the stonemasons that helped build the cathedral.

Back then it was really amazing to see that huge, magnificent structure in a little town out in the middle of the prairie. It was much larger than any of the churches in Winnipeg, which by comparison, at the time, was a large metropolis. It was the third largest city in Canada. This is the same cathedral mentioned in John Greenleaf Whitter's poem "The Red River Voyageur."

> The voyageur smiles as he listens
> To the sound that grows apace
> Well he knows the vesper ringing
> Of the bells of St. Boniface.

When Mama reminisced about her childhood, it was an idyllic time in her life. It reminded me of Louisa May Alcott's *Little Women*. Just as in that story, Mama and her sisters all got along with one another, even as adults they all lived near each other, with the exception of Aunt Cee and Uncle Bill who lived in Vancouver, BC. They were all very close. I never heard them ever speak unkindly to one another. My dad loved Mama's family.

They all went to St. Mary's Academy in Winnipeg, a boarding school nearby. My Grandmother had gone to the academy also. They were weekly students. In that same French tradition, Dad agreed to Mama's wish that my sisters and I also go to boarding school. We attended the Ursuline Academy in Chatham, Ontario, as monthly students. Since Chatham is two hours from Detroit, we came home one week-end each month. We loved it there and have many wonderful memories.

Mama graduated from Manitoba Agricultural College in 1921 and taught the primary grades at King George V School in Norwood, Manitoba. On July 10, 1926, Mama married Cyril Gustave Muller in

St. Boniface. He was a city engineer in Winnipeg. He came from a well respected family in the Winnipeg/St. Boniface area.

They separated for a few years before their divorce was final in 1936. After that, Mama would always refer to Cyril as "The Skunk." She never referred to him by his name, just "The Skunk."

It was years later, when I was researching the family that I found his name. I said to Mama one day, "Does the name Cyril mean anything to you?" She looked askance at me, and I started laughing.

"What more do you think you're going to find when you dig up our relatives?' Mama said. Actually I found very little to embarrass the family on the French Canadian side.

When they separated, Mama moved to Chicago and sang on the radio from the Palmer House. She had years of formal training as an opera singer and was known as the "Voice of French Canada." Mama once sang on the radio with Guy Lombardo and the Royal Canadian Orchestra. The band touted they had "The sweetest music this side of heaven."

The following articles appeared in the Winnipeg newspapers (this would have to be the late twenties or early thirties.) Mama sang this very beautiful lullaby from the opera *Jocelyn* by Benjamin Goddard.

As the "flickering shadows softly" came and went, a hush fell over the gathering as Madame Elissa Brault-Muller mounted the stand and began the beautiful strains of "Berceuse de Jocelyn" by Goddard. Her rich voice rolled across the silent multitude and echoed far and beyond the shadowing fringe of trees. As the last notes died away on the quivering air, unstinted applause burst from the audience. Many did not know the words, but all knew the sentiment.

Mme. Eliza Breault-Muller, who is known to radio listeners throughout Manitoba as one of the soloists on the "French Hour" will be the featured artist Wednesday night. She will sing the "Berceuse" from "Jocelyn" by Goddard.

A special drop fare of 5 cents will prevail from 7 to 10:30 p.m. Wednesday to make it easy for Winnipeg citizens to attend the Night of Community Song. Provencher cars will take community singers right to the Old College grounds on Provencher avenue.

All Winnipeg and St. Boniface are invited to participate in the Night of Song, to come and sing.

In the 20s and 30s Mama sang at weddings and funerals of friends and family. Her "Ave Maria" by Franz Schubert was so beautiful. I feel so blessed that I was able to hear Mama's beautiful soprano voice before it was compromised by age.

When Mama got upset with our antics, especially mine, she would speak to us quietly through clenched teeth. We knew then and there that we had gone too far. I don't remember who I was more afraid of, Mama or Dad with his swearing and all. Mama had wonderful expressions that she used when appropriate, for instance if Mama didn't feel she was dressed properly, she would say that she looked like the "Wreck of the Hesperus," the ship in Longfellow's poem, or if she hadn't agreed with someone, she would tell us that they could "go cook a radish," or that they had "such crust." If she liked someone, she would refer to them as "a good egg." When Mama got excited she would use expressions like "good gravy!" When she got mad, she'd say things like, "good heavens" or "my God" or "good grief," usually in French. I won't go into what Dad would say, but his expressions were priceless.

One of the funniest quirks about Mama was that she was uncomfortable talking about certain things. For example she never referred to the bathroom by name, it was either the restroom or the ladies' room, or mens' room, whichever was appropriate. Her chest, she referred to as, her balcony, and her derriere was her grand piano. She had a wonderful sense of humor. One time, she must have been in her eighties, her bra strap broke. Mama, who was well-endowed, said, "The balcony has gone down to the mezzanine." When her sister Anna died, Mama told us she died from liver cancer. I found out years later it was colon cancer. God forbid Mama would ever talk about anyone's colon! For years she told us Dad died from a rare form of bone cancer. It was prostate cancer.

Growing up, Mama lived quite comfortably. Years ago when I was doing oral history of Mama's family, I asked her what tasks she had to perform when she was a little girl. "Tasks!" she said, "What tasks?""You know, like doing dishes or vacuuming.""We didn't do any of that, Scholastique did all the housekeeping; all we had to do was play," she said. Scholastique was the housekeeper.

Sometime in the 30s, Mama and Aunt Mac were having lunch in a Windsor restaurant. Windsor is primarily an English speaking town, just across the Detroit River. Mama and Aunt Mac sat down near two young gentleman who were speaking French. Mama and Aunt Mac were always well dressed, small in stature, and very attractive young ladies. Sitting down and looking over the menu, they overheard these two gentlemen making lots of comments about them, in French. Mama and Aunt Mac kept speaking to each other in English. They were enjoying the nice compliments the men were giving them. When they were through eating, Mama went over to their table, and in her perfect French, thanked them for all the complimentary things they said. Mama said, "Their mouths fell open. They were clearly embarrassed." Mama and Aunt Mac left the restaurant smiling.

I had to run to answer the phone one day. It was Mama, and she wanted to know what took me so long.

"I was out in the garden," I told her.

"Out in the garden?" She said. "You don't have your hands in the dirt, do you?"

"Yes, I do." I told her.

"Why are your hands in the dirt? If you must work in the dirt, be sure to wear gloves or you'll get arthritis."

By coincidence, I have arthritis in my hands, and when Mama died at age 95, she had very little arthritis in her hands, or anywhere else for that matter. Perhaps she knew something.

Mama and Dad were always in love with each other and both were affectionate people, with each other, and with us.

When Dad died, Mama was 57 years old, Dad was 58. Marguerite, Joanie and I were all teenagers. For such a fragile looking person, Mama was very strong. She had nursed Dad through six months of pain and anguish until he finally, mercifully, died of cancer.

She maintained full composure throughout the whole ordeal and the funeral. She said that her years with Dad and us were by far the happiest years of her life. Coming from a woman who not only had an idyllic childhood, came from a well-to-do family, married a city engineer, divorced him and then married my dad, a Detroit police officer, that was quite a compliment to my dad, and well deserved. It was a wonderful thing to hear.

Mama and "the aunts" always wore beautiful, expensive, fur coats. You can hardly live through a winter out on the Canadian prairie without a fur or two! Marguerite had bought a really cute, rabbit fur jacket, and while visiting Aunt Cee and Mama, asked Mama, "How do you keep your furs from shedding?"

Mama replied condescendingly, "I wouldn't know. My furs don't shed." Mama never liked Marguerite's jacket because rabbit isn't exactly mink. Mama stressed her point when we were visiting Dad's cousin Howard in Royal Oak, and his Golden Retriever joined us in the living-room. Mama looked at the dog and said to Marguerite, "You know, that's the same color as your fur jacket."

A short time after Dad died, his cousin Bob, Howard's brother, who was a recent widower, wanted to take Mama to lunch. Mama was a bit uncomfortable about Bob, and wanted me to accompany her. I reluctantly agreed. Bob picked the Canopy, a very nice restaurant in Brighton. During lunch, Mama asked Bob what Ruth had died from. Bob and Ruth had been avid golfers. Bob said that Ruth had died from cancer, and he had taken her ashes and spread them around the golf course. "For heaven's sake Bob we're eating." Mama said

Many people have wonderful memories of helping their mothers bake cupcakes or Christmas cookies. They have handed-down, wonderful recipes, and stories of working in the kitchen together. I don't have that. In fact, the only hand-me-down recipes from the family was Mama's French Canadian tomato soup, and Aunt Cee's Scotch shortbread, which no one seems to be able to locate. Aunt Mimi made excellent banana bread, but no one can find that recipe either. Joanie remembers Aunt Mac's wonderful soups. The French Canadians aren't exactly known for their cuisine!

We do have memories of a wonderful mother whose idea of a picnic at the lake was linen tablecloths, and napkins, silverware, china dishes, and a pressure cooker filled with wonderful beef roasts, potatoes, carrots and the best gravy in the world; this was one of Mama's better meals. The only thing missing from our picnic table was candles. People walking up from the lake and passing our picnic table always wanted to know what smelled so good.

I have memories of a mother who always set the table with linens, be it breakfast, lunch or dinner, and don't ever mention paper plates or plastic dinnerware to Mama.

Mama had wonderful tea parties with her grandchildren. She taught them all to play bridge.

I remember Mama taking us to the Detroit Symphony once a month on Tuesday evening at the Masonic Temple. Our next-door neighbor Delbert Flemming drove us.

Mama took Joanie and me, on the bus, to the Olympia Stadium to hear the "Kids on Keys." Hundreds of kids played in unison on beautiful grand pianos. It was 1955, so I was fifteen and Joanie sixteen. It was wonderful.

I have memories of a woman who sang French lullabies to us like "Do-Do Baby" when we were going to sleep at night. Marguerite's children and grandchildren called Mama, Grandma DoDo. Mama babysat for them a lot because Jim and Marguerite both worked. The other children referred to her as Grandma Babe.

Mama helped our Girl Scout troop learn piano for our music badges. Mama was an accomplished pianist. She also taught us French for our language badges.

I have memories of a woman I would try all my life to emulate, but I never quite got to the degree of my mother's wonderful temperament. I remember that she was always and ever the optimist and would say, "It's always darkest before the dawn," and Mama also said, "There's never an excuse for rudeness." I have memories of a woman who was gracious, kind, and understanding, a woman who, in all the 55 years I knew her, was never depressed, no matter how difficult the situation. I remember a very strong woman who was a devout Catholic, who practiced what she preached. Mama was never rude to anyone, ever, even if they deserved it. Jim loved Mama, and she loved him. I would describe Mama as having a happy heart.

When Aunt Cee passed away Mama was 85 years old. They had lived together for the past twenty five years. Mama decided she wanted to paint again. She was an artist but hadn't painted in years, so we encouraged her to take up her oils again. She liked to use oils and loved painting landscapes. Not only had it been quite a while since she had painted, she then had macular degeneration to contend with, but we still encouraged her, and she painted a nice piece of scenery with a river running through it. It was not her best work, but was wonderful for a woman considered legally blind.

I took her to Howell to a very nice framing studio where we were greeted at the door by a rather young receptionist and her husband, the owner, a well dressed man in his early to late fifties. He started to show Mama some frames. He looked at the painting and made a snide remark about it. I glanced at Mama. She didn't flinch. I thought, thank goodness she didn't hear that remark. We continued looking at a few more frames, then Mama thanked the owner and said good bye.

We stopped by the receptionist on the way out, and Mama said to her in a louder than usual tone, "Well, tell your father, thank you very much," and we left. Outside I said to Mama, "You know Mama, he's not her father, he's her husband."

Mama replied, "Oh, I know that." I loved it. Mama was a master of the subtle put down. She was always dignified and polite.

In 1986 Mama and I attended her grandson Billy's graduation. Billy had Down Syndrome There must have been fifty mentally challenged young adults graduating. Mama and I were sitting near the back. As we're watching the ceremony, I turned to Mama and told her,

"I can't take this anymore, I have to leave."

"You ought to be ashamed of yourself. These are all God's children," she said.

"No, Mama, it's the rocking back and forth every which way. It's making me nauseous."

Every graduate was incessantly rocking, without stopping, during the ceremonies. I went outside to get fresh air and calm my stomach down. I have severe motion sickness.

Mama baby-sat the kids every now and then. She lived in Brighton at the time, which is about twenty minutes from the house. On this particular day, our friend Doug had come over. I was about to leave and take Mama home. Doug offered to drop her off, since it was on his way. He told Mama he had a pick-up truck. Mama told him that would be fine. Doug has a good sense of humor, and he's quick. Mama was about to get in the truck, when Doug offered to help, but she struggled a little and got in. Doug said,

"You're pretty spry for an old gal."

Old gal. I thought. Mama's not going to like that

"Who told you my age?" Mama asked.

"Diane talks in her sleep,"

Mama got a kick out of that. She said, "Doug you're terrible."

None of our other friends could have gotten away with that,

For years when I was growing up Mama played bridge with her sisters and some French ladies who lived in the area. The first prize was always a lovely, English bone china cup and saucer. My sisters and I inherited many of those cups and saucers won by Mama and her sisters. The booby prize was usually a beautiful hat pin, or lapel pin.

Marguerite was visiting Mama at Marycrest Manor Nursing Home in Livonia, in the last year of her life, and she asked Mama where she got the sweater she was wearing, because it was not familiar to her. Mama, in her 95th year was having bouts now and then with dementia. She told Marguerite that her mother had given it to her. Marguerite said, "Mama, your mother died sixty years ago."

Putting her hands together as if in prayer and looking up to the heavens, Mama replied, "Dear Lord, I want to thank you for giving me a daughter who knows everything."

Mama was one classy lady. I miss her every day.

6

Mama and the Landfill

When Jim and I moved to rural Hamburg, we had to get used to many things. Being from the city, we had no idea about septic tanks, septic fields, or landfills. Most people call it the "dump," but it sounds so crass.

This particular day, if memory serves me, I was taking Mama home after she had spent the weekend with us. I had a few errands to take care of and decided, since the dump was on the way, to take a couple bags there. I loaded the kids into the backseat of the car, and Mama in the front. Off we went. As we neared the dump, I explained to Mama that it would just take me a minute to unload the garbage bags. Mama couldn't believe that this is a job I had to do, plus she had never seen a landfill before.

A "dump" conjures up images of broken couches, mounds of garbage, flies, lots of flies, especially in warm weather, rats, and odors so strong from rotting trash it radiates into the air. Sometimes trash flies around when strong winds kick up which only adds to the character of the landfill.

Hidden away off M-36, down a beautiful, winding, tree-lined road, (looks can be so deceiving) I made a right turn at the curve, and there it was… with mounds of trash twenty feet high or more. At the bottom was a large heap of strewn garbage bags and other such items that for whatever reason didn't make it onto the pile.

When it rained you really had to wear boots or you would sink ankle deep in slush or worse. To the right side, before you got to the heap, used furniture was lined up alongside appliances, TVs, and lamps. This was for the convenience of any one wanting these discarded items.

To use the township dump, residents had to go to the Township

Hall and buy a ticket for $10.00. It had ten punches on it, one punch for each bag of garbage. The old man who ran the "dump" punched your card. He was known as "the Candy Man" because he gave candy to the children and treats to any pets in the car.

You parked your vehicle as close to the pile of garbage as possible; you got out and started hauling your bags of trash to the heap. Take one bag at a time, swing it back and forth a few times to get some momentum going, then fling it in the air towards the heap. As you can imagine, men were a lot better at this than the women. That's probably why you didn't see women there very often.

This was only my second time there. Why I went the second time I'm not sure, but more importantly, why I brought Mama defies reasoning, or as Jim later said laughing, "What possessed you to take your mother there; what were you thinking? She's not my mother, but even I know not to take her there."

Mama always was a city girl. While I was taking care of hurling the trash, the Candy Man approached the car and leaned in the window to talk to Mama and the kids.

When I got back to the car, the Candy Man was handing the kids candy, and Mama was thanking him and smiling. Things are going pretty well, I figured. I got in the car, and Mama immediately wanted me to roll up the windows as I drove out. The smile was gone from her face. Mama turned towards the kids in the back seat and said in the low, soft voice, between clenched teeth that she only used when she was upset, "Give me that candy."

"But Grandma."

"Give me that candy."

"But Grandma, he's the Candy Man! He gives everyone candy when they come here."

"He's filthy, he works in this filthy place all day, and you're not going to eat anything he gave you. I'll buy you candy."

Mama turned to me, again with her teeth clenched, and in that low tone of hers, said, "I can't believe you come to a place like this and you bring the children. What kind of a place have you moved to that doesn't have trash pick up?"

"We don't have trash pick-up out here, Mama. We're out in the country. This is a rural area."

"Well, this is no place to take the children."

We stopped at the Dairy Queen and Mama bought us all ice cream.

7

My Aunts

Mama was the youngest of five daughters. Celina Philamene, (Aunt Cee) was named after both her grandmothers. There was a little boy, Amable Zeno Domina, who died at thirteen months. He was born one year after Aunt Cee. Margaret Bella Clara, (Aunt Mac) was named after her Aunt Marguerite. Emelia Marie, (Aunt Mimi) was named after her Aunt Emelia, and Anna Rosina (Aunt Anna) was named after her mother, Rose Velina. My mother, Elissa Magdeleine (Babe) was named after her Aunt Elisa. The youngest was a little boy, Philias Domina, named after his father, who died at eight months old, when Mama was five years old.

My aunts were much older than my sisters and I. My first cousins were born in 1918 and 1921, whereas my sisters and I were born in 1937, '39 and '40. Consequently, we did not have the kind of family that had big picnics and get-togethers playing sports and such because of that great gap in our generation.

My aunts were polite, refined, respectable and very approachable. Proper manners ruled the day in our family. The aunts were also kind and loving. In fact, genteel is probably the best description for them. I can't say enough about these remarkable women I have always admired. They dressed in the latest fashions and always wore hats. As my mother would say, "A hat completes the ensemble".

My aunts lived a couple miles from us when we were growing up, except Aunt Cee who lived with Uncle Bill in Vancouver, British Columbia. They had gotten married September 27, 1920, lived in St. Boniface a couple years, and then Uncle Bill accepted a position with the Canadian Pacific Railroad in Vancouver.

Mama told me Grandpa was very sad to see Aunt Cee move so far away. They lived in a lovely apartment at 1183 Pacific, facing the

Pacific Ocean with the mountains in back, not very far from beautiful Stanley Park. They both lived in that same apartment until Uncle Bill died in 1960 just before my wedding. Imagine renting for 40 years!

Since the family never talked of such things, it was believed that Aunt Cee had a benign tumor on her uterus and consequently had to have a hysterectomy. She was never able to have children.

When Aunt Cee, and Aunt Mac were born, Benjamin Harrison was President of the United States, and Sir John A. MacDonald was Prime Minister of Canada. Aunt Cee was a very devout Catholic, as were all the aunts. I never heard her ever speak ill of anyone. A couple years ago, Dave asked me, in front of his wife Lisa, "Who was or is the nicest person you've ever known?"

Without hesitation I said, "Aunt Cee."

"See, I told you," he said. "Every one loved my Aunt Cee".

At age 95, Aunt Cee was taken to the hospital with pneumonia. She was in critical condition, and because of her age, was not expected to survive. When Julie and I went to visit her she was in an oxygen tent. Julie start to cry, which was unusual for her. I asked her why this was upsetting her so. "No one I loved ever died before," she said. Aunt Cee died the following day.

One time Aunt Mimi got upset with the three of us for wearing slacks to go Christmas shopping at Northland Center, just outside Detroit. Northland was a milestone for shopping centers in the country after World War II. It opened in 1954 and had a J.L. Hudson store with four levels. At that time it was the largest shopping center in the world, and Hudson's was the second largest department store in the country next to Macy's in New York. Coming back to Aunt Mimi, she was a strict Catholic and shared her views generously with the family whether they wanted to hear them or not.

We were teenagers, and Aunt Mimi thought it unseemly for us to wear slacks for other than playing. My dad liked Aunt Mimi a lot but referred to her as, "The Pope's Assistant." She had opinions on everything.

My aunts and Mama always set the most beautiful tables. Limoges china, sterling silver, cut glass, beautiful linen tablecloths and napkins, or as Mama and her sisters referred to them, serviettes. We never had a children's table. My parents always had us eat at the dinner table with the adults. At formal meals we had wine with the adults, only ours was watered down.

My children always remembered Aunt Cee's wonderful Scotch shortbread. Her husband, Uncle Bill (William Wallace Oakley) was born in Edinburgh, Scotland; maybe she got the recipe from him. Their way of cooking really hit home with me when I was invited to Jim's house for dinner. His mother cooked like a chef. Her meals were fabulous. It was then that I realized what I was missing. To this day I've never tasted anything that comes close to my mother-in-law's cooking.

Aunt Cee came to live with Mama in 1961, a year after Uncle Bill died. Aunt Cee and Mama always got along. She lived to be 95, and with the exception of the hysterectomy, Aunt Cee was never ill or in the hospital until she succumbed to pneumonia and passed away one month after her 95th birthday. Her mind was always sharp, and she never once missed mass on Sunday. She was the only one of my mother's sisters who remained a Canadian citizen.

Aunt Mac was engaged to a Scotsman, Sergeant Auld, who was killed in World War I. She never dated or married after his death. She was about 25 years old when he was killed. She joined her parents in Detroit around 1926. She lived with them in an apartment at 1721 Collingwood near 12th Street, on the west side of Detroit. They were beautiful apartments with hardwood floors and marble window sills. All the apartment buildings were brick, and some had beautiful bay windows. It was a wonderful neighborhood with stately elm trees lining the streets. This was the same neighborhood that thirty five years later was near the center of the 1967 Detroit race riots.

Grandpa Brault died March 3, 1935, at Visitation church just after receiving communion. He is buried in Holy Sepulcher Cemetery at Beech Daley and Ten Mile Road, in Southfield. Most of Mama's relatives are buried there except Aunt Cee who is buried in Vancouver next to Uncle Bill, and Mama who is buried next to Dad in Grandlawn Cemetery at Seven Mile and Telegraph Rd.

After Grandpa Brault passed away, Grandma Rose bought a house at 15494 Pinehurst, and Aunt Mac, Aunt Anna and Mama moved in with her. It so happened that my dad was renting a house next door. That's how Mama and Dad met. When they decided to get married, my dad exchanged a piece of property on Birwood for a down payment on the house on Pinehurst. When the house was completed on Birwood, Aunts Mac and Anna moved in, as well as cousin Edmo. They lived within walking distance from us.

Aunt Mac lived on Birwood until 1965 when Aunt Cee, Aunt Mac and Mama rented an apartment together at Sevlen Manor on the corner of Seven Mile and Telegraph. Aunt Mimi and Uncle D rented an apartment there, as well as Edmo and his wife Lulu. There was a swimming pool at the apartment, and visitors were welcome to swim on Tuesdays. My kids loved it, especially when their cousins were able to join them.

At the time of her death in 1977, from a stroke, Aunt Mac had worked at New York Central Railroad in Detroit in the accounting offices for 42 years and retired at age 82. She passed away two years later. Aunt Mac was Joanie's godmother.

When Aunt Mimi was born, Grover Cleveland was President of the United States and Sir John Thompson was Prime Minister of Canada.

Aunt Mimi married James Edouard Desilets (Uncle D), on September 14, 1920, a week before Aunt Cee got married. Their only child, a son, Louis Emile was born on June 21, 1921, in St. Boniface, Manitoba. They moved to Detroit in 1926, and lived in an apartment on Byron around the corner from my grandparents. Louis went to Visitation High in Detroit. He died in Detroit in 1941 of a neurological disorder. He was 20 years old. He was my godfather. Aunt Mimi and Uncle D visited his grave at Holy Sepulchre cemetery every Sunday until Uncle D died in 1973; he was 82 years old. Aunt Mimi and Uncle D celebrated their 50th Wedding Anniversary in 1970.

In 1948 my Aunt Mimi and Uncle D went to Three Rivers, Quebec, to bring home Louis Gil, Uncle D's brother's youngest son. He was named after the first Louis. Uncle D's brother had died, and his wife had a nervous breakdown, and since Louis was the youngest of five boys by at least ten years, there was no one to help bring him up. Aunt Mimi and Uncle D brought Louis back to Detroit but were unable to adopt him because of their age, but they were able to raise him.

Louis started kindergarten, but since he could only speak French, Aunt Mimi would put him on the school bus with a note pinned to his pocket that said his name and address. Louis was close to my age, and as adults, he and his wife Lynn attended many of our neighborhood picnics. Louis was a lot of fun. He died in 1991, at 47, having suffered from leukemia for 15 years.

Louis always had a good story to tell. One he told Jim and me was about a day when he was coming home from Cooley High School. He got off the Puritan bus a couple blocks from home so he could smoke a cigarette. As he was walking along Puritan Avenue, he flicked his cigarette up in the air behind him, in front of one of the stores. His house is only two or three minutes away. When he got home he heard sirens blaring down Puritan Avenue. He looked down the street and saw the awning on the store where he'd flicked his cigarette was on fire.

My dad felt sorry for Louis, probably because his mother, like Dad's, had not been able to raise him. Dad took our bike that we had grown too big for and fixed it up, painted it red, and gave it to Louis. It was similar to a chain driven Mercury tricycle and had a longer body than most tricycles. Louis was thrilled. His wife Lynn told me years later that Louis was so proud of that bike because it was the fastest bike in the neighborhood.

When Aunt Anna was born in 1896, Grover Cleveland was President of the United States, and Sir Mackenzie Bowell was Prime Minister of Canada. Aunt Anna was my godmother.

Aunt Anna married Big Edmund Lafrance January 18, 1918. They had a son Edmond Ernest Eli, born October 11, 1918. We always referred to Edmond Ernest as Edmo, as opposed to his father who was referred to as Big Edmo. Sadly, Big Edmo came down with influenza and died five months later. He was 24 years old. Mama said St. Boniface Cathedral was so packed for his funeral because all the churches and other public places had been closed during the epidemic. People were discouraged from meeting in large groups for fear of contaminating one another.

Big Edmo's younger brother Ernest Lafrance died September 3, 1918, in World War I. He was 22 years old. Anna's mother-in-law, Evangeline Lafrance, was a widow. She came to Anna a short time after Big Edmo died and signed over his insurance policy because, as she said, "That would be what he would have wanted."

Aunt Anna was only 21 when Big Edmo died, and her baby was five months old. Aunt Anna and little baby Edmo lived next door to Grandma and Grandpa in an upstairs flat that the grandparents owned. Anna never remarried, and she never dated. Edmo got lots of attention when he was little. He was right next door to his Grandma, Grandpa and two aunts who all doted on him.

I have explained how proper my aunts were, Edmo was not. He was always joking and horsing around. We just loved him. While he was using his crutches he would tease the aunts by using them for balance while kicking his legs around off the ground. Edmo was a big man. He would get such a rise out of the aunts, we could not stop laughing. Of course they were afraid he'd injure himself more. His ankle had been so badly broken that the doctors had seriously considered amputating his foot. So you could see why he would get such a rise out of them.

Even though Edmo was a veteran of WWII, the aunts still felt so protective of him. My sisters and I always got a kick out of him. The only one he could really rile was Aunt Mimi when they played bridge. They were all very good players. I don't know if Edmo was a good player, but every time they played cards with Edmo we knew something was going to upset Aunt Mimi. We were never sure what was upsetting her because everything was in French. Her sisters kept telling her, "He's just teasing," but he could always get under her collar. It was funny. Aunt Mimi was never upset for long. She really loved Edmo.

Nobody could stay mad at Edmo, and before the day was out Aunt Mimi was good again only to wait for the next bridge game. Edmo just couldn't help himself. He actually teased all the aunts the same way, but probably because Aunt Mimi was somewhat feisty and the others weren't, they either laughed or just ignored him.

In my aunts' lifetimes airplanes were invented, phones and radios came into use. They went from horse and buggy to automobiles. They travelled by train extensively throughout Canada. It was very luxurious compared to the way we travel today. They were all taught by nuns at private schools. Aunt Cee was the first of my aunts to wear slacks. She was in her 80s when she bought a pant suit. She looked so cute.

My sisters and I loved our aunts. They were wonderful people, and they all got along so well with one another. We always loved visiting with them.

8

My Cousins

Edmond Ernest Elie Lafrance (Edmo), and Louis Emile Desilets were my only first cousins. Edmo was the only child of Aunt Anna and Uncle Edmond (Big Edmo). Louis was the only child of Aunt Mimi and Uncle "D".

Louis was born in 1921 and died of a neurological disorder in 1941. He was my godfather. My sisters and I never got a chance to know him.

He was born in St. Boniface, and moved with his parents to Detroit in 1926 when he was 5 years old. He graduated from Visitation High School in 1938 and attended the University of Detroit until he was bedridden. Edmo would visit Louis after he got sick, and played the piano to entertain him. Louis died a few months later. He is buried in the family plot at Holy Sepulchre Cemetery in Southfield, Michigan.

Edmo was born October 11, 1918 in St. Boniface and died of an acute coronary thrombosis on January 8, 1972.

Edmo's father, Big Edmo, as he was referred to, died before Edmo was a year old. His mother never remarried. He grew up with four doting aunts and loving grandparents. The family was bilingual.

Edmo arrived in Detroit on Feb. 2, 1937. He came to live with his mother, his Grandma Rose and his Aunt Mac. He became a naturalized citizen February 13, 1943. Dad sponsored him and signed his United States citizenship application.

Edmo was educated in the schools in St. Boniface with the exception of the two years he attended Visitation School in Detroit, 1926-1928. It was at this time that his grandmother Evangeline Lafrance died at her home, at 161 Dumoulin, in St. Boniface. Edmo then went back to St. Boniface schools and then to St. Boniface

College, the only French-language university in Western Canada. He majored in Liberal Arts and Business Administration.

Edmo joined the army in 1941. He fought in the Battle of the Bulge in Belgium, and since he was fluent in English, French, German, and Russian, the army stationed him in Neufchateau, Belgium, in the southern region of Belgium where French is the primary language. He was assigned as chief translator and interpreter, translating war damage claims of citizens in the surrounding area. This is where he met and later married Marie Louise (Lulu) Jullion. Her mother's maiden name was Wilvers.

Lulu was a Belgian war bride. When she came to America after the war, she could only speak French, but because she would be living with her mother-in-law and Aunt Mac, who were both fluent in French, it worked out quite well. In fact, Dad and the three of us were the only ones in the family who didn't speak French. The Lafrances and Aunt Mac, all lived at 17342 Birwood in northwest Detroit.

I remember the first time I met Lulu. The family had gathered in the living room, at the Lafrances' residence. When we were kids we always referred to it as Mac and Anna's, or mac and bananas. Lulu came down the stairs. I was six at the time. My first impression was of a beautiful, young, blond woman with a soft voice and a lovely smile.

Edmo began piano lessons at age five. He played classical music beautifully, and also played boogie-woogie and jazz. I don't think there was anything he couldn't play. He was so talented. Later in life he played the pipe-organ at St. Ives on Lasher Rd. in Southfield. I regret never taking the time to go to Mass there to hear him play. When he'd visit us at The Ursuline Academy, everyone wanted him to play boogie-woogie. I always looked forward to his visits, although there weren't many because, at that time, his mother was dying of cancer.

The following story is written in Edmo's own words:

Ginger Snooks and the Honey Cart

I heard this story, which is true, from my grandfather. Somewhere in it lies a lesson, but I'm not sure what kind.

In 1900, the city of Winnipeg, Manitoba, Canada, had a mayoral election. Politics in those days were very much like politics today. Possibly they used a little more imagination than they do now.

At the time in question, Winnipeg had only the barest facilities in the way of sanitation. Commodes were of the exterior type and were emptied twice weekly by a civil servant who drove a cart carrying a wooden vat type affair, drawn by a middle-aged horse.

One of these civil servants was a gentleman named Ginger Snooks, his actual name. Mr. Snooks was a heavy-set man, about 50 years old, who had never been known to wear anything but leather clothing. He took special pride in his buckskin jacket which had fringes across the shoulder line at the back, and at the elbows.

My grandfather's family was living on Hargrave Street at the time. Mr. Snooks would visit the rear of the premises on Mondays and Thursdays. On these visits he would sometimes step into my grandmother's kitchen for a cup of tea, and he and grandfather would discuss politics. Their views were similar.

Certain persons in Winnipeg looked down on Mr. Snooks because of his calling, and were not above poking fun at him.

As a joke, these persons decided to nominate Mr. Snooks as a candidate for mayor in the forthcoming elections, and accordingly, his name appeared on the ballot. Ginger Snooks came within 47 votes of being elected mayor of the third largest city in Canada . . .

Many times as these stories are repeated, they tend to lose their accuracy. In this case, Ginger Snooks actually ran for city council in Winnipeg. The rest of the story is fairly accurate.

When Dad died, Edmo would come over to our house and help

Mama sort through Dad's things, and he had a lot of things. We had two bedrooms on the second floor, the rest was the attic.

In the attic you could see the ceiling of the back bedroom, my bedroom. Edmo climbed up and was walking around on top of the ceiling being careful to walk only on the joists. Dad had stored some stuff up there.

As I was straightening out my bedroom, I heard a loud crash and an even louder WHOOAA! "Sacré Bleu!" I looked up, and there was Edmo's big foot sticking out of my bedroom ceiling. He wiggled it around for more attention and laughs. We couldn't stop laughing.

Edmo was Marguerite's first choice to walk her down the aisle when she married Jim Kirby, but he couldn't accept because he had broken his leg falling from a tree he was trimming, so Uncle "D" walked her down.

On my wedding day, as Edmo walked me down the aisle, I was so overcome with emotion I started to cry. While, Edmo was walking with me he was whispering funny things to me under his breath, but all I could think of was that I was marrying this wonderful man that my dad would never get to meet, and he was not here to walk me down the aisle.

Edmo and Lulu were Steve's godparents. Edmo also walked Joanie down the aisle on her wedding Day.

He played classical music so beautifully, and he new most of the music by heart. His signature song was "Ronde Alla Turca" by Mozart. To this day when my sisters or I hear it, Edmo immediately comes to mind. He was such a gifted pianist.

He was one of those men who never grows up. They just make everyone happy. Of course, when he played bridge with Aunt Mimi and would tease her, was probably the exception, but Aunt Mimi never stayed mad at Edmo, nobody could.

Sometime after Dad died, Edmo told Mama he had a neighbor who was a handy man and that he would bring him over to help her fix up the house. He told Mama when Ed Lowe showed up, to speak loudly because he was almost deaf. In the meantime, he told Ed Lowe to speak up when talking to his Aunt Babe because she was quite hard of hearing. When they met they were shouting at each other, until Mama figured out what Edmo was up to.

Another time Mama and Lulu were going shopping at Northland. This was in the fifties when people dressed up to go shopping. Mama and Lulu, of course, looked very nice as they always did, and Edmo had to drive them to Northland, since neither of them could drive. Edmo had been painting something in the house, and was still in his painting clothes when he drove them. He parked the car, helped them both out, always the gentlemen, and then proceeded to follow them into Northland. That must have seemed better to him than waiting for them in the car. Lulu kept telling him to go away and to leave them alone and quit following them. After a few minutes of this Edmo said to them in a loud voice, "But ladies, all I want is a dime for a cup of coffee."

Steve was born at 4:00 a.m. at Detroit Memorial Hospital, the old St. Marys, in downtown Detroit across from Detroit Receiving. The hospital always closed their doors after visiting hours, and absolutely no one could get in. Emergencies could be dealt with across the street at Detroit Receiving. In fact, during my three day stay at the hospital, all I heard were sirens day and night.

I was in a private room and Steve was in a little bassinet next to my bed, and who showed up in the wee hours but Edmo. I asked him how he got in. Believe me, no one could get into that hospital during the night. The staff was very strict about that. Edmo said to me, laughing, that he could get in anywhere he wanted. At that time, he worked as a dispatcher at Detroit Police Headquarters downtown. He had just gotten off work, and came to visit his new godchild. He stayed for a while, we talked, and then he went home. He was so thoughtful.

When Steve was 5 years old, Edmo won a child's race car that you sat in to pedal. He gave it to Steve. Steve was so happy with it. He would ride it up and down Grandville, until a couple months later, the boy down the street, who belonged to a large family whose parents never seemed to watch their kids, broke it. Steve sure did enjoy that car while it lasted.

Lulu passed away, at her home in Grand Rapids, from colon cancer. Mama, of course told us that Lulu had died of lung cancer. Lulu was cremated. Her memorial was held some time later at her parish church, St. Thomas the Apostle.

It was a lovely sunny day. The family decided it would be nostalgic to walk to church on the same streets that Lulu walked every Sunday. I was one of the lectors.

The Lafrances are a family of heroes. Edmo received the following information from the Veterans Affairs of Canada, concerning his Uncle Ernest Lafrance who served in World War I. Ernest was killed in action in France on September 3, 1918, with the Canadian Field Artillery. He was a gunner. He was awarded the British War and Victory medals, which were given to his mother in 1921. He is buried in plot 1, Row A, grave 3, Drury Crucifix cemetery, Drury, France. Drury is a village some twelve miles Southeast of Arras.

Edmo served in WWII as a sergeant in the 9th Armored Division, and fought in the Battle of the Bulge. He worked as a chaplain's assistant in the European Theater of Operations, and assisted with chapel duties, played the pipe-organ for church services, and handled correspondence and paper work. He was also chauffeur to the chaplain. His vehicle of transportation was a jeep.

He was demoted to private when he went AWOL to marry Marie Louise Jullion. He was awarded the American Campaign Medal, recognizing his performance in the American Theater of Operations during WWII, three Bronze Stars, they are the fourth highest military award and the ninth highest by order of precedence in the U.S. military, the Good Conduct Medal, and a WWII Victory Medal. His Honorable Discharge was given at Camp Atterbury, Indiana Dec. 31, 1945.

André, Edmo's son, served honorably in the Vietnam War. He was in the Third U.S. Army Co. B, 5th Aircraft Maintenance Battalion. He was mainly involved in helicopter rescue missions. He was a sharpshooter (M-14 Rifle). NDSM, VCM, VSM. 2 O/S Bars and a Good Conduct medal.

Edmo didn't live to see André graduate from Western Michigan

University with a BA in English, or Josianne graduate from Aquinas College also with a BA in English.

André became a school teacher and married Carol deMoor, also a school teacher. They have two children, Andrew Jerome and Kathryn Marie Louise. Andrew (Andy) married Kristy. They have a daughter Jaslyn. Kathryn (Katie) married Denis Rice, they have a son Mason Kennedy.

After several years of marriage, Carol and André divorced. Years later, André married Penny Jepson. They live in Battle Creek with Penny's granddaughter Zoe.

Josianne never married. She lives in Grand Rapids in the sorority house she lived in while in college. Lulu bought the house, and Josie renovated it and lives there now.

9

My Hometown

As I walked down Grandville to say goodbye to my neighbors, I began to realize that I was leaving my hometown for good. We were taking the children out of their familiar surroundings, out of their school, St. Suzannes, that they loved, and from all their friends, to start new friendships on Hamburg Lake, forty miles northwest of Detroit.

I was born in Detroit in 1940. I lived at 15494 Pinehurst for the first twenty years, then married Jim Wrobleski in 1960 and moved to an upstairs flat on the east side at 20153 Keating near State Fair and John R.

My son Steve was born while we lived there and was baptized at St. Rita's Church. We were there four years, then bought a house at 9976 Grandville near West Chicago and Evergreen. It was while we were living there that Dave and Julie were born. They were baptized at St. Suzanne's Church. We lived there nine years.

As a child growing up on Pinehurst on the west side of Detroit, there were elm trees in front of every house in our neighborhood. In fact, they were everywhere in the city. When the trees became overgrown their branches would reach down and lightly touch the top of the cars as they drove down the street. It was like driving through a tunnel of trees. They were magnificent. We used to hide behind them when we played Hide and Seek, or Cowboys and Indians.

In the fall we would rake the leaves into great piles by the curb and play in them until Dad came home. When he lit the leaves, the plumes of smoke permeated the air with an unforgettable aroma. That aroma was one of the wonders of my childhood. To this day, whenever I smell burning leaves, I remember my childhood living on Pinehurst.

Since St. Francis de Sales was just down the street, my sisters and I would come home for lunch like clockwork at 11:20 and return at

12:20. Mama would have a nice hot, bowl of soup waiting for us on cold winter days.

In the mid-forties, when we were little, Mom and Dad would take us to the Masonic Temple near downtown, to see current movies. This Masonic Temple is the largest in the world.

It was just after World War II, and we didn't have a car, so we would take the Trumbull streetcar to Cass Avenue near downtown. The Trumbull line went downtown and then returned to the other end of the line at Birwood and Fenkell, just a couple blocks from our house. The tracks turned off Fenkell onto Birwood and the streetcar would have to be turned around to face the opposite direction. I don't remember how that occurred, but I do remember that one time during this process it tipped over. The Trumbull streetcar was taken out of service in 1951. By 1956 all the street cars in Detroit were gone. What a shame, because they all ran on electricity.

My best friend Mary Ann Froslie and I would take the Fenkell bus downtown via Twelfth Street, when we were twelve. We would have a Sanders hot fudge sundae and then go to Hudson's mezzanine and buy Nancy Drew books. As soon as we got home we read our newly bought mysteries in one day, and then traded with each other, so we actually got two books for the price of one. I remember my first Nancy Drew book was book seven titled *The Clue in the Diary*.

J.L. Hudson's Department Store was the centerpiece of the downtown shopping area. Its Christmas displays are what I remember the most. In their windows they had moving displays, with little elves helping Santa, and Santa laughing. Other windows showed children ice skating. It all looked so real.

The holidays didn't start until the Hudson's Thanksgiving Day Parade. It was the only commercial free Thanksgiving Day Parade to be televised nationally. Hudson's subsidized the whole thing. The Christmas season didn't begin until the end of the parade when Santa stepped out of his sleigh, said a few words, waved to the crowd, and then took up residence on the twelfth floor of Hudson's, in their vast toy department, to await the children with their Christmas lists.

This store was the second largest department store in the country after Macy's in New York. Hudson's had the world's largest flag. It was unfurled in front of Hudson's during patriotic events. It was 3,700 square feet and covered five stories. It was eventually given to the Smithsonian Institute. Hudson's was also the first department store to have air conditioning. When Hudson's Northland shopping center opened in 1954, it was the largest shopping center in the world.

You have no idea what a wonderful experience it was to grow up in a great city like Detroit. Detroit has public swimming pools, beautiful, tree lined boulevards and 137 beautiful parks, and some of them have rivers that run through them. It is the only city in the country to have an island in the middle of an international seaway. Belle Isle is a little jewel in the middle of the Detroit River. It is the largest island city park in the country and is larger than Central Park. There is a little river meandering through it that you can canoe on, and in winter ice skate on.

Jim used to take me there when we first started dating. He worked at the canoe shelter and after school he took me there with my friend Mary Ann Palutis, who had introduced us a few weeks earlier. Jim would row us to a tiny island in the middle of Belle Isle, and we would do our homework until he was through working. Then he'd take us home.

Bob-Lo Island is located twenty miles south of Detroit where the Detroit River meets Lake Erie. Bob-Lo Island was the ultimate summer playground for the residents of Detroit for over a hundred years. In its hey day, the island housed an amusement park with one of the world's largest dance halls, an elegant restaurant, and a hand-carved carousel. There were two large steam boats, the Bob-Lo boats, complete with dancing and other entertainment, to ferry you to and from the island, which was not accessible by car. There was also a moonlight cruise to Bob-Lo. It circled the island and returned to Detroit. Dinner and dancing as the band played, made for a wonderful evening. Detroit gave me many great memories.

The only time I didn't live in Detroit growing up was from 1952 to 1954 when my sisters and I went to boarding school, The Ursuline Academy in Chatham, Ontario. We loved it there, but of course missed our friends in Detroit.

A favorite place to visit when I was growing up was the Detroit Zoo. It was the first zoo in America to feature animals in open exhibits. It allowed the animals more freedom to roam.

The Michigan State Fair was held in Detroit in late August. It was the nation's oldest state fair. It began in 1849. Jim took me there when we were first dating in 1957.

On Jefferson Avenue downtown, stands the historic Mariners Church. On November 11, 1975, it's bells rang twenty nine times in honor of each sailor lost in the sinking of the *Edmund Fitzgerald*. This was immortalized in the last verse of Gordon Lightfoot's ballad, "The Wreck of the Edmund Fitzgerald":

In a musty old hall in Detroit they prayed,
In the Maritime Sailors' Cathedral
The church bell chimed 'til it rang twenty-nine
For each sailor of the Edmund Fitzgerald."

The church did that for every sailor whose ship sank on the Great Lakes, and over the years there have been many. Also, along the Detroit River there is a unique post office: The J. W. Wescott offers mail-in-a-pail. The mail boat brushes up to the much larger vessels on the river, a rope with a bucket is lowered from the ship to the smaller boat, where messages, mail and other items are placed inside it, and raised back up. It's a floating post office with its own zip code, 48222.

Jim and I graduated from Cass Tech high school which was one of the largest high schools in Michigan at that time. It was a college prep school, considered one of the best in the country. It required a B+ average for admittance. In 1958, there were three grades 10, 11 and 12. The student population was over 2,000 Many famous people graduated from Cass Tech: Ellen Burstyn, John DeLorean, Dianna Ross, Della Reese, to name a few, and Lily Tomlin who went to school when I was there. Her name then was Mary Jean Tomlin. She was voted most popular girl in her senior year. She was a lot of fun and was also captain of the cheerleaders. Charles Lindberg was born in Detroit, and his mother taught chemistry at Cass Tech.

In the fifties when I went to Cass Tech, the ratio of white students to black students was close to 50-50. The three years I went there, I never saw or heard of any fights or disruptions between the students. I had a dress design class where the teacher and I were the only white people in class. I had very nice friends there. Several of them were black, but it was the fifties, so I knew I could never invite any of them to my house and vise-versa. It just wasn't done back then. We each had our hang-out after school. The black students had the Bungalow on Grand River Avenue, and we had Ginny's on the opposite side of the school, on Henry Street. We didn't mingle much outside of school.

Everyone got along, probably because we all had a goal. We wanted a good education. The students at Cass Tech were referred to as the brightest and the best. Remember, these were students from all over the Detroit metropolitan area. They came from diverse backgrounds and economic situations. Several students were from the projects. Some of the graduates that went on to college remarked that Cass Tech was harder than college. Their marching band performed at President Obama's 2013 inauguration.

My wedding day was set for September 3, 1960. That summer, just before the big event, the elm trees really needed trimming. Jim worked for the City of Detroit at that time and unbeknownst to me, had the crews begin trimming the trees a few days before our wedding. I was panic stricken thinking, why couldn't they wait until after our wedding? If they didn't get done by Friday, I was going to have to walk to church from my house which was only a block and a half away, but what if it rained?" Jim finally told me he had requested that the crews do our street. He knew they'd be done on time. The street looked beautiful and the weather was perfect. All went well.

Those beautiful American Elms are gone now, thanks to the elm bark beetle. I've only been down Pinehurst a few times since the trees were taken down. I hardly recognized the street. It's so bare without those elms. I feel sorry for the people living on my old street now; they will never experience the sights and smells of those stately giants. The city did start to plant some trees, but with budget constraints, what they did plant could never compare to those mighty elms.

It's funny how you tend to remember those beautiful scenes from your childhood, but sadly as we grow older those places sometimes fall on hard times. Belle Isle is no exception. There are several beautiful structures on the island including the Detroit Yacht Club, and the beautiful Scott fountain that Jim and I danced around in the moonlight the night of our high school prom. The conservatory that used to house one of the largest orchid collections in the world remains. There are fishing piers, nature trails, a mile and a half long beach, walking and biking trails, a band shell, and a petting zoo, and all this only three miles from downtown Detroit. That island contains many wonderful memories for me.

Detroit is the only place in the country where you look south to see Canada.

You can't talk about Detroit without mentioning Motown. Motown music began in the 1960s. It's an African American music style. It combines gospel, soul, and rhythm and blues. Smokey Robinson, the Four Tops, Martha and the Vandellas all came from Detroit, and all were big Motown stars, as were the Supremes, the Temptations, Gladys Knight and the Pips, Aretha Franklin and Della Reese, to name a few.

In 1962, Jim and I went downtown to the Detroit River to see the sunken ship the *Montrose*, a British ocean vessel. We couldn't believe that a ship had sunk in the Detroit River. All our lives we'd heard stories of the great ship wrecks in the Great Lakes, and over the years there had been plenty, but in the Detroit River?

The British ship collided with a loaded barge. The ship had rolled over on its side. You could see half the ship out of the water. I couldn't believe that the Detroit River was that shallow, or was it that the ship was that wide? The water was 30 feet deep where the ship sunk. One of the newspapers remarked that this incident involving the *Montrose* became the first time a British ship was sunk by an American ship in American waters since the War of 1812.

In 1964 Jim and I bought a house at 9976 Grandville near Rouge Park, a beautiful, 1200 acre park with the Rouge River running through it. When I was little, Dad took me to the Brennan pools at

Rouge Park to swim. They had two diving boards. Dad always dove off the highest one. He loved to swim, and so do I. The Mounted Police had their horse barns at the Park. Years later when Steve was in Cub Scouts we had our Cub Scout picnics there. When the kids were older we'd ride our bikes through the park. It was less than a mile from home.

I was driving through the park one afternoon in the station wagon with the kids, and our Bassett Hound Flower. When I pulled up to a stop sign, a gang of motorcyclists drove up beside us. They were not the good guys in white hats either. I got real nervous when I saw them and told the kids to look straight ahead until we got out of the park. I glanced over at the bikers and saw that they were looking at our car and laughing. I looked back at David who was five years old at the time, with the cutest face, dimples, blond hair and the biggest blue eyes you ever saw. There he was making all kinds of silly faces at them, and next to him was our large English Basset Hound with her doleful look. I couldn't wait to get out of there. . .

Detroit is showing some signs of revival. We have Ford Field, the new Lions football stadium, the new Comerica Park baseball stadium, and soon to be completed, the Little Caesars' Pizza Arena, home of the Red Wings.

During World War II, President Roosevelt referred to Detroit as "The Great Arsenal of Democracy" because of the rapid conversion of much of the auto industry in Detroit to produce armaments. I'm praying that in my lifetime Detroit will be brought to her former grandeur, and everyone will fall in love with her again. As Alexander Pope said, "Hope springs eternal."

10

Christmas Traditions

Holidays sharpen our memories and tend to link the present with the past. Our dining rooms are filled with lively conversations. This is the time of year when families grow together. The hymn that best expresses this is "We Gather Together to Ask the Lord's Blessing."

All my Christmases were white when I was growing up in Detroit. Since my Dad was a policeman, we were never sure until just before Christmas, whether or not he would be able to spend it with us. The tradition in our house was that Christmas, including a turkey dinner, would be at our house because my two older sisters and myself were the only children in the family. Aunt Mimi had Thanksgiving at her house, and Aunts Mac and Anna had turkey dinner at their house on New Years Day.

We hung our stockings on the fireplace, and we would get such nice gifts in them. They were filled with jewelry, small toys, playing cards, small bottles of perfume, and what I remember most was a tall cardboard candle filled with the most delicious chocolate coins wrapped in gold foil.

Since Mama was French Canadian, we followed the tradition among the French to celebrate Little Christmas, January 6th, also called Epiphany, or Twelfth Night. We kept the creche up until Epiphany. Mama and Dad would give us each a small gift.

To this day my sisters and I still talk about Aunt Mimi's gifts. Aunt Mimi didn't have a lot of money, but that never stopped her from giving us Christmas presents. We all got identical gifts, practical gifts like gloves and tams or scarves. Our other aunts gave us lovely gifts that were more expensive, but we don't remember them as much as Aunt Mimi's. The one we remembered the most was the year she gave us each snuggies. As funny as that gift seemed to be at that time (cotton underwear, light peach in color, that practically went down to our knees), we all remembered how they came in handy when we were sledding or ice skating. They really were aptly named: snuggly and warm.

Aunt Mimi was a bit feisty in comparison to Mama's other sisters. They all had wonderful personalities. They were well-bred women with exquisite manners, and all got along well with one another, but Aunt Mimi was a bit more outspoken. We remembered so many things about Aunt Mimi that we still get a kick out of, and we all still miss her.

Dad's police detail, when I was little, was the New York Central Depot near downtown Detroit. It would be the equivalent of having a police detail at the airport nowadays. Trains were the main transportation back then.

One Christmas Eve when I was about eight, we had a terrible snowstorm and all the trains were grounded. Dad had been talking to a family from St. Louis who had a daughter about my age, eight years old, and they were preparing to sleep on benches in the depot Christmas Eve. They were stranded at the depot and wanted to get home to St. Louis for Christmas. Well, that wasn't going to happen, so Dad called Mama and asked if he could bring them home to spend Christmas with us until the trains started running again. How could Mama refuse? They were a very nice family. They had Christmas dinner with us, and if I remember correctly, Dad took them back to the depot the day after Christmas when the trains started running again. They kept in touch with us for years.

At Christmas the depot was always crowded with travelers. Christmas carols blared out over loud speakers, and beautiful decorations were everywhere. I remember one Christmas when Dad came home from work and said "If I hear 'O Little Town of Bethlehem' one more time. . . " and then he ended that sentence with a few choice swear words. The family took that under consideration, and in deference to Dad, no one sang or played it for the rest of the season. We teased Dad about it after Christmas was long past.

One Christmas, Dad told us he was going to give us a gift that would answer any questions we would ever have: *The Books of Knowledge* and *Grolliers Encyclopedia*. Joanie read all the *Books of Knowledge* the first year we had them. We loved those books. Joanie still has them.

A couple of weeks before Christmas, the Shriners always had a Christmas party for all the children of all their members at the Masonic Temple downtown. I remember there was a beautiful ballroom with chandeliers, and that's where the Christmas Party was held each year.

The room looked magical with decorations everywhere and a large Christmas tree with what seemed like a million lights on it. Near the Christmas tree stood a very formal looking chair I knew was for Santa. I kept my eye on that chair even while we ate. We looked forward to that party every year. After dinner Santa would arrive and give out gifts grouped by age. We received the greatest gifts and lots of them, too. There were dolls and doll furniture, wood-burning sets, board games, coloring books and cut-out books, jewelry making kits, tea sets, puzzles of all kinds, and stuffed animals. We each received so much stuff that I don't remember all of it. The trunk of the car was full when we left for home, and so were our stomachs.

We also went to the Policeman's Christmas Party, and it was pretty much the same story—lots of food and tons of presents. I think we received more presents than anyone else in the neighborhood. My sisters remember one Christmas when between us we had at least ten dolls and one or two doll carriages.

There was another Christmas I remember, but not fondly. I believe I was seven when Dad gave me a dollar to go to Kresge's Dime Store to buy a gift for Mama. I must have seen something that I really liked at the store and bought it for myself, but then all I had left was twelve cents, so I bought Mama a little bottle of perfume. When she opened her gift she graciously commented on what a thoughtful gift it was. I felt so ashamed. I couldn't look Dad in the face because I knew, he knew, what I had done. My parents did not believe in corporal punishment, which probably explains why I'm alive today... I think I punished myself more than Dad ever could have. I had never felt so guilty in my life.

Years later, after we were married, Jim and I, like all couples, tried to meld our family Christmas traditions as best we could. It started with Aunt Mimi having a family Christmas party in the basement recreation room of the apartment building where Mama and her sisters lived. Then after Aunt Mimi passed away, Mama and Aunt Cee hosted the family Christmas party. This was held each year on the Sunday before Christmas.

After a few years I hosted the party at my house. We were about 35 people in all. Then a few years later Mama and Aunt Cee decided to host a Christmas brunch at a lovely hotel in Novi, Michigan, the Sheraton Oaks. It later became known as the Double Tree. It was on the corner of Novi Road and I-96 service drive. It was more centrally located for most of the family.

Mama and Aunt Cee paid for the party because they wanted to give us each a gift, but were getting too old to shop or even to know what their children and grandchildren wanted, so the party became our Christmas present each year. We had a separate room at the hotel set up with a Christmas tree that had loads of decorations on it. The hotel was known for its wonderful Christmas brunches, and the Christmas atmosphere was just great. Each table in our room was adorned with beautiful Christmas decorations. Santa would come in to talk with the children. We bought gifts for all the children eighteen years and under. After we ate, Marguerite would hand out the gifts. Aunt Cee passed away in 1985, and we kept up the tradition for ten more years until Mama passed away in 1995.

My nephew Tony had a couple Christmas parties at his house in Warren. My grandson Seth was about five when we went to Tony's house for Christmas. Tony had tables set up in the basement with white tablecloths, and had the buffet set up on the bar. Seth went downstairs to see what it looked like, and immediately ran back upstairs and told me, "Grandma, come and see! There's a restaurant down here." After Christmas at Tony's, Marguerite took up the gauntlet and made arrangements at local restaurants, with each family paying their own share.

One of the last Christmas parties we had was held at Tina and Nasser's house in Dearborn. She has a lovely home that can accommodate thirty or so people quite easily. It wouldn't have mattered if she could have accommodated a hundred people, because the day of the party, there was a blizzard that brought just about everything to a standstill. Only seven or eight people were able to make it. Some of the families were coming from Ann Arbor, Grand Rapids, Kalamazoo, Rochester, Redford and Livonia. Naturally only the ones living nearby were able to make it. Lots of food went to waste that day.

Now, since my two sons and their families live down south, the family has decided that, in lieu of the Christmas party, we would have a family picnic in July at Marguerite's house. That pretty much ended the tradition of the Family Christmas Party in Michigan.

Coming back to my immediate family, my children opened their gifts on the Sunday before Christmas, which was the Family Party, and then on Christmas Eve they opened their presents from Santa. Sometimes in between the Christmas Party and Christmas Eve, Jim would let the kids choose one gift from under the tree to open. On Christmas Eve he played with the kids in the basement while waiting for Santa to appear. He kept telling the kids to listen for the jingle of Santa's bells so they could get a quick glimpse of him. Our next door neighbor Denny would place the bags of gifts on the patio outside the family room, ring the bells, and then high-tail it back to his house. Try as they might, the kids never did see Santa.

On Christmas Day we always hosted a Christmas Open House for neighbors and friends, and the kids had a few more gifts to open. The neighbors tell me to this day that they remembered how good my Egg Nog was. Recipe follows:

Diane's Ultimate Eggnog (serves 25)

1 doz. eggs, separated	I pint (I use 1/2 pint) whiskey or rum
3 c. sugar, divided	1 tsp. nutmeg
1 pt. whipped cream	1 quart half n' half

Separate eggs and stir yolks with whiskey, 2 cups sugar and 1 tsp nutmeg. Let mixture "ripen" in refrigerator 12 to 24 hours. Just before serving, add half n' half to mixture. Beat egg whites, adding one cup sugar while beating, until sugar is dissolved and egg whites are firm.

In separate bowl, whip cream. Fold egg whites and whipped cream into yolk mixture. Sprinkle with nutmeg. Makes 25 servings. It will fill a punch bowl.

Note: I use 1/2 pint Southern Comfort.
Enjoy!

Jim, who was just a kid at heart, loved to watch the kids open their gifts, and this was his way of extending Christmas for as long as possible. He also did all the Christmas shopping for the kids. He loved toy stores and after our kids grew up, Jim and I would visit our neighbors Butch and Cindy and watch Brett and Brandon open their gifts and play with them. The kids loved it. Years later after the neighbor kids were grown, they would tell us how much fun they had when we came over on Christmas.

It wasn't long until our grandchildren came along, and Jim was once again in seventh heaven. It was now back to the toy stores with any excuse he could find, whether Christmas, birthdays or whatever the occasion would be.

Juniper, spruce, and pine are found in most homes at Christmas time. The aroma of pine that welcomes you at the door brings back wonderful memories of Christmas past. Now we spend our winters in Tennessee, and it's here that I use Yankee Candles with either pine scent or apple-cinnamon to replicate the scents of Christmases past.

No matter where you are, the meaning of Christmas remains the same.

All our Christmases bring back such wonderful memories. Christmas has always been our favorite holiday.

11

Route 66

In June 1952, I was in sixth grade at St. Francis de Sales school in Detroit. I couldn't wait for summer vacation to begin because Dad was taking us on our first vacation as a whole family. We had gone on a previous vacation, five years earlier, to Niagara Falls with Uncle "D" and Aunt Mimi, but Dad wasn't able to join us.

Our vacation was going to take us to California on Route 66. I could barely sleep the night before our big trip. My sisters and I each had our own duffel bags for our belongings. I had packed my duffel bag weeks before in anticipation of our exciting adventure. It has been more than sixty years since we took that trip. and my memory fails me sometimes, but I believe Mama and I had the only cameras. I had a Brownie camera, and I lost it down Grand Canyon or actually in the Grand Canyon.

We had always complained to Dad how everyone went on vacation and all we ever did was go on picnics, or to the lake, or to Howell to visit Dad's Aunt Anna. Finally in 1952, the year my Dad retired from the Detroit Police Force, he told us he would take us on a vacation that we would never forget. How right he was . . .

Dad had planned the whole trip to enable us to see as many National and State Parks and as many places of interest as possible. Dad was going to fit it all into a three week adventure. We visited 18 of the 48 states and 12 of the 58 National Parks.

Grandma would not be going on the trip with us. We had to pack our 1950 Ford coupé with luggage for five people, and we also needed room for a three person tent. The back seat of the Ford was very small, and since Mama was under 5 feet tall and I was the youngest and the shortest, (I don't remember how tall I was then) the back seat was designated as our space. In the middle of the back seat we had luggage and what-not, almost piled to the roof, so you can see why Grandma didn't join us on our adventure. The car did have a very large, accommodating trunk, thank goodness. Remember, this was 1952, so there was no air conditioning in our car, and we also didn't have a radio!

A little introduction to the people in this journal that I kept. Dad was 54 years old and just under 6 feet tall. He was the greatest dad in the world. He was lots of fun, and very understanding, but he didn't have a lot of patience. He was also very outgoing, and as the saying goes, "never met a stranger." Mama was 52, a well educated, and well bred woman who had only camped once before. Mama had a wonderful personality and was always very pleasant to be around. When I tell friends about our trip, they can't believe that Mama agreed to go on this adventure. My sister Marguerite was 15 at the time, and like my Dad, almost 6 feet tall. Next was my sister Joanie, 13 years old and a quiet type of person, and lastly, myself, 12 years old. Marguerite and I have the same outgoing personality; neither one of us is very quiet.

A description of our tent: I think it was the same tent Mama and Dad took on their honeymoon in 1936. I'm not sure about that, but it sure looked like it could have been. It was a canvas tent with one double cot, and one single cot, a center pole and a front flap where you had to duck down to get in. When it rained it leaked in the center where the pole was. There was no floor in the tent.

During our whole trip I kept a journal, and what follows is the unabridged, journal of a 12 year old girl. This was a wonderful journey. Comments are interjected as needed.

My Vacation 1952 Diane Stuhlfaut

June 28, 1952 "Eastern Standard " 100 degrees Saturday
We left home this morning at 4:45. We went to Toledo on U.S. 24 and in Toledo we changed to U.S. 25. We entered Toledo at 6:00 A.M. and we went through. We passed such cities as Troy, Dayton, and Cincinnati. We entered Kentucky at about 2:00 P.M. We went to Louisville on U.S. 42 and from there we took US 31E and that took

us to Mammoth Cave National Park. We camped there for the night. We all took showers in the Bath House. We went to bed at 10:P.M. Mom and I slept in the car.

Note: The campground was in the woods. I remember the wonderful fresh smell of the trees, and the outdoors. These were beautiful, tall pine trees.

June 29, 1952 "Central Standard " 98 degrees Sunday

I woke up with mom at 5:10 A.M We cleaned ourselves for the trip ahead and for church. We packed the tent and we left for mass. We went to 9:00 mass at Mammoth Cave Chapel. Then we bought tickets for the tour of the cave. It took us two hours to go through the cave, it was very interesting. A bus took us to the Cave, and when we got off the bus we lined up to get our pictures taken. We went in the cave at 10:A.M. and came out at 1:30 P.M. We got off the bus, a man was selling the pictures for 40 cents a piece, so we each got one. We went to the Hotel to eat lunch. We left Mammoth Cave N. Park at 3: P.M. We visited Abraham Lincoln Memorial Historic Park. There we saw the log Cabin he was born in. While we were riding we saw the house he lived in during his childhood. After we saw this we tried to make Missouri before night. But we didn't make it. We stopped at a gas station and the attendant told dad if he wanted to camp, Pine Knob would be just the place. We rode six miles up a dirt road, then we came in view of Pine Knob. There was 1 General Store and two houses, a Creek and a lake. The people who owned Pine Knob were Mr. and Mrs. Shane, they were very nice, they let us camp on the park near the Creek. It was very hot that day, so dad and I sat in the Creek as it was only a couple feet high. Mrs. Shane told us that she was a straight descendant of Daniel Boone. We ate and then went to bed.

Note: I loved seeing Abraham Lincoln's log cabin, and I remember there was a spring near his cabin, and the water was so clear and smelled so fresh like a little creek of running water. I was told it was the same spring that Lincoln's family used to fetch water for use in their cabin. We continued on our journey to Pine Knob. At Pine Knob the people there were amazed at all the items Dad pulled out of the trunk. They were equally amazed in the morning when Dad was able to put everything back in the trunk. Dad had very little patience putting up the tent each night. It got the best of him more than once. This happened at Pine Knob.

In the midst of the peaceful sounds of the evening, the chirping of the crickets, the croaking of the frogs by the creek, all of a sudden the wonderful sounds of the outdoors were interrupted by my dad and his colorful language or phraseology, damning the tent all to hell and gone, as only he could do. Finally it was up, and he carried on like nothing had ever happened. Do you remember the dad in the *Christmas Story*? Well that was my dad, although I must say he never used any profanity worse than J.Cs, G.Ds, hell, S.O.Bs or bastards. Mama lived to be 95 years old, and I never once heard a swear word come out of her mouth.

June 30, 1952 "Central Standard" 108 degrees Monday

We left Pine Knob at 7: A.M. We rode for about 2 hours then we crossed the Mississippi into Illinois then to Missouri. We were only in Illinois for two Minutes. We went straight through Missouri it was 108 degrees for about 5 1/2 hours then it started to rain, and after that every thing was cool. We rode 2 hours on flat land, then we came to pretty hills full of trees. It rained for quite awhile so we had to get a Cabin in Kansas called Camp Joy Cabins. The rain stopped early in the morning. We all slept well.

Note: We picked up Route 66 in St. Louis. Route 66 was also known as the Will Roger's Highway. It was one of the original highways. Route 66 was established on November 11, 1926. This highway became one of the most famous roads in America. Route 66 served as a major path for those who migrated west, especially during the Dust Bowl of the 1930s. The Gateway Arch wasn't completed until 1965. I saw it years later from a plane. The Mississippi is the largest river I've ever seen. I was surprised how brown it was. I thought it would be blue like the Detroit River. Then I recalled the nickname "Ole Muddy." There were large barges on the river that we could see from the bridge. It was so hot in the car even with the windows down and the wind blowing in at us.We had toothbrushes and little plastic containers that held our manicure sets. They all melted. When that rain came, what a relief. . .

July 1, 1952 "Central Standard " 100 degrees Tuesday

We woke up at about 6: A.M. and it was very nice outside. After we packed and were ready to go I stepped out of the house and saw a big June Beetle about 3 inches long. It had big pinchers, dad put the bug on his key and it hung there till dad shook it off. It took us about an hour to get out of Kansas then we entered Oklahoma. On the way it started to rain so once again everything was cool. We passed over two dried up lakes. They were big lakes too. We went to Claremore, Oklahoma to see Will Rogers Memorial. After we visited the Memorial I bought a Pennant and some post cards. When we went through Oklahoma City we saw lots and lots of oil wells. All the dirt around Oklahoma City was red. It started to get dark so we stopped at a gas station and dad ask the man where we could camp and he said in his yard, so we did. I went to bed at about 11: P.M. I had a very good sleep too.

Note: When Dad told us we were going to visit Will Roger's Memorial we wanted to know who Will Rogers was. Dad was so upset that none of us had ever heard of Will Rogers. He said, and I paraphrase; "What in the hell do they teach you in school nowadys, God damn it. I can't believe you don't know who the hell Will Rogers is." He was one of my dad's favorite entertainers. It was really interesting to learn about this wonderful man. Dad was right. After we had taken in all the information about Will Rogers, I was really glad Dad had us stop. I learned that Will Rogers was a comedian, a humorist, social commentator, Vaudeville performer, actor, and one of the best known celebrities of the 1920s and 30s.

July 2, 1952 "Mountain Standard " 103 degrees Wednesday

Mother woke me up at 6: A.M. We cleaned up and then woke up the others. The lady who owned the gas station showed us how to milk a cow. We entered Texas at 9: A.M. All the land is flat and just a little hilly. Mother stopped in Armarilla, Texas to buy us some clothes. We each got a shirt and shorts. Out side of Armarilla dad bought us a dinner. It wasn't very hot today. We have been riding through the panhandle of Texas. It was 1:55 P.M. when we saw the mountains in Texas, they were the first mountains I ever saw in my life. We entered New Mexico at 1:10 P.M. All there is in New Mexico is Mts. & plateaus. We stopped in Albuquerque to get some Indian stuff. We stopped at a little town called Grant we ate in a café and then we went to bed. I didn't sleep to good, as trains were near by.

Note: I didn't really like milking the cow very much because, for one, I didn't realize how big, cows were up close, and also the odor. Not only did the cow reek, but the stench in the barn was overpowering. I was also afraid the cow might get mad and maybe kick me. The lady laughed and was very patient with me. Marguerite and Joanie milked the cow also.

We saw lots of Burma Shave signs along the highway as we traveled. These were red signs with white block lettering. They were close to the highway. The signs were humorous jingles that were placed at approximately 100 feet apart along the highway. Each sign showed one line of a four-part rhyme until the last line which said, "Burma Shave." We'd read each sign out loud in anticipation of the punch line. It was fun. A few examples:

Within this vale of toil and sin
Your head grows bald,
But not your chin.
Burma Shave

Dinah doesn't Treat him right
But if he'd shave, she might
Burma Shave

Before I tried it, the kisses I missed
But afterward-boy! The misses I kissed.
Burma Shave

In the desert with canvas bag

I remember, in Texas, and perhaps in some of the other western states, Dad would get lots of silver dollars for change in lieu of paper currency.

On the desert there were signs warning drivers to fill up on gas, because gas stations were at least a hundred miles apart. The signs would tell you exactly how many miles to the next gas station. Also, it was required of all drivers to fill a large canvas bag with water and attach it to the hood ornament on their cars before setting out into the desert. Later in the day the owner of the gas station where we stopped for gas told Dad that we could pitch our tent next to his gas station in the middle of the desert. One thing about the desert, it cools off at night and actually has a bit of a breeze.

July 3, 1952

"Mountain Standard " 90 degrees Thursday

This morning mom woke me up at 6:45 and we started off once more. We entered Arizona at 7:15 A.M. Today we saw the Painted Dessert and the Petrified Forrest. We were in a little town in the mountains went the tire got a flat. We saw the largest meteor Crater in the world. In the museum they had lectures on the meteor Crater. We ate dinner and then started for Grand Canyon. On the way we saw a sign that read "Look out for the Snow Plow." We entered Grand Canyon at 5:25 P.M. And we entered Grand Canyon N. Park at 6:15 P.M. We drove over a mountain and there wasn't hardly any fencing. It was about 1/2 mile deep. I think Grand Canyon is very pretty. We went to the tower and bought some film. We looked out the tower window and we saw the Colorado river. We slept in Grand Canyon National Park. We all slept well.

Note: This was an unforgettable experience. It wasn't just the scenery, but my poor dad, in the heat, changing that flat tire. More colorful phraseology. . . We felt sorry for Dad because it was really a tough job. We tried to help him all we could, but he was really in a bad mood. He had to unpack our whole trunk to get to the tire. We were able to help him pack it back up again though. Then Dad carried on like nothing had ever happened. I guess he just had to let off steam once in awhile.

The Painted Desert is like a rocky badlands with beautiful color striations - from deep lavenders and rich grays, to reds, oranges and even pink. The Painted Desert lies within the Petrified Forest National Park. This is one of the world's largest concentrations of petrified wood. The tree stumps and fallen trunks looked like marble.

The Meteor Crater is nearly one mile across and 2.4 miles in circumference and more than 550 feet deep. This was the result of a collision between a piece of asteroid and the Earth. We learned that it hit the earth at 2,000 miles per hour. I looked down from the rim of the crater and was amazed at its size.

Grand Canyon is one of the few places on Earth that has a real wow factor. Awesome, sells it short. It overwhelms you through its immense size. Approximately 277 miles long, up to 18 miles wide in some spots, and 1 mile deep. This day was worth the whole trip.

July 4, 1952

"Pacific Daylight Saving" 93 degrees Friday

Dad woke me up at 7:15 this morning, we ate, packed and left. We stopped on a village, on top of a mountain called Williams. Mother bought us each an Indian bracelet. We entered Nevada at 7:55 P.M. We saw Hoover Boulder Dam. It is very beautiful. We crossed the Nevada Dessert and mom took our picture. It isn't very hot, as the sun is setting. We entered California at 9:20 P.M. Right now we are on the dessert near Tehachepi. We are sleeping in the middle of the dessert, it is very nice and cool. We all slept good.

Note: The bracelet Mama bought each of us was very pretty. It was nickel with turquoise. This part of the trip, driving through the desert, I could have done without. It was nothing but flat land with no color except grey brown. I tried to sleep through some of it, but it was god-awful hot in the car and not really conducive to sleeping.

My sisters and I each had a canteen that we filled with water each morning. This particular day I drank all mine right away. After awhile I was still thirsty and asked Joanie for a sip from her canteen. She said only if I paid her a quarter. I complained to Dad. and he said it was her water, and she could do whatever she wanted with it. More whining from me. I did give her a quarter though. Like everything else in the car, the water was warm, too.

Out the window there was nothing to look at but the miles and miles of road ahead. For a twelve year old it was quite boring. Every now and then we would see a diner or a trading post—I'm talking maybe 50 to 100 miles apart or more—and once in a great while a roadside zoo. That did break up the monotony of the desert, somewhat.

July 5, 1952 "Pacific Daylight Saving" 92 degrees Saturday

Mom woke me up at 7: A.M. We packed and left. We are still crossing the dessert. We saw an exstinct volcanoe. I saw a freight train that had 86 cars on it. It is 6:10 Mountain & Pacific time. We saw another extinct volcanoe, it had lava all over. We saw a part of the dessert where the picture "The Three Godfathers" was made. We went to a Trading Post and mom bought us each a polo shirt. We went through Pasadena, L.A., Hollywood & Beverly Hills. But we didn't see any movie stars. We saw Hollywood and Vine in L.A. Dad drove us up to Ventura to see the Pacific Ocean. It was to foggy and cold to go swimming. We passed Santa Paula and then we crossed the mountains and camped in a man's Trailer Court near Bakersfield. We all slept well.

July 22, 1952

Bakersfield had a bad earthquake. The mountains that we crossed, one of them fell.

Note: What I remember about the desert was that we could actually see the San Andreas Fault. Years later, flying over the desert, it was even more remarkable to see it from a plane. The White Wolf Fault is the best known and largest fault to cut across the San Joaquin Valley. Its notoriety is due to the fact that movement along this fault was the cause of the 7.7 magnitude 1952 Bakersfield Earthquake which was the third largest recorded quake in California. This quake had several severe aftershocks. We had only been home three days when the earthquake struck. We thanked the Lord that we were not there when it happened .

July 6, 1952 "Pacific Daylight Saving" 92 degrees Sunday

Mom woke me up at 8:A.M. and we packed and left. We went to 10:A.M. Mass at St. Anne's Church in Portersville. Now we are climbing the mountains, we are almost at the top. Mom is very worried and scared. We stopped at a mountain spring and we all filled up on water. When you're riding if you look down out the window you can see almost a mile straight down. Our elevation is 5,000 feet. Sequoia N. Park is on the top of the mountain. It is 82 degrees up here and 92 degrees on level land. We are now 7,000 feet elevation. Today in Sequoia National Park we saw the largest tree in the world. We saw Mt. Whitney. We went through General Grant N.P. and also Kings Canyon N. Park. We are sleeping on top of a mountain 6,000 feet elevation. We are at Sunset Camping Grounds, Kings Canyon N.Park. Joanie and I are going to sleep in the car tonight.

Note: The giant Sequoias were just magnificent. This forest contains the largest trees on Earth, and some of the oldest trees on Earth. The forest did not disappoint. I remember the winding roads up in the mountains that led to the Sequoias, and the elevation was very high. My stomach was queasy so I closed my eyes in hopes my stomach would settle down. All the mountainroads that we took throughout the trip were two lanes that seemed to be quite narrow and didn't have guard rails. Because the road hugged the mountainside, the drivers would creep around the curves and beep their horns to warn any oncoming traffic. I found it very scary. At one curve, Dad honked his horn, and the RV in the oncoming lane, that we couldn't see, honked his horn. Dad got out and talked to the other driver. It was decided that Dad would back up to an appropriate spot to let the RV go by. Boy! the language Dad used when he got back in the car, priceless. . . I remembered the driver of the RV, because it was the first time I'd ever seen an albino.

Crosses were placed by the side of the road all along the roads up in the mountains throughout our whole trip, to indicate someone had died there. That was the first time I'd ever seen that.

July 7, 1952 "Pacific Daylight Savings" 80 degrees Monday

Today I woke up at 8:A.M. We packed and left. We saw four baby fawns on the mountain top while we were riding. While we were in Yusemite we saw alot of snow. The weather is warm. We saw El Capitan, and Bridle Vale Falls. Today it is about 80 degrees in the mountains. We went through a tunnel 2 miles long and when we came out we could hardly hear each other. We saw Glacier Pt. We slept in Yosemite N. Park Campgrounds. I went waiding in an ice cold current stream. It was melted ice and snow from the mts. Was it ever cold.

Note: Yosemite National Park was so beautiful. Mother Nature at her best. Bridal Veil Falls and El Capitan were awesome. The scenery was spectacular. Dad was not a religious man, but I remember a couple years after our trip he said, "If there is a heaven, it's Yosemite Park."

July 8, 1952

"Pacific Daylight Saving" 85 Degrees Tuesday

This morning Dad woke us up at 7:A.M. We packed and left. We rode through Stanislaus National Park. We unpacked at the house of friends we made the at the Campgrounds the night before. They lived in Oakland, so we went of the Bay to San Francisco. On the Bay Bridge we saw Treasure Island and Alcatraz. Now we are in San Francisco, we ate at the Fishermans Warf. We went to the Cliff House and we saw Seal Rock. We rode on a Cable Car Through San

Francisco. We went over the Bridge again and came to Oakland, we didn't have to hard a time to find 1807 38th Avenue. And we ate and went to bed.

Note: I loved San Francisco and especially the cable cars, but all the while I was there I kept thinking about earthquakes. At the campground the night before, Dad struck up a conversation with a man from the city of Oakland who just happened to be a policeman just like Dad. He invited us to spend the night at his house. He had children around our ages. We ate dinner there, and Dad pitched the tent for us in their backyard, and Mama and Dad slept in the house. They were very nice and friendly people. Mama and Dad kept in touch with them for years.

July 9, 1952 "Pacific Daylight Saving" 83 degrees Wednesday

Joan woke me up at 9:A.M. We packed and left. We went through Sacramento and we saw the Capital Build. We are riding on the mts. again. Most of them have snow on the tops. We went through Reno Nevada and now we are on the Nevada Desert. We pitched are tent at 11:P.M. but the wind blew it down, so dad, Joan, and I slept in our beds under the tent. I had a very good sleep.

Note: We went through Donner Pass on our way to Reno from Sacramento. I do recall that we were up in the Sierra Nevada Mountains. The roads were not that great, and we were at an elevation of about 7,000 feet. Again, I had to close my eyes to avoid motion sickness. Reno is in northern Nevada, and it sits in a high desert valley (Black Rock Desert) at the foot of the Sierra Nevada mountain range.

July 10, 1952 "Mountain Standard" 80 degrees Thursday

This morning Dad and mom woke me up. We packed and left. We left before the sun came out. I went to sleep in the car and when I woke up, they said I had been sleeping one hour. We went through

Elko. We entered Utah at 2: P.M. We saw the great salt desert, and also the great Salt Lake. We entered Salt Lake city and we ate dinner at some friends of ours. I took a bath there too. Then Golda took us all around Salt Lake City. We saw the Capital of Utah and the famous Mormen Temple, and their Tabernacle. Inside the Tabernacle we saw the 2ⁿᵈ. largest organ in the world. Then Golda rode up a hill and showed us the city, it was big. We went through three parks and then she took us home and we went to bed. We set up a tent in their backyard just for fun, and Joan & Marguerite slept in the tent with the twins Joan and Jean. Butch slept in his bedroom and I slept with mom and dad in the twins room as there was three bed there. We all slept well.

Note: The Great Salt Desert was fascinating. As far as you could see it looked like snow. The Christiansens were neighbors of ours from Pinehurst. They didn't live on Pinehurst very long before they moved to Salt Lake City. They were members of The Church of Jesus Christ of Latter-day Saints (the Mormons). When we were inside the Tabernacle, Dad told us that the acoustics were so good that if you dropped a pin in the back of the tabernacle you could hear it way up front.

In the evening Golda took us up the mountainside just outside the city. It was so beautiful looking down at all the lights. I liked Salt Lake City very much. It is surrounded on three sides by the Wasatch Mountain Range.

July 11, 1952 "Mountain Standard" 80 degrees Friday

Today I woke myself up at 9:10 A.M. And I went riding with one of the twins (Jean). Then we went to the Carnival with Butch and Jean, we had lots of fun. Then we met Joanie my sister there and she gave us some money for more rides. The twins are going to be 8 yr. on July 22. Butch will be ten in Sept. We left there house at 4:10 just after we had dinner. We entered Cache National Park. We entered Idaho at 8:05 P.M. We saw Big Bear Lake. We passed a lot of cows in the middle of the road and some in people's gardens eating flowers and grass. We passed quite a few pretty mountains. We rode over some of them. We entered into Wyoming at 9:20 P.M. we are still riding. We stopped at a motel in Wyoming for the night.

Note: Cache National Forest is in northern Utah and southern Idaho. Big Bear Lake is in the Cache National Forest in Idaho. It is called the "Caribbean of the Rockies" because of its unique turquoise-blue color, the result of suspended limestone deposits in the water. I don't remember this part of the journey. Perhaps I was sleeping.

July 12, 1952

"Mountain Standard" 65 degrees Saturday

Mom woke me up at 7:30 A.M. we packed and left. On the way we saw a great big cloud in the valley, I suppose that was because are elevation was 5,000 feet. We are now riding in a cloud. We passed through Jackson Hole, Wyoming. We saw the Grand Teton mts. Their were clouds over them but some you could make out the outlines of the mountains. They all had snow on them. On the road we saw a dead black cub. We are now in Yellowstone National Park. We are entering it from the south entrance. We saw 3 moose. We passed the continental devide in Yellowstone National Park at 11:20 A.M. We saw the Hot Springs. I saw a black bear by a mans car. We saw a fish hatchary. We also saw Yellowstone Lk. We saw mud volcanoe and many geysers . And dragons mouth which was near by. We saw Mud Geyser, mud pots, and Yellow Stone falls. We also saw Artists point and Yellowstone Canyon. It was raining out too. I saw Upper Falls. So far I have seen 8 bears. We drank water that had 67 minerals in it, it tasted very salty. We saw a natural glass mt. And a bunch of hot springs and 1 petrified tree. We saw roaring mountain volcano. We saw 3 elks, and Old Faithful. We are camping for the night in Old Faithful Camping Grounds.

Note: The Grand Tetons are unique in that the east side of the mountains have no foothills. They just rise up majestically from the valley floor. This was just the beginning of a day full of wonder. There is nothing on earth like Yellowstone National Park; it is simply stunning. What a treasure. I was mesmerized by Old Faithful. This geyser has a margin of error of ten minutes. Today it will erupt every 65 minutes after an eruption that lasts less than 2.5 minutes, and 91 minutes after an eruption lasting more than 2.5 minutes. The geysers, the falls, the spectacular scenery in the midst of the Rocky Mountains, there are no words to describe its wonder. Grizzly bear, black bear, elk, moose, and bison roam freely throughout the entire park. Park Rangers were getting rid of the wolves in the 1950s. Wolves were reintroduced to Yellowstone in 1995. Everywhere you look it is so beautiful. Even though Dad always had a revolver on him when we traveled, and he kept it under his pillow at night, I was still glad I slept in the car. I was frightened by the thought that those bears could come into our camp ground.

July 13, 1952 "Mountain Standard" 65 Degrees Sunday

This morning mom woke me up at 5:00, we went to mass at Old Faithful Lodge Recreation Hall. Then we went over to Old Faithful and we saw it shoot up at exactly 7:25 Mountain Standard time and 9:25 Eastern Standard time. We saw mt. Sheridan. We are on Sylvian Pass, elevation 8,532 feet. We are now in Shoshone National Forrest. We left Yellowstone National Park . Then we saw a free Zoo $2.00. We saw Buffalo Bill dam. We went through 6 tunnels. We saw Buffalo Bill's museum. We went through Greybull and the historical places like General Custer's last stand etc. We passed a real bad muddy road, I was very scared. We passed through snow and clouds, we are still on the Big Horn Mountains. We saw three deer while were in Big Horn National Forrest. We went to a place called Dayton, Wyoming and the man there told us there was a pretty camping place at the bottom of the mountain so we went there and here we are in *the same place ready for the night. This Tongue River Canyon is five miles from Dayton.*

Note: Sylvan Pass is the only way to exit Yellowstone from the East Entrance. Wyoming had the worst roads of our entire trip. Many of them were dirt roads.

Buffalo Bill's Museum is in Cody, Wyoming. Greybull, Wyoming, is in the heart of the Big Horn Basin. We saw the Battle of Little Big Horn (Custer's Last Stand). This area memorializes the battle between the U.S. Army 7th Cavalry and the Sioux and Cheyenne Indians' last efforts to preserve their way of life. The battle took place in Montana and the Little Big Horn National Monument is in Sheridan,Wyoming.

July 14, 1952 "Mountain Standard" 70 Degrees Monday

Dad woke us up at 6:50 a.m. and he fixed a flat tire while we packed. We ate and left. We went through Sheridan. We stopped for dinner at a little restaurant called (Dinner Bell) in Gillette. We lost one hubcap on the way from the camping grounds. We saw Devil's Rock or Devil's Tongue. We entered South Dakota at 7:30 p.m. We saw Deadwood, South Dakota. We camped at Black Hills National Forrest just outside of Deadwood, it is called Tomahawk Camp.

Note: Poor Dad with another flat tire and even more swearing when he realized he'd lost his hub cap.

We stopped to see Devil's Tower. It is a monolith in the Black Hills. You can see it for miles. Devil's Tower takes up 1,347 acres around its base. It just rises up out of the ground with nothing else around it. I was fascinated. Film Director Steven Spielberg used this location in his 1977 film, *Close Encounters of the Third Kind.*

Deadwood reminded me of the old west. It was named for the dead trees found in its gulch.

July 15, 1952 "Mountain Standard" 74 Degrees Tuesday

Mom Woke me up at 8:00 this morning, we ate packed and left. We went back to Deadwood, to mt. Moriah to see the graves of Wild Bill Hickock and Calamity Jane. On Wild Bill's grave it said:

Wild Bill Hickock Died Aug. 2, 1876

and on Calamity Janes' grave it said: Calamity Jane or Mrs. M.E. Burke Died Aug. 1, 1903 Age 53 years
We saw preacher Smiths Grave and Potato Creek Johnnies' grave. We went through a gold mine in Lead city. We had a real good dinner then we started off for Mt. Rushmore. We went to Mt. Rushmore and I bought a pair of Indian moccasins, and three pennants. We're starting through the Bad Lands. We just passed through Wall South Dakota. We entered The Bad Lands National Monument at 9:10 P.M. Eastern Standard time to 10:05. We stopped at Kadoka and we camped at (Rainbow Camp and Cabins).

Note: In the beginning, Deadwood was a lawless town. Wild Bill Hickok was murdered there. He is buried in Mt. Moriah Cemetery. The Homestake Gold Mine in Lead closed in 2002. It was the oldest, largest, and deepest mine in the Western Hemisphere, reaching more than 8,000 feet below the town of Lead.

I loved Mount Rushmore. We had our picture taken there with a Lakota Sioux Indian. He told us that he had modeled for the Indian on the Buffalo nickel. I believed him because he looked just like the Indian depicted on the obverse side of the Buffalo nickel. I think we had to pay a dollar to have him be in the picture with us. The Indian moccasins that I bought had beautiful beads on them.

The Badlands were kind of depressing. It reminded me of the surface of the moon. Badlands National Park is composed of 244,000 acres.

July 16, 1952 "Central Standard" 103 Degrees Wednesday

Dad woke me up at 8:10, we packed and left. We crossed the Missouri river but we are still in South Dakota. We stopped at a park in Whitelake, South Dakota and had a picnic. We went through Soux City. We are on U.S. route 18. We entered Iowa at 6:30 Eastern standard time. We camped on a ladie's property in Iowa., we all had a good sleep.

July 17, 1952 "Central Standard " 80 Degrees Thursday

Mom woke me this morning at 7:45. We packed, ate, and left. We passed through the Biggest Little Town in Iowa. (Ventura). There is an overcast in the sky,
We are crossing the Mississippi river. We are now crossing the . Mississippi river. We are mow entering Wisconsin at 3:50 P.M. We went through Madison, the capital of Wisconsin. We camped in a town near Watertown. It rained almost all night.

July 18, 1952 Central and Eastern Standard 83 Degrees Friday.

Dad woke me up this morning at 5:30, we packed, and left. We went to Milwaukee, and saw some houses that dad use to live in. We saw lake Michigan and the Millar High Life Brewry. We had breakfast, visited the Milwaukee museum and, left for Chicago. It is raining today. We ate dinner in Kenosha, Wisconsin. We saw an old friend of dads (Mel Jorgenson) in Kenosha. We went through Zion, Wackegon, North Chicago and Chicago. We've had rain all day, now it is getting worse. All the streets have water about 6 in. deep. It stopped raining but the streets are still flooded. In Chicago we saw the largest hotel in the world, (The Stevenson, it has 2,345 rooms. We drove on lake shore drive in Chicago but we couldn't see the skyline as the the fog was so dense. We entered Indiana at 7:10 P.M., We entered Michigan about a half an hour later. We ate at a

Restaurant in Three Oaks, Mich. There we slept near a little town. We all slept good.

Note: I don't remember too much about Mel Jorgensen except he used to bring us gifts at Christmastime when we were little. I wish I had paid more attention to the places where Dad lived in Milwaukee. I also wish I would have taken pictures of those places (remember; I lost my camera at Grand Canyon.) I know he lived there with his mother and step-father when he was a teenager, or maybe even younger.

July 19, 1952 "Eastern Standard" 84 Degrees Saturday

I woke up at 5:00 A.M. and we left for Detroit. We went through Ypsilanti, and we got home to find that our little black kitten was lost. I showed Grandma and Aunt Anna my souvenirs. We all agreed it was the best time of our lives.

Note: The beginning of the end for Route 66 came in 1956 when the National Defense and Interstate Highway bill was passed in June of that year.

12

The Ursuline Academy

My sisters and I attended the Ursuline Academy in Chatham, Ontario. It was a two hour drive from home. During the beginning of my first year at "The Pines" I was occupied with familiarizing myself with the rules, learning the routine, and meeting the other students. The academy was divided into three divisions. The Mother Superior was Mother Angela Claire. Third Division consisted of K through four. Second Division, that's where Joanie and I were, consisted of grades five through eight, and First Division, where Marguerite was, consisted of nine through grade thirteen. Grade thirteen in Canada is the equivalent of Freshman college.

Each division had its own recreation room that held tables, chairs, lockers, books, and a record player. That's all I can remember. First Division had private rooms that were on the third floor. Mother St. Bride supervised the girls in First Division. Second and Third Divisions had their dormitories on the second floor. The nuns that supervised the girls in Second Division were Mother St. Albert and Sister Mary of Lourdes. Sister was a novice and would take her final vows in a year or two, and then would be addressed as Mother Mary of Lourdes. The school was obviously run by Ursuline nuns.

The Ursuline order was founded in Italy. They were the first order of teaching nuns ever in the Roman Catholic Church. They were also the first Roman Catholic nuns in America. They settled in Quebec City in 1639. In 1727 they became the first Roman Catholic nuns to settle in the United States, in New Orleans, Louisiana. Their patron saint is, of course, St. Ursula.

In Poland, in WWII, the Ursulines offered asylum to Jewish children. The nuns never refused to take in a child. Thousands of Jewish children were rescued by the nuns. They also were able to rescue Jewish women from the death camps by disguising them as Ursuline nuns.

Marguerite began her first year of high school at the academy in 1951. Joanie and I followed in 1952. Joanie was in eighth grade and I was in seventh grade. Some students were classified as yearly (mostly students from other countries like Central and South America, the Caribbean countries and Bermuda). My sisters and I were monthly students. There were also weekly students and daily students who lived in or near Chatham. We would go home one weekend a month, either by train, or bus, or our parents would pick us up.

Our uniform was a navy blue, gabardine skirt that covered the knees, and a bolero to the waist with a white blouse that had a Peter Pan collar. The younger students in Third Division had to wear knee high navy blue stockings. The rest of us had to wear nylons. Marguerite told me that some of the girls in First Division would take a pen or eye liner and run it up the back of their legs to make it look like seams. Panty hose weren't around until the late fifties.

The building itself was a four story brick building, more than a hundred years old. It was surrounded by tall, mature pine trees, hence the nickname, "The Pines." The floors, staircases, and windows were highly polished wood. For an institution of learning it was really nice inside and very homey. There was a beautiful chapel on one wing of the building that had a pipe organ. This was on the first floor, and that side of the building also housed the nuns' convent which was separated from the school and dormitories by the visitors parlor.

Towards the back of the building was the music department, classrooms, and dormitories. "The Pines" was under the auspices of the Western Ontario Conservatory of Music. Our parents enrolled Marguerite in violin, Joanie in piano, and I took singing lessons. The school put on cantatas. I remember one Christmas we performed the *Nutcracker Suite*. Our orchestra and glee clubs won many medals and trophies for the academy. Mother Marguerite was head of the Music Department.

We attended mass every morning in the chapel, except Tuesdays, when we were allowed to sleep in before breakfast. As we walked down the long corridor toward the chapel, the beautiful voices of the nuns softly singing the wonderful Gregorian chants wafted through the halls. It was majestic, this praise to God in song. It was how I imagined what the music of Heaven would sound like.

We wore our navy blue uniforms and mid-length white chapel veils to Mass. As we entered the chapel, the nuns were chanting, standing facing each other across the chapel, under the stained glass windows on either side. We were in the middle, and our pews faced the altar. It was glorious. We would sit and quietly meditate until Mass began. I have heard the Gregorian chants sung by many different monks and priests over the years but they never could compare to the heavenly voices of those nuns at "The Pines".

It's amazing to me how saintly I always felt in that chapel, but I never seemed to be able to carry that feeling with me throughout the day. I usually talked too much in class or played tricks on fellow students or just committed small infractions during the day. I tried to do the right thing, but sometimes you have to let go and have fun. The nuns were very tolerant of me.

When Mass was over, the white veiled students marched down the aisle and out of the chapel. We then headed downstairs to the refectory for our breakfast before school started.

The refectory was on the first floor or the lowest level like a half basement, what we would now refer to as a daylight basement. The dining hall consisted of many tables all covered in white linen tablecloths and white serviettes, as napkins are referred to in Canada. We ate six to a table, family style. All our meals were home cooked by the nuns. We had an apple orchard on the back of the property, and when apples were in season we had homemade apple pies. For the most part the meals were very good. We had fresh table linens starting on Sunday, and if anything was spilled on the table during the week the nuns would help us put a small bowl of water underneath the spot and pour lots of salt over the spot, let the salt soak up the water, and in doing so, absorb the stain. We usually let it sit overnight. That seemed to do the trick.

We started and ended all our meals in prayer. The atmosphere at mealtime was very relaxed. The nuns kept watch over us to ensure that we used proper English and etiquette at all times. After breakfast we headed to our classrooms that were scattered between the first and second floors. After lunch we had an hour recreation either inside, or out on the property in back. After dinner we had an hour of recreation followed by homework in the study hall.

We got snacks during the day, cookies and such, but the one thing I really didn't like was when we were served peanut butter and honey sandwiches. Marguerite loved them. I never could get used to them. We also had a small room where Mother Bursar, as we called her, had snacks to purchase: pop, potato chips, cookies and the like. Also there were holy cards, rosaries and stories of the saints to purchase. We used the holy cards as book marks and would write nice little notes to our friends or to our favorite nuns on the back of the cards. Mother Bursar was an elderly, eccentric nun. When she climbed the stairs, she would pick up part of her habit, and we could see those ugly black shoes that she wore, along with white long johns. When we'd see her climbing the stairs we'd point and chuckle, to ourselves, of course. All the other nuns wore the standard black oxfords and black stockings.

In the dormitory Joanie and I were in, there were two long rows of ten or fifteen beds, with dressers between each bed. For privacy, each bed was shielded from the others by a white curtain that the students pulled shut for undressing and then pulled the curtain back so that only the foot of the bed was exposed. We brought our own bed linens to school which had to be white, and we had to have white, chenille bedspreads. In each dormitory, one nun had a bed. My dormitory had Mother St. Albert. Marguerite was in First Division, and all those students had private rooms and private showers.

The second floor also had the bath tubs, maybe fifteen in a row. The tubs were the old fashioned type with claw feet. Between each tub was a table to put our night clothes on, and a white curtain surrounded each tub. I loved those tub baths, but I was never able to spend as much time in the tub as I would have liked. At home I always loved to read a book in the tub. Usually my baths lasted an hour or until the water got cold or I fell asleep and dropped the book in the tub. Actually, that only happened to me once, but I do love long tub baths followed by a quick shower.

During the day we could hear the chapel bells chiming, announcing the Angelus at precisely 6:00 am, 12 noon and 6:00 pm. If you were near the chapel you would hear the nuns saying the Angelus. It's a prayer said in Latin. Angelus Domini meaning "Angel of the Lord." They also said Vespers in the evening.

The first floor of the school consisted of the parlor where guests were greeted. It was beautifully decorated in the traditional style. It was to this room that we were called when our parents or other guests arrived for a visit.

Joanie and I were in a split class of seventh and eighth graders and our teacher was Mother Patricia. She was a real character. Joanie and I laugh every time we talk about her. She was probably in her late fifties, small in stature, but had a large and domineering personality that was really a façade,. A more pleasant demeanor would come through every now and then. No one was really afraid of her, but she did command respect.

Our classroom was on the second floor and this particular day we were having a fire drill. As soon as the alarm went off, Mother Patricia quickly opened the window, which was a feat in itself since they were wood windows, floor to ceiling, and quite heavy. But Mother Patricia managed to get that window opened, hiked up her habit and climbed out onto the fire escape, poked her head back in and shouted, "Last one out turn off the lights and close the door." Off she scurried down the fire escape.

Mother Patricia also had the habit of throwing chalk at anyone who wasn't paying attention. She never seemed to miss. One time her chalk found its way to my head. I don't remember what I was doing, but I had all I could do to keep from laughing out loud. All the other girls were smirking and trying not to laugh.

Mother Patricia was born in Michigan, and even though we were in Canada, she always let it be known that things in the U.S. were better, to the eternal consternation of the Canadian students. Joanie thought Mother Patricia favored the American students.

The postulants, young women joining the convent on a trial basis, and the novices, those nuns who have not yet taken their final vows, would play baseball on the grounds in the back of the academy. In order to run the bases, the nuns had to hike up the skirt hems of their habits and pin them to their waist with long straight pins. It was fun to watch them play. We had a lot of fun cheering them on. Once in a while we played baseball with them.

We had swings out back and benches to rest. There was a beautiful rose garden that one of the nuns tended to, and we had a grotto of St. Bernadette of Lourdes that was along a beautiful, tree-lined path that led to the apple orchards out back. There were benches along the path. It was here that I learned to meditate. My godmother, Aunt Anna, my mother's sister was dying of cancer, and I would contemplate many things including my beloved aunt, the lives of the saints, and I prayed a lot there. I thought for a long time that I might like to become a nun, an Ursuline nun. I wanted to emulate Mother St. Albert; she was such a good person, and lots of fun. She had a wonderful demeanor and was always smiling.

The nuns were very good to us. They never used corporal punishment. What they did do was increase our homework, or in my case do the times tables 1 through 12 hundreds of times. A call home to your parents usually did the trick of keeping you in line. At least it did it for me. . .

Late one night Joanie was either not feeling well or was homesick. Sister Mary of Lourdes heard her crying. Joanie told me she was homesick the first few weeks we were there, so maybe that was the problem. In any case, Sister went down to the refectory and brought back hot chocolate and cookies for Joanie and stayed awhile and talked with her until she felt better.

Father Tierney, an elderly priest, had a small room on the premises. He said mass everyday and heard confessions on Saturday. One day poor old Father Tierney slipped on a rug in his room, and for days afterward he had two big black eyes. We referred to him irreverently as the The Raccoon.

There was a song, I don't know where the melody comes from,

we used to sing about the boarding school, but never when the nuns were around:

At the boarding school where I go, everything is growing old. Long gray hairs are in the butter, and the bread is green with mold, (song softly) is green with mold.
When the dogs die we have hot dogs. When the cats die, catnip tea.
When the nuns die I am leaving, spareribs are too much for me,
    (sung softly) too much for me.

On Saturday if we had a good report with no demerits we could wear our street clothes and go into town, to either shop or take in a movie that the nuns approved of, of course. Chatham is a wonderful town, very English or British if you prefer. The Thames River meanders through town with an occasional bridge to cross.

After the movie there was a wonderful little English Fish and Chips place that served the best fish and chips. They were served on newspaper that had been shaped into a cone. Some type of vinegar was sprinkled on the fries. Those were the best fish and chips I've ever had. I would love to taste them again. The only ones that ever came close were those served at the Michigan State Fair. Also in town were lovely china shops and little stationery stores.

I really liked Chatham. My sisters and I went back to "The Pines" for a visit in the eighties, and were surprised at how much the town had grown.

13

My Michigan

I have lived in Michigan all my life. I love it here, not just for its beauty and diversity, its four beautiful seasons, but those beautiful deep-blue lakes; actually they are inland seas. It is a true water wonderland, but also because I have a long family history here.

In the summer of 1701, Antoine de la Mothe Cadillac, Sieur de Cadillac, leading fifty soldiers, fifty traders, and some artisans, and two priests, left Montreal, went up the Ottawa River, across Lake Nipissing to Georgian Bay (part of Lake Huron) down the St. Clair River and Lake St. Clair, then finally to the banks of the Detroit River, where he built Fort Pontchartrain and founded the city of Detroit. Among those fifty traders were my ancestors Georges (Bro) Brault and his brother Jean. They are the ancestors on my Mother's side.

From 1707 to 1818 the Brault (Bro) family handed down the license of voyageur from father to son, uncle to nephew. It was the law that only licensed traders, the voyageurs, could trade with the Indians. The Coureur de Bois, on the other hand, were lawless traders, who were renegades and traded freely with the Indians.

The voyageurs toured the lakes, spending much time at Fort Michillimackinac. The French flag flew over the fort until 1761. It was here that the sturdy voyageurs, among them my ancestors, paddled huge 35 foot canoes, known as bateaus, from Montreal to rendezvous with the Indians to exchange furs. These hardy voyageurs wintered in the frozen north of what would later become the state of Michigan. Although these men had early connections to Michigan, they never settled here. They always returned to New France (Quebec). It was not until 1926 that the French side of my family decided to live here permanently.

It's hard for me to believe that Mama's relatives were some of the first white men to see Michigan, which then was a primeval forest surrounded by the most beautiful blue, inland seas, and some of the largest white pines in the country. The White Pine is our state tree. It was called the Tree of Peace by the early Indians. Some pine trees have reached 500 years of age and in pre-colonial days, reached over 300 feet in height.

Mama came to Detroit around 1935 to be with her family who left St. Boniface, Manitoba, in 1926. My father was born in Bay City. An area known for its German influence. Three of my dad's grandparents came to Michigan from Germany. Gottlieb Sautter and his wife Mary Zeigler Sautter came from the province of Wurttemberg, and settled in Sebewaing which is located in the thumb area of Michigan. Heinrich Schindehette came from the city of Kassel and eventually settled in Bay City.

Heinrich was 22 years old when he answered the call of General Lewis Cass "to come forth in this time of peril," the Civil War. He enlisted in the Michigan 24th, the famous Iron Brigade. It was known for its strong discipline, its unique uniform, its tenacious fighting ability. Some say it was the most famous unit in all the armies of the Union. They suffered the highest percentage of casualties of any brigade in the war. Originally called the "Black Hat Brigade" because only the soldiers of this brigade wore the regular army's dress black hat with a black plume instead of the more typical blue cap. It was the only all-western brigade in the eastern armies of the Union. When President Lincoln said, "Thank God for Michigan," he was referring to the Iron Brigade.

My dad's maternal grandmother Samantha Diamon came from a New England family that traces its roots back several generations to Connecticut and western New York. Samantha's grandparents, John and Sarah Diamon, left western New York state and settled in the Territory of Michigan in 1818, before the Erie Canal was built.

Jim and I were both born in Detroit and met at Cass Technical High School (Cass Tech). Jim lived on the east side by Dequindre and 8 Mile Road, and I lived on the northwest side by Fenkell and Meyers.

Jim's four great-grandparents were among the first wave of

immigrants who came to Michigan from Poland. They settled in the Polish enclave of Hamtramck in 1879. Hamtramck was founded by Polish immigrants, and is a city completely surrounded by Detroit.

I'm very proud of the fact that Michigan was the first English speaking territory in the world to ban capital punishment.

Minnesota calls itself the Land of 10,000 Lakes, but Michigan has over 11,000 lakes, and depending on their minimum size, you could say that Michigan actually has 69,798 lakes. That would include small lakes of a couple of acres in size. From the surface of the moon, an astronaut gazing back at earth finds the Great Lakes the most instantly recognizable feature on the North American continent.

I love our state motto: "Si Quaeris Peninsulam Amoenam Circumspice," translates to: "If you seek a beautiful peninsula, look about you."

14

Love at First Sight

My father died from cancer February 20, 1957. I was sixteen years old and heartbroken. I didn't think I could ever be happy again. He was a hard working, wonderful man of integrity, honesty, and full of love for his family, the type of father everyone would like to have.

I was a junior at Cass Tech High School in downtown Detroit. It was a three year college prep school. It was considered one of the nation's pre-eminent schools. A large school, seven stories, and in 1957 it had an enrollment of more than 3,000 students. The students were required to choose a curriculum path. Mine was Dress Design. Jim's was Architectural Drafting. The building itself was 831,000 square feet. It was the largest school in Michigan at that time.

Many famous people graduated from Cass Tech including John DeLorean, Ellen Burstyn, Diana Ross and Lily Tomlin who I went to school with, and at that time was known as Mary Jean Tomlin. In 1957, she was voted Most Popular. She was also captain of the cheerleaders.

More famous people came out of their music department than any other department in the school. It was here at Cass Tech where the top scholar was more honored than the star quarterback. Stories went around that students who went on to college found their classes there to be easier than those at Cass Tech.

In the fifties, Cass Tech's ratio of black and white students was close to 50:50. For such a large school, there were never any fights, in school or out, at least none that Jim or I could remember. In my Dress Design class only the teacher and myself were white. I considered several of the black students my friends. We got along just fine. We had lunch together, did many things together but that's as far as it went. I could never have invited any them to my home and vice-versa.

We never fraternized after school. The black student's had their hang-out, the Bungalow on Grand River Avenue, and we had ours, Ginny's on Henry Street.

I was on the 5th floor talking to my friend Mary Ann Palutis, waiting for my class to begin. I saw a gorgeous, tall, dark, and really handsome guy walk by. I told Mary Ann, "That guy is gorgeous; I'd love to meet him. In facr I'd love to marry him.." "You mean Jim Wrobleski?" I was surprised that she knew him. She made arrangements for us to meet. I was so anxious to meet this guy I could barely concentrate on my schoolwork.

A week later Mary Ann introduced us at Henry's, the coffee shop across the street. He was everything I thought he would be and more: Smart, funny, great sense of humor, and even better looking up close. I was definitely in love. School was about to let out for the summer. I found out that Jim was going to summer school so he could graduate the following January. I was also going to summer school to make up classes I dropped because of my dad's illness. That would allow me to graduate in June on schedule.

Mary Ann found out which locker Jim had, and we made sure I got the locker next to his. Remember, this was a school of over 3,000 students, so what were the odds of me accidentally getting a locker next to Jim? I mean *right* next to his?

When Summer school started, and while I was at my locker, Jim showed up. He was surprised at the coincidence. I'm thinking to myself, "This is going to be easier than I thought." Like casting out a line and immediately reeling in a big fish . . Jim never did like that analogy. Plus, when I retold this event, and I did often, I used to add, "Doc-dee-doe," as I impersonated his coming down the hall towards the lockers. He'd smile, but I knew he didn't like it. (I can tease too.) But he was a good sport.

Jim had a part time job at the canoe shelter on Belle Isle. This is a wonderful little jewel of an island in the Detroit River near downtown. It's actually a lovely park with a little river meandering through it. After school, Jim occasionally took Mary Ann and me to the island, paddled us out in a canoe to a smaller island on this little river and dropped us off so we could do our homework. A couple hours later when work was over he would pick us up and take us home. That was the beginning of a glorious summer.

We went on dates to the beach, bowling, the drive-in, picnics, and lots of parties where we both loved to dance the "Funky Chicken." That was the rage in the late fifties. We were falling in love. Before it was just me falling in love; as the summer progressed it was definitely "we" falling in love. I thought of my dad dying and thinking how I could never be happy again, and now I was in love. I would give anything if my dad could have met Jim. He would have loved this guy.

Mama, and Grandma, and my sisters all loved Jim. He was a real gentleman, and since none of us drove, and with my dad gone, Jim took over and drove Mama to the grocery store or wherever she needed to go. Mama was crazy about him, and he thought the world of her. He helped with things around the house, and I was falling deeper in love. It was at this time that Jim gave me a lovely plain, gold band to signify that we were now going steady.

My sister Marguerite was getting married that August and her fiancé asked Jim to stand up at their wedding. We were both in the wedding party, and we had a great time.

Whenever Jim was on his way to my house, I would sit on the front steps and wait in anticipation for him. I would look down the street towards Puritan waiting for his car to turn the corner unto Pinehurst. The feeling that I got when I saw his car is hard to describe. It's like a warm tingly feeling in the pit of my stomach. I think it's what people describe as butterflies in your stomach. All I know was, I got a wonderful tingly feeling all over that I hoped would never end. On the days when he couldn't come over, I felt blue and lethargic the rest of the day. I really was head-over-heels in love with this guy.

It was towards the end of my senior year when Jim took me to the prom. It was held at the Veteran's Memorial, an impressive building on the Detroit River downtown. I wore the bridesmaid dress from Marguerite's wedding. After the Prom, Jim and I went with friends to Belle Isle and danced around the beautiful Scott Fountain that stands by the river's edge. It was so romantic as we listened to the music from our car radios and danced under the moonlight. It felt so good when he held me in his arms to dance. The subdued lights from the fountain only made it more dreamy. This was the most wonderful day of my life. I felt like Cinderella at the ball. Then Jim told me I was beautiful, and that he loved me, (Beauty is in the eye of the beholder.) If I could fast freeze in time at one special moment, that would be the one.

An old saying in Detroit was, "You went to Belle Isle to watch the colors changing on Scott fountain, or to watch the submarine races - depending on how old you were...

Love at first sight does happen. It sure happened to me.

15

Wedding Bells

Jim graduated in January 1958 and I graduated in June 1958. That year there was a recession going on, and I knew we couldn't get married until we had a decent car. So following high school I attended Felt and Terrant Ltd. Business School downtown. Jim was attending Lawrence Tech. I wanted to learn to operate a comptometer.

A comptometer is a a key driven, paperless calculator that is extremely fast, depending on the operator. As soon as you maintained 95% accuracy or better, they graduated you. I reached 99.2% in three months. They gave me a gold pin that I still have.

Diane and Jim

While Jim was at Lawrence Tech, I got a job at American Standard Offices in Dearborn, in the Cost Accounting Department. It was a good paying job, especially when you figure there was a recession going on.

On New Year's Eve of 1958 Jim proposed to me at a party and clumsily put an engagement ring on my finger. Things were really looking up. I couldn't wait to see what 1959 would bring.

I bought a black, 1954 Crown Victoria from Mama's friend, Pat Hogan. We decided that would be a good car for us. Now mind you, I didn't know how to drive yet. Well, don't think the guys at American Standard didn't tease me about that. They wanted to know if I had a twin sister… Jim's dad co-signed for me because I was only nineteen at the time. That's the car we took on our honeymoon.

While we were dating, I told Jim how much I loved the song the Four Freshman sing, "I Remember You" that said in part, "When the angels ask me to recall the thrill of it all, then I will tell them I remember you." He recalled that moment years later and told me how much it meant to him.

In the spring of 1959 we took rides in the country. In summer we picnicked and swam at Kensington Park. We picnicked at Warsaw Park, in Shelby Township just off Dequindre Rd. where we danced to live music at the Pavilion, mostly polkas. I have lots of fond memories from when I was a little girl. We would go to Warsaw Park for the Policemen's Picnics.

We swam nights and week-ends at Walter's Beach on either Cass or Elizabeth Lakes, I don't remember which. In fall we went to Yates Cider Mill on Avon Road in Rochester for cider and donuts, and to Greenfield Village in Dearborn to watch the muzzle-loaders, and to walk around the village. This is the largest indoor/outdoor history museum complex. It's founder was Henry Ford. Imagine, Henry Ford, once said, "History is bunk;" go figure. The property consists of famous homes, machinery, exhibits and Americana. Jim and I both loved history. He is a Civil War buff. In winter we tobogganed down the hills on what is now the property of the GM Tech Center on Van Dyke in Warren.

In 1960, Jim and I are started planning on getting married later that year. We picked Labor Day week-end, September 3rd. This was the first time in our relationship that we started arguing. Should we invite 50 people or 100? Why doesn't your mother want to invite your Dad's brothers? On and on it went. Why don't we just elope? Finally Jim, who was so even tempered, just started laughing and said "Just think, at this time next month we'll be married." At that point we just sat back, took a breath and re-grouped.

Our big day arrived and it was a beautiful, perfect, sunny, seventy degree day, with just an occasional cloud in the sky. Jim and I had been practicing abstinence before our marriage and this made our day all the more special.

Father O'Neal married us at St. Francis de Sales Church at the corner of Fenkell and Pinehurst on Detroit's west side. It stood just down the street from where I grew up.

My nehew Mike Kirby married Tammy Ohl at this same church years later and Fr, O'Neal married them also..

I loved my cousin Edmo very much. He took me down the aisle, but all I could think of was how much I wished my dad could have been there to walk me down the aisle.

Joanie was my maid-of-honor, and Mary Ann Palutis, naturally, was one of my brides' maids. Marguerite was pregnant at the time, so she was not in the wedding party. At that time pregnant ladies were never in the wedding party. I've always regretted the fact that she was not my matron-of-honor. Joanie was Marguerite's maid-of-honor, I was Joanie's maid-of-honor and Marguerite was suppose to be my matron-of-honor.

We were married September 3, 1960. I had been laid off from American Standard a month before my wedding. The choice they gave me was to move with the company to Cleveland or get laid off. I wasn't about to leave my family, and Jim didn't want to leave his family either. It turned out to be a blessing in disguise. American Standard had to pay me severance pay, my two weeks vacation and unused sick days. That took care of the wedding and honeymoon, plus we had $100 left and bought a black and white TV with it.

We went to Washington D.C., Williamsburg, Gettysburg, the

Shenandoah Valley and the Blue Ridge Parkway on our honeymoon. We also saw Harpers Ferry and Richmond, Virginia.

It was in Virginia where we first saw, "Whites only" and Colored only" signs on the drinking fountains. This really bothered us. When we were driving through Virginia, we experienced some car trouble and pulled into a little town called West Point. Three black fellows took Jim into town to get our car fixed, and an old black lady who ran a restaurant, invited me in for a wonderful chicken dinner, while waiting for Jim to return. The woman and her restaurant looked like they didn't have much money, but in spite of that, she would not let us pay for the dinners. She was adamant. I never forgot her or the town. They had been so good to us, and by the way, the chicken was some of the best I've ever eaten. Our honeymoon lasted one week.

Jim had been hired by the City of Detroit as a tree trimmer, and I got a job in December at Excello Corporation in their Accounts Receivable Department. I loved working there. That's where I met Lori Guinean.

When Lori got married she wore my wedding gown. She wanted me to be a bridesmaid, but I was pregnant with Steve at the time. As it turned out, Steve was born two weeks early, on October 10, and Lori's wedding was early November, so I could have been her bridesmaid. Her husband, Dick Enos and Jim became best of friends, and remained so until Dick passed away in April, 1991. Sadly, Lori passed away April 2015. I was in Tennessee, so was unable to attend her funeral.

16

Working Women in the Fifties and Sixties

Not many professional jobs were open to women in the fifties. There were receptionists and typists and such, but all were under the "rule" of men. There were very few exceptions. By 1956, 35% of all adult women were members of the labor force, and nearly one quarter of all married women were working. Only two out of five women with husbands and school-age children worked outside the home.

In 1958, upon graduating from Felt and Tarrant Business School as a comptometer operator, I interviewed for my first position. At that time you were expected to wear a hat and gloves to an interview. I remember very clearly my interview at Campbell Ewald, a large advertising firm that included General Motors as one of its clients. I filled out the application form which included age, marital status and religion. During the interview I was asked a few questions. I thought everything was going well until the interviewer came to the section on marital status. He then preceded to tell me that he wouldn't be hiring me. I asked why not. I thought if the interview didn't go well I wanted to know the reason. It seemed the distinguished firm of Campbell Ewald had a policy of not hiring young married women, especially Catholics, because they generally started families right away.

Shortly after I got married I was interviewed by the personel department of Excello Corporation in Detroit for a position in the Accounts Receivable Department. On their application form they wanted the date of my last "menses," along with religion and marital status. I didn't put anything down because I didn't know what menses meant. When told, I was embarrassed, even though I did write it down, I was very uncomfortable. It was not part of a young lady's vocabulary. I was told to come back for an interview with Ted Kleinhans, the supervisor of the Accounts Receivable Department. I did get hired, and Ted Kleinhans and I got along famously. He said he enjoyed the interview and wanted to know when I could start. His priority was a person's ability to do the job and how well they would fit in with other employees. Evidently my religion didn't bother him. He turned out to be a wonderful gentleman and a great boss.

The policies at Excello were very chauvinistic. The men could smoke at their desks, but the women could only smoke in the ladies room. Women could not wear slacks or pant suits to work. That was pretty much standard everywhere. Women had to take a fifteen minute break in the morning and one in the afternoon. Women had a limit on the hours they could work each day, and they were also limited to the number of hours of overtime they could work per week.

Men were not affected by these rules. There was a large disparity in income between men and women holding the same position. Women were laid off first, even if they had more seniority because the thinking at the time was that men were the main breadwinners, not women. I don't remember any women in supervisory positions at Excello. (1960-1965).

If you got pregnant you were not allowed to work past the first trimester, and you lost your pension. That happened to me twice. Years later they had two class action suits, both pertaining to loss of pensions. I missed out on both.

After my second son David was born, I quit and stayed home for fifteen years to raise my children. I went back to work in 1980, and was surprised to see that comptometers were being phased out of the work place. Calculators were taking their place. It was a whole new world out there, so I returned to college and then the work force a few years later.

Whenever I hear people criticize the feminists, or women's libbers, I remind them of what Betty Freidan, Gloria Steinem and others in the women's liberation movement did for all of us. Many young women today have no idea what these and other women had to endure to correct the injustices toward women in the workplace. The types of injustices that I've mentioned occurred frequently, from the largest corporations on down. Surprisingly, little has changed since the 1960's in regard to pay equity.

Census statistics released September 16, 2010 showed that women still earned 77% of what men earned, based on the median earnings of full-time, year round workers in 2009. Both men's and women's earnings showed slight increases from 2008 to 2009, with men's at $47,127 and women's at $36,278, a difference of $10,849.

On average women continue to earn considerably less than men. In 2015 full-time women workers earned 80% for every dollar the men earned. $51,212 and the women earned $40,969. a difference of $10,243.

Two years before Steve graduated from high school, I enrolled at Washtenaw Community College. My field would be accounting and general business. My goal was to eventually get my bachelors degree. Two years later I graduated with honors and received my associate degrees in Accounting and General Business. At that time Dave was in high school and Julie was in middle school. I got a job at McNamee, Porter and Seeley, an engineering firm, where I worked for five years.

Then I moved to another job where I was able to work during the day and go to school in the evening. It took me years of evening classes to complete my bachelor's in history, with a minor in general business and then a master's in public administration.

17

Jim's Parents

I first met Jim's parents, Frank and Louise, when we started dating. Frank seemed all right, but I immediately got the feeling that Louise didn't like me. Jim kept telling me that she did, but I wasn't buying it. Mama said of Louise, "Jim's an only child; no one will ever be good enough for her Jimmy." (as Louise liked to call him.)

In the beginning, Louise started calling me Gloria. I'm pretty sure she knew that wasn't my name. I told Jim about it. He said he had gone out with Gloria a couple times. So I asked Louise about her, and she said she always wanted Jim to marry Gloria because her dad owned a bowling alley, and my dad was just a policeman. I said to her "What about Jim's dad? He's 'just' a policeman?" "Oh, yeah, that's right," she said, and started to laugh. Gloria's name was never brought up again.

Louise had many good traits. The one I liked the best was her sense of humor. She also had a great laugh, and tears would roll down her face when she had a good laugh going. She was very honest. You could say, brutally honest. She was the best cook I ever knew. To this day I know of no one who could equal her skills in the kitchen. She could have been a chef, and she would have been a good one.

We had been married two years when Louise told us how much she worried about Jim. She said she didn't think he would know a good girl from a bad girl. Jim said "I still don't." I was sitting in on this conversation, about eight months pregnant with our first child. I just rolled my eyes.

My mother-in-law was a character. She had a wonderful disposition that Jim inherited from her. She was also quite comical. One day, I asked her how she met Frank. Looking over at him, she said, "Naturally I had to latch onto something like that during the

Depression." Then she laughed that infectious laugh of hers, where the tears ran down her cheeks.

I would describe Louise as lacking in sophistication. She was just the opposite of Mama, but surprisingly they both liked each other and got along well with one another. Mama said "She's a diamond in the rough."

Louise was honest to a fault, and didn't seem to have any filter for that trait. She once told me, out of the blue, that "Joanie has it all over you and Marguerite for looks." When I told Marguerite and Joanie that, Marguerite and I couldn't stop laughing. I don't think Joanie knew what to say. But that's Joanie, quiet and reserved.

Steve was born two years after we were married. I had to quit work. The rules at Excello and just about every large company was that you had to quit by the end of your first trimester. Since I didn't show much, I quit at six months.

When Steve was six months old, I went back to work at Excello, and Louise took care of Steve. Steve looked so much like Jim when he was a baby that she refused to call him Steve. She called him Jimmy. She just would not call him Steve. We finally settled on "Little Tiger." That, she was okay with. I guess you could say, I just took baby steps with my mother-in-law and eventually she came around . . . or was it me that came around?

Steve remembers his Grandma Louise fondly. She stood in long lines with him waiting for her "Little Tiger" to see Santa Claus. She took him to the zoo. She played so much with him that she told me she didn't like putting him down for his nap because she still wanted to play with him.

By the time our "Little Tiger" was two, Louise had taught him his colors, numbers and letters. She would dress him in beautiful boucle´ outfits, usually white, because Steve had that beautiful olive skin like his dad.

Louise had a brother Charlie who was one year older than she. He was an auto mechanic and a barn stormer. He died of tuberculosis on May 9, 1937. Jim never knew much about his Uncle Charlie except he had a wife named Althea, and a son. They lived in Texarkana, Texas.

Louise never knew her own mother. I believe she died in childbirth. Louise didn't have a birth certificate. She said she was born on a farm in Ohio, and her dad remembered that the peaches on the trees were ripe, so he made her birthday August 26, 1900. Louise's birth was recorded as 26 August, 1900 in Newark, Licking County, Ohio. She passed away on July 14, 1974, in Algonac, St. Clair County, Michigan. Her death certificate lists cause of death as brain ataxia.

Louise and her brother were raised by a step-mother who didn't seem to pay much attention to them. Louise never said much about her childhood. When she was older, she lived with her aunts in Zanesville, Ohio.

One time while Jim and I were visiting my in-laws, Louise took me downstairs. She was cleaning out some items in the basement. They had a very nice finished basement. I remarked about these two lovely, expensive frames on the wall. One frame contained a picture of an Englishman in his riding gear on a horse. The other frame contained a caricature of dogs playing poker. She told me there were drawings behind the pictures. Then she took the pictures off the wall and gave them both to me. I asked her if she was sure she didn't want them. Actually, exquisite might better describe those frames. Louise told me that they were wedding gifts from her first marriage, so she really didn't have any use for them. Wow! ! ! That marriage thing came as a surprise.

On the way home, I asked Jim if he knew his mother had been married before. He was real surprised. He had no idea. When we got home we couldn't wait to see what was under the pictures within those frames. Jim started to remove the picture from the frame, and low and behold, there was a most gorgeous piece of artwork in a chalk rendering of fruit, that had been hiding behind those dogs. Jim said he remembered those dogs since he was a little boy. In back of the other frame was a beautiful chalk drawing of a hunter's prize of ducks on a line that was carried home from a successful day of hunting. It was in an unusual frame. We had them both restored. They are beautiful.

Jim wondered about who his mother's first husband was, and when did they marry and divorce. I told him I'd start digging. This is what I found on the 1920 U.S. Census: Louise's first marriage was to Harold Koch, in Lucas County, Ohio. They probably lived in Toledo. He was six years older than she. I don't think they were married very long. Jim was surprised when I told him. He still couldn't get over the fact that his dad was not her first husband. However, Louise was Frank's first wife. He married Geraldine Gregory after Louise died.

Louise came to Detroit during the Great Depression and worked at a boarding house on the east side of Detroit. That's where she met Frank. He was a Detroit police officer, and single, and lived at the boarding house. They married in 1932. Jim was born in 1940. Louise told me she had had seven miscarriages before Jim was born. Jim was an only child. Louise absolutely doted on her "Jimmy." When I married Jim, surprisingly he was not spoiled, and was a very "low maintenance" guy.

Louise told me her favorite singer was a country singer from Tennessee, Eddie Arnold. Her favorite song of his was "Make the World Go Away." To sum up Louise, she possessed good, old fashioned, common sense, honesty and a complete lack of pretense. She loved children, not just her son and grandchildren but all children. She was child-like in a lot of ways. I didn't like her much when I first met her, but after I got to know her I really loved her.

To sum up Frank, he was a good person with a good sense a humor, but many times his drinking clouded his judgement.

After Frank retired, he had a lovely ranch home built along the St, Clair River in Algonac. It was brick. I think it was the last bricklaying job he did after he retired. I asked him why Algonac. He said there use to be a trolley that ran from Detroit to Algonac, and then on to Port Huron when he was young, and he'd take it as far as Algonac and go fishing. He wanted to live there someday.

Steve spent a lot of time in Algonac with his grandparents. He would go fishing with Grandpa, and Grandpa's cousin George Polanowski. I think baseball was Grandpa's favorite sport. He had an acre or two behind the house that abutted the Algonac State Park, and Steve remembered playing catch a lot with Grandpa there. He remembered going with Grandpa to the landfill on several occasions.

He also told me that one time when he was staying with his grandparents, Grandpa drove to the bar in Algonac. Steve waited in the car, and after a couple beers, Grandpa had Steve drive him home. Steve was eleven years old. Steve said Grandpa told him what to do and off they went down North River Road to home. Steve loved it. It was only lately that Steve told me this. I asked him why he hadn't told me that before. Naturally he figured we wouldn't let him spent time alone with Grandpa anymore.

Another time we were all visiting Jim's parents, I was about eight months pregnant with Julie. We were all out back when we heard several motorcycles pull up out front. As I rounded the corner of the house, I could see Grandpa putting Steve, who was six at the time, on the back of one of the motorcycles. These were motorcycle gang members. Not the nice guys in white hats. I ran over. I was so scared. I just blurted out to this big, burly guy in a black, leather jacket with long hair and tattoos, "I don't allow my children to ride motorcycles because I'm so afraid of them, but thank you so much for wanting to take him." I was talking real fast and out of breath. As I talked, I took Steve off the motorcycle. I was so scared I was actually shaking. Years later Steve told me he was really disappointed because he wanted a ride on that motorcycle. Needless to say I was pretty upset with Frank. He had a little too much to drink that day and didn't remember a thing.

I remember one time when we were visiting Frank and Louise, Dave, age seven, and Julie, age four, sang a song for them. David continued to entertain. He had his music on a stand in front of him. He wouldn't quit. Finally Grandpa started to remove the music stand, and David kept singing and following the moving music stand right out of the room. Louise laughed so hard tears were running down her face.

Julie never remembered much about Grandma Louise because she had been bedridden for a couple years and died when Julie was just five.

Frank was born May 22, 1904, in Hamtramck, Michigan. The oldest of four brothers: Harry, Bruno, Raymond and Walter. He had an older sister Rose. Frank's parents and grandparents all came from the Silesian region of Poland that was under German control. All of

Jim's Polish relatives were part of the "second wave" of immigrants from Poland which took place between 1860 and WWI. They were in search of a better economic life. The German/Poles tended to be better educated and had more skilled craftsmen than the Russian or Austrian/Poles. Jim and I had no relatives that entered this country through Ellis Island. They were all here before 1892, the year it first began accepting immigrants.

All that I was able to find out about Frank's siblings, was that Rose, born April 1902, was married to Harry Walney. She became an alcoholic. Frank's brother Harry changed his last name to Sparrow. Wrobel in Polish translates to sparrow, or near the sparrows. Last I knew, he was living in Wyandotte, Michigan. Nor do I know anything about Bruno except that he was born 1908. I believe he lived in Hamtramck. The only brother I met was Ray who was born in 1909, and his wife Gabby, short for Gabrielle. She was born in Montreal. He was a lithographer in Washington, DC, and they had several children. They lived in the Watergate building in Washington. Two or three of their daughters became nuns. I liked Jim's Uncle Ray and Aunt Gabby.

Walter, the youngest, born in 1910 or 11 was a bachelor and lived in California. He died there in 1966 or 1967. He had terminal cancer and went to Mexico to get Laitrelle treatments. It was illegal in the United States. It was the same treatment Steve McQueen, a popular movie star at that time, received in Mexico. Neither survived. Frank and Louise went to California to see Wally before he died.

When I asked Frank about his parents, Frank told me his mother and father died within two weeks of each other in 1917; other than that he didn't seem to remember much. I tried unsuccessfully to obtain death certificates for them in Hamtramck and Detroit. Then I tried Lansing, and was excited when I saw an envelope in the mail from Lansing. I told Jim I couldn't wait to open it. To my utter surprise or shock, I don't know which, I read Jim's grandmother's death certificate first. It said cause of death was homicide, gunshot to the head. We didn't know what to make of it. Then I couldn't get to his grandfather's death certificate fast enough. Suicide. . . We were both stunned. I asked Jim if he had any inkling about any of this. "No" he said, "but Mom and Dad sometimes talked in whispers with other relatives. Maybe that's what they were whispering about." Knowing Jim's mother, she would definitely keep something as tragic as this from her Jimmy.

Jim went with me to the Harlan Hatcher Library at the University of Michigan. We went through lots of Detroit newspapers for April 1917. Finally, we found two articles in the April 13 Detroit Free Press and an article and an obituary from the Detroit News, dated April 23.

The following is the first newspaper article:

SHOOTS WIFE, MOTHER OF 7

Dodge Motor Worker Sends Bullet into His Own Temple Notifies Police, Is Taken To Hospital and both will Probably die.

Because he refused to divide $16 which he won by betting on Cleveland in the opening baseball game, and she would not drop divorce suit proceedings. Willian Wroblewski and his wife Margaret are dying in Samaritan Hospital. Wroblewski shot her twice through the head and then shot himself once in the right temple in their home on 112 Lumpkin Avenue, Hamtramck, Thursday night. Wroblewski offered to compromise by splitting his winning if his wife would withdraw the suit. She refused. Mrs. Wroblewski is 40 years old, the mother of seven children. Frankie, eight years old, witnessed (actually, Frank was 13) the tragedy. He says his father entered the bedroom and asked for the revolver. His mother told him where it was.

SHOOTS WIFE AND SELF

Wroblewski picked up the revolver, shot her twice through the head, then pointed the weapon at his own temple and pulled the trigger.The husband then walked down-stairs and called the police. "Better come send a wagon right away " he said. "I got her this time." A year ago he had made an unsuccessful attempt on his wife's life. Mrs. Wroblewski was rushed to Samaritan Hospital. The patrol then returned to the station with Wroblewski. He walked into the station, told Police Chief Whalen he had shot his wife because she made trouble. He began to tell of family quarrels, but fell in what police mistook for a drunken slumber, upon the floor.

Murderer May Die

Efforts to waken him proved fruitless. He had not told the police he shot himself. Doctor X.A.Jones was called. He found a small hole covered by hair, on the man's right temple. He was taken to Samaritan Hospital, where he has slight chances to live. Wroblewski was a Dodge Motor Works employee. Mrs. Wroblewski kept a little dry goods store with the help of her children.

The following is the second newspaper article:

WIFE SHOOTER IS DEAD IN HOSPITAL

William Wroblewski Succumbs to Wound: Mother of Seven Will Probably Die.

After lingering 21 hours from wounds ordinarily instantly fatal William Wroblewski, Dodge factory employee who shot his wife and himself Thursday night in Hamtramck died at 11 o'clock Friday night in the Samaritan Hospital. Margaret Wroblewski, the wife still lives showing little change although her vitality puzzles the nurses, as she has three bullet wounds in her skull and another bullet in the back of her brain. Wroblewski shot his wife in the head in a bedroom over the little dry goods store she kept at 112 Lumpkin avenue, Hamtramck.Thursday night. Then he shot himself in the right temple. After examining both victims Dr. X. A. Jones said Thursday night neither could live more than a few hours.

The two oldest of the seven Wroblewski children, Margaret who is 16 and Mary who is 14 were at their parents bedsides Friday.

(Jim and I had no idea who Margaret and Mary were. Maybe William was married before.)

The following appeared in the Detroit News. An article and an obituary, Both dated April 23, 1917:

WIFE SHOT BY HUSBAND APRIL 12, DIES SUNDAY

Seven children are left orphans by father who shoots mother and then commits suicide. Mrs. Margaret Wroblewski, 112 Lumpkin street, Hamtramck, who was shot by her husband William on April 12 died as a result of her wounds at the Samaritan hos-pital, Sunday. Wroblewski, after shooting his wife shot himself in the head and died before medical aid arrived. The couple are survived by seven small children.

The following is the obituary:

WROBLEWSKI, Margaret. April 22 at Samaritan hospital. Mother of Rose, Frank, Harry, Bruno, Raymond, and Walter. Daughter of Mrs. Helen Rozmarynowski. Funeral to take place from residence of her sister, Mrs. Polanowski 1016 East Hancock, Wednesday at 9 a.m. Sweetest Heart of Mary Church.

After Frank's parents deaths he lived with his mother's sister. Mrs. Polanowski, cousin George's mother. Frank joined the Merchant Marines at an early age, then joined the Detroit Police Department on October 1, 1930. He was assigned to the 15th precinct and retired from Recorders Court effective July 5, 1956. He received several citations; one for an arrest of a concealed weapons charge, one for the arrest of an armed robber, and one for arresting five juveniles in a stolen, getaway car. There could have been more but that's all I found. Frank and his cousin George Polanowski were also bricklayers.

I thought back about Frank and how difficult life must have been for him to have not only lost both parents but right in front of him, when he was only thirteen.(the newspaper had incorrectly reported his age as eight). There were no psychologists to help these poor children. I told Jim, "No wonder your dad drinks, after going through all that." It explained a lot of Frank's behavior, and I felt so sorry for him and his siblings.

Louise told me, in the last years of her life, that the only thing she regretted was the time she spent worrying. "I'd say ninety percent of the things I worried about never happened."

Louise is buried in Woodlawn Cemetery, 19975 Woodward Avenue between 7 and 8 Mile Road. It is one of the most beautiful cemeteries. It was established in 1895 and immediately attracted some of the most notable names in the city: Booth, Hudson, Groesbeck, Ford and Dodge,

Frank died on Jim's 58th birthday. He and his second wide Geraldine are buried in a little rural cemetery just outside Algonac in Starville, Michigan, called Maple Grove Cemetery.

18

Starting Out

When we finally set a date for the wedding, Louise bought whole rooms of beautiful, brand new furniture for us. It was Danish Modern, which was very much in vogue at that time. She had it shipped to my house on Pinehurst, because Marguerite had gotten married, so now we had an empty bedroom upstairs.

After we were married and moved into the upstairs flat that Louise found for us, I got a job at Excello Corp. This is when I realized she lived too close to us, about a mile away. When I'd get home from work and open the door to our flat, I could see she had moved things around. This happened several times. I was in tears. I kept asking Jim to get the house key back. But he just couldn't. I was crying to Mama, literally crying on the phone about it, and Mama said, "Don't say anything, just keep moving everything back the way it was, and eventually she'll get the message." Mama was so wise. That did the trick, but it took several months.

Our flat had beautiful, hardwood floors. There were French windows in the living room. All the rooms were large, including the formal dining room, an eat-in kitchen, a ceramic tiled bathroom, and two spacious bedrooms. There was a little niche in the hall off the dining room where you kept your rotary phone, and a shelf below for your phone book. There was a little porch off the kitchen, in the back of the house, and in the summer during the Michigan State Fair we could hear the barkers on the midway. The Fairgrounds were about a mile away.

We loved the place, and the landlords, Mr. and Mrs. Ellis. There was one stipulation, no children. That was fine with us, we would deal with that when the time came.

We shared the basement with the owners, Mr. and Mrs. Ellis.

They were a nice middle age couple with no children. They lived on the first floor. They kept the whole place, immaculate inside and out. We never had any complaints, and neither did they.

Louise also filled our pantry full of food and some of her canned goods. She canned everything. She filled our kitchen with a sixteen piece place setting of plain white dishes, two complete sets of silverware, brand new Revere Ware pots and pans with the copper bottom. Boxes full of groceries. She did like to shop, but this was fantastic, just the kind of thing a young bride dreams of. She didn't miss a trick. She also filled our linen closet with tablecloths, towels and bedding, all brand new.

She crocheted a beautiful tablecloth for our new dining room table.

We settled in, and in 1961 we bought a deep red, four cylinder, 1961 Pontiac Tempest. It was Motor Trend magazine's 1961 Car of the Year. One of the many innovative decisions John DeLorean (Cass Tech alum) brought to the Pontiac Tempest, was the four cylinder engine. We loved that car. Deep red, leather bucket seats. Fast and zippy. Unfortunately, we only had it for a year or two when Jim, while driving with his buddy Jerry Czermendy, rolled it. Neither were injured, but I couldn't say that about the car.

Well, the time came two years later when we told the Ellis's that we were expecting. They said it was okay for us to continue living there, which we did for two more years. Then we found a cute, brick bungalow on the west side of town at 9976 Granville, right down the street from St. Suzanne's church and grade school. It was the perfect location just like Pinehurst. The kids would be a block and a half from the church and school. Dave was born three years after Steve, and Julie was born three years after David.

We paid $11,300 for the house. In the nine years we lived there, Jim finished the basement, and had a new roof put on, took out the ribbon driveway and put in a full driveway, We added a two car garage. Jim finished the attic with a large bedroom for the boys with lots of closet space.

One of the things that sold us on the house was the corner living room windows and the covered porch. The house was small but well built, with a slate foyer, marble window sills, and casement windows.

In a 1972 we bought property on Hamburg Lake. We started building our house in 1973. We moved in on November 13, 1973.

19

Man's Best Friend

Our first family pet was a pedigree English Bassett Hound, named Flower, given to us by our friends Dick and Lori Enos. I'm not sure why they were giving her up.

We found Flower to be a laid back, family friendly dog who was very affectionate. I was pregnant with Julie at the time, so I think my guard was down when I agreed to take a dog the size of Flower. I'd never had a dog, but Jim had Brittany Spaniels growing up, so he was fine with us having a dog. Steve, who loved animals, really wanted a dog, so Jim and Steve prevailed. This dog, however, was eighty pounds. You couldn't help loving her when you saw her sad face. She was precious. She looked just like the Hush Puppy dog in the commercials. They are wonderful pets for children.

As I said, I was pregnant with Julie. Actually eight months pregnant.

On this particular day, the dog ran out the front door before I could close it, and ran right out in the street. The car coming honked at her, and she froze, right in the middle of the street. She laid right down and wouldn't budge. I kept coaxing her to come, but she wouldn't, or couldn't, move.

I tried to pick her up, but it was no use. The driver of the car couldn't drive around her, so he reluctantly got out of his car, asked if the dog bites, and picked Flower up for me, and put her down gently on the front lawn. I was so embarrassed. I thanked the man profusely.

Flower's papers declared her, "The Duchess of Flowerdom." The family guessed that was because she was tricolored and had the perfect shape of a lily on her back. The neighborhood kids called her the "locomotive."

We were living in Detroit at the time, so Flower was not allowed out of the yard without a leash, however, every now and then someone would open that front door, or the backyard gate, and before you knew it, out flew Flower, all eighty pounds, with her ears flapping like she was going to take flight.

Everyone loved that dog, and got a kick out of the fact that we thought she'd make a great watch dog because of her loud, low bark. She loved to lay in the vestibule, so when people would come in our house, they'd have to step over her. They didn't want to wake her up.

To this day, I think Bassetts are the best breed for young children. These are very gentle animals, they are so friendly, love attention, and because they're built like a tank, they love children playing with them, and horsing around with them. When Steve or David would leave the house to play with friends down the street, the dog would howl like you wouldn't believe. A loud, long, low howl. I think it's called baying, as in baying at the moon. As you can imagine, we had the kids play at our house most of the time.

Flower was in the house the day I called the kids in for supper. I couldn't have been on the porch calling the kids for more than a few minutes. When I came back in, there was Flower, licking her chops. She had eaten the entire pot roast that had been sitting on the table. Jim was in the shower or he could have stopped her. I never thought Flower could reach the top of the table, but then I remembered her putting her paws on the kitchen sink..

When we moved out to the lake, Marguerite offered to take Flower because she had a fenced-in yard on a corner, a good place for Flower. Marguerite's son Billy, had Down Syndrome. They were good companions for each other. We knew this would be a good place for our Flower. No one on Norene Court had fences. Poor Flower would have been hit by a car the first day.

When you live out in the country, you get an occasional abandoned litter of puppies or kittens. We had only been living out there six months when Steve came home with a little, stray puppy not more than six weeks old. She was all dirty and had gum in her hair. She looked like the dog Benji from the movies. We named her Ginger because of the color of her coat. We had that dog for thirteen years.

She seemed to be Julie's dog, because wherever Julie was in the neighborhood, Ginger would be there with her.

Julie would paint Ginger's nails, and spray her with perfume, or put body powder all over her, to the boys utter consternation. Jim loved the fact that Ginger only ate generic dog food. He tried different brands, but Ginger still favored the generic.

In back of our house, and across Strawberry Lake Road, there's a little cemetery, naturally called Hamburg Cemetery. I heard a lot of barking one morning, and it sounded like Ginger's bark. I looked out the window, and there she was with her incessant barking as the people were entering the cemetery for a burial. I couldn't get to her fast enough. She just kept on barking. I was mortified. I apologized in a whisper to the people sitting by the casket. That was the first and last time she ever got out to disrupt a funeral.

I decided one day to start exercising, and bought a leash for Ginger so we could walk around the lake together. I never realized until Ginger was two years old that she had never been on a leash. You should have seen the spectacle that transpired when I tried to get the leash on her. Even though Ginger was only forty pounds, I could not wrestle that leash around her neck. She reminded me of a cat with catnip. Well, I finally gave up, and exercised without her.

Unlike most dogs, Ginger hated to get in the car. It appears the only time she had gone in the car was to the vet, and not without a struggle. We could understand that.

We got Ginger when Julie was in Kindergarten. Ginger was killed by a hit-and-run on M-36. It was Julie's senior year. We had that wonderful animal for thirteen years.

Then there was Steve and his friend Mike Wiles who found a lost poodle, but couldn't find the owner. Steve named him Fred, as in the dancing team of Fred and Ginger. He lasted two years. He drank someone's anti-freeze.

Steve used to talk about how smart that dog was. "If he only knew his real name," Steve said, "he could probably do many things that his prior owner had already taught him." For instance, when Steve's alarm would go off in the morning, Fred would jump on the bed and pull the covers off him.

That dog was not only impervious to storms, but actually would not "come in out of the rain," literally. During a thunder and lightening storm I kept calling for Fred. When a bolt of lightening flashed across the sky I could see Fred sitting like a sphinx in the middle of the road. His ears pinned back by the wind and facing the storm head on. He ignored me when I first called him, but as the lightening flashed again, he looked right at me, but still would not come in. He was unbelievable. You had to be there.

Jim got Fred a close-shaved hair cut. It was summer, and we wanted the dog to be comfortable. We never had his hair cut in those strange styles that you see on some poodles. It reminded me of something Gilda Radner once said on *Saturday Night Live*. "I wonder if other dogs think poodles are members of a weird religious cult." I wondered if male poodles got an inferiority complex having to walk around with those strange hair cuts.

After his haircut, the kids in the neighborhood didn't recognize Fred, except for Jeanette Liggett. She said "I'd know Fred anywhere. It's that attitude of his; he's so cute." She was right. He wasn't a big dog, but he was all about attitude.

One day, Louise called me at work to tell me that Fred had died right by the school bus stop. I asked her if she could take the dog's body away from there, so when the neighbor kids got off the school bus they wouldn't see Fred. I asked her if she would put Fred in the back of our house until Jim or I got home, (preferably Jim, I thought). When I got home from work, Louise had already buried the dog in her garden out back. Louise also loves animals. I knew what a hard thing that was for her to do. In her usual way, she brushed it off as nothing.

Ever since Fred died, whenever we went to the farmer's Market, Jim would wangle me over to the puppies. I kept telling him that with both of us working, a puppy would be too much work, plus I would feel bad leaving a puppy home alone all day. Being so young, it would get separation anxiety.

This went on for quite awhile. Then one day, as we were driving to Howell, Jim had to go in a feed store for something. I stayed in the car. In a few minutes, Jim came back out and told me he wanted me to see something in the store. "A feed store, really?" I said. But he insisted I see something in there. Sure enough, as soon I entered the store I heard dogs barking in the background.

As we approached the area where the barking was coming from, I could see several dogs in cages, but no puppies. I could tell that Jim was already becoming attached to a beautiful English Springer Spaniel. Evidently this dog did not like being in a cage, because he wouldn't stop barking. Sure enough, that's the dog Jim wanted. I kept telling him that with both of us working how is that suppose to help the dog?

Jim purchased some items, then we left. In the car Jim kept talking about that dog, so finally I told him to go back, and if the dog was still there, we'd take him. Well, I thought Jim was going to break the speed limit. We were back there in no time. Of course the dog was there, still barking. You could hear him all over the store. We purchased a leash, signed some papers, then took him home.

Would you believe? As soon as we got in the car the dog finally shut up. As I was looking at the packet the store gave us concerning the dog, it stated that his name was "Dusty." He was ten months old. It gave the owner's name and phone number and the name of his vet.

We called the owner. He wasn't home, but his dad talked to us. He told us his adult son owned the dog, and really loved him, but was getting engaged, and his girlfriend was allergic to dogs. We told him we lived on a lake and had two small grandsons who visited us often. We also told him that our yard was not fenced. The dad couldn't have been more pleased. He was sure the dog would be happy with us. We gave him our address and told him his son could come and visit Dusty anytime.

The boys loved Dusty. Jim took him everywhere. He turned out to be a wonderful dog. When we'd take our 2 1/2 hour drive up to the cottage, Dusty sat in back and enjoyed every minute of the drive.

Dusty is the only dog we had that had seizures. I was with him both times they occurred. He could have had others that we were not aware of.

When Jim was becoming more debilitated with Parkinson's, he would walk with Dusty to the Hamburg Post Office. It was about a mile or more, there and back. That was great exercise for both of them. As Jim's Parkinson's progressed, he would walk with Dusty around the lake or the neighborhood. I felt comfortable at work knowing Dusty was at home with Jim.

I called Dusty into the house one afternoon. Opening the side door expecting Dusty to come in, I saw him standing by our car, and not moving. I called his name. Nothing. I went over to him and petted him, but he wouldn't budge. He leaned his body against my leg, and we slowly walked into the house that way. I knew he was blind. He was perfectly fine when I had let him out, now this. I was really concerned.

We took him to the vet that specialized in neurology, and was told that he probably had a brain tumor, and at thirteen he'd had a good life, and he should probably be put down. All that for $1,000.00.

The weeks and months after Dusty died were hard on Jim. He didn't go outside anymore except to walk down to the road to get the newspaper, or sit on the porch to watch the sailboats. He use to go everywhere with Dusty because Dusty could bring him back home. Now he wasn't sure he could even find home.

Jim's instincts were correct when he picked such a fine dog. Dusty truly was a wonderful companion. He was always by Jim's side.

It was at this time that I started thinking about retiring from the Environmental Protection Agency. I really loved my boss, Chet France. He was very understanding. Every now and then I had to take time off for doctor's visits, or just go home to help Jim out, as he was becoming more and more debilitated. I loved my job at the agency and all the people I worked with, especially, Ines Storhok, Rita Parsons and Julia Mac Allister.

Marguerite and I meet with them for lunch each year when I'm home from Tennessee.

20

Steven James

Steve, our oldest child, was born at 4:05 am October 10, 1962. We picked the name Steven because it means strength, and James after his dad. He sure lives up to the characteristics of the Libra. He is charming, kind, gentle, and understanding. I mention gentle because Steve is what some would describe as a big man. Like his father and brother Dave, he is 6ft 2in, but more husky. Steve possesses all those rare qualities plus the patience of Job. He takes after his dad who was a very patient and kind person.

St. Suzanne's Catholic Church was down the street from our house. When Steve was five he saw Fr. Fontana going into Mary Pat's house across the street. Steve ran in the house so excited and said to me, "You'll never guess whose visiting at Mary Pat's house, God." He knows that churches are referred to as houses of God.

When I told Fr. Fontana, he loved it. "That's the best compliment I could ever receive, being mistaken for God." He said rather proudly, "I've got to tell the other priests. I bet that's never happened to them."

Once we had moved to Hamburg, stray dogs kept coming to our house, thanks to Steve. At 3:00 one morning the doorbell kept ringing. Jim couldn't get downstairs fast enough, thinking there was an emergency. He was amazed at what he saw. At first it looked like a short man with dark glasses. Turned out to be a large Alaskan malamute with black fur around his eyes standing on his hind legs looking in the front door window with his paws unintentionally pressing against the doorbell, and obviously looking for Steve. Another time there was a beautiful little husky puppy, so small he couldn't climb our front steps, but we could hear him crying. Steve took care of him while putting up fliers in town to find the owner.

From the back of our house you could see Strawberry Lake Road, which, like most roads in the country, was not well traveled. Just on the other side of it is Hamburg Cemetery. It's not a very large cemetery. I think Steve was twelve at the time when I looked over at the cemetery and saw our little dog Ginger gently pushing a small object across the road towards our house. It was a newborn bunny. Steve immediately ran to the cemetery and found two more little bunnies. They could hardly have been a day old. He immediately called Scott, one of his classmates whose dad was a veterinarian, but the dad was out of town for the week-end. Steve was able to get instructions from Scott on what to do to keep the bunnies alive until Scott's dad got home. Steve hardly left their side the whole week-end. He was feeding them with an eye dropper and massaging them. He got a heating pad for them and did everything his friend had told him to do. The first day he lost one, the second day the next one died. I was praying that he could keep the last one alive; he had worked so hard, but it was not to be. The last one died early Monday morning. Scott's dad called Steve when he heard what he was trying to do, and told him he couldn't have done a better job himself.

We had a small Jet Wind two-man sail boat that Steve practically lived on in the summer. He loved the water. He would wear a tee shirt with his bathing suit whenever he sailed because his ruddy skin tans easily. In the winter Steve and his buddy Mark Waters made their sail boats into ice boats and sailed all winter long on the lake.

He loved baseball and was an excellent player. He's left-handed so he's a natural as first baseman and also an excellent pitcher. Everyone likes to yell and heckle the pitcher but nothing like that ever fazed Steve. At one particular game as the heckling was going on, a fellow a couple seats down from us wanted to know if the pitcher was deaf. Jim and I got a kick out of that.

In the following, Steve writes about his experience in the Brighton. Olympics:

The Brighton Olympics started in the summer of seventh grade. Getting the Brighton Argus and seeing the entire form for the sport you would like, was the start of a fun summer. For me it was ping pong, horse shoes, swimming and badminton. Those four games were my favorites. Playing horseshoes with my dad in the side yard helped me get competitive. Having two buddies that had Ping-pong tables, (Mark Waters and Curt Bennett) was what I needed to sharpen my game.

My swimming capabilities were getting better when mom and dad bought me a sail boat. I wanted a sail boat because some of my other friends on the lake had one. Our lake did not allow motors, so sailing was what everyone did on the lake. I could swim, but I was not a good diver at that time.

The Swimming Olympics were a freestyle swim that was familiar to me. To start the race you had to dive in. So when the starting gun went off everyone dove in but me. Diving was not my forté, so I did a "cannonball" and then started to swim like crazy to catch up to the rest of the field. Being able to pass several swimmers and ending up taking third resulted in a bronze metal. Everybody said, if I knew how to dive I would have won easily. The next year I did learn how to dive, and took the gold.

Horseshoes was an easy gold medal because kids my age really did not get into horseshoes. Badminton was a gold medal as well. Once again, playing in the side yard that summer with dad and my buddies helped dearly in winning the gold.

Ping-pong was the hardest medal to win. That was because of my nemeses Donnie and Ronnie Cash. I took silver both years. Don beat me the first year, then Ronnie beat me the next year. We became friends and kept playing, and eventually we were teammates in bowling. Those years created a desire for competition that has remained with me throughout my life.

In middle school, Steve worked in that little cemetery near us with his friend Bill Kapp, cutting grass and raking leaves. That was seasonal work, so when he was sixteen he worked as a cook in the Edelweiss German restaurant in town. He was in tenth grade and no longer working in the cemetery when a terribly sad event stunned our little community. A classmate, Linda Evans, who we carpooled with for sports events at the school, was killed in a car accident. Steve and Bill told the sexton of the cemetery, who happened to be Bill's Uncle Dale, that they would like to volunteer to help straighten up the cemetery before the funeral and have everything looking really nice for Linda's funeral. Steve thought it would be more personal if her friends took care of the preparations instead of strangers.

In high school, Steve started dating the girl across the street. What follows is the story of Kathy, according to Steve:

We moved from Detroit to Hamburg when I was in the sixth grade. At that time the 6th grade was a split shift school year. I noticed this blond girl across the street and found out she was my age but was going in the afternoon to school. I had the morning shift. In fact that first year everybody my age had the afternoon shift except me.

We saw each other from time to time but I was afraid to approach. Then as the summer came, a kid up the hill named Bill Kapp and I started to hang out and play baseball with the other kids. Come to find out Bill was a cousin to Kathy. I asked about her and Bill said she was "okay" for a girl.

The years passed and we started talking every now and then. We rode the same bus but never in the same seat. I started noticing around 9th and 10th grade that she was a pretty girl. The real ice breaker was the purchase of my first car. Once that happened, new freedoms opened up for me.

In the past, I noticed Kathy had gone out with fellas that had cars, and I didn't, until now. Then low and behold I started driving her to school and back. Every now and then we went to McDonalds or Dairy Queen. She started coming to my basketball and baseball games. Then we started to just hang out together, and when the summer came we went out on the sailboat and then we went to a movie and all of a sudden we were boyfriend and girlfriend.

A year or so went by and it was starting to get a little mundane for both of us. Other people were vying for our attention.

Working more hours started taking up more of my time. Sports, and hanging out with my buddies, Mike and Wally took its toll on our relationship. We remained friends afterwards. Although I have not seen her in over 30 years I found out she also had moved to North Carolina and coincidentally just down the road from me, in a small town called Lincolnton. I always wondered if I would ever run into her, but frankly, I'm not sure if I would recognize her.

Steve was six feet tall and two hundred pounds in ninth grade. The football coach wouldn't stop calling, practically begging Steve to play. Steve liked football but was already on the schools traveling Bowling League. His bowling average is over 200. (2016) .He ended up lettering in baseball and basketball.

The four years Steve was in high school he had a woodworking class that he loved. Freshmen year he made assorted wood items like a small bookcase, a spice rack and book ends. Sophomore year he made a beautiful mahogany coffee table; junior year an award winning mahogany grandfather clock, and in his senior year he out did himself with a sewing center that was a replication of one found in Family Circle magazine 1979 issue. I don't remember the month. It was such a work of art. Again, all mahogany, closed, it looked like a beautiful buffet, opened it was a complete workstation.

Steve and Dad

The whole family, all his friends, and the neighbors knew he was a lead foot. My father had a lead foot too, but he was a policeman and could get it out of his system racing around in scout cars. Butch, one of our neighbors saw Steve speeding down the highway, and the next day when he saw Steve, told him "If I see you speeding like that again I'm telling your dad."

Steve has always loved cars, in fact today he lives in Charlotte, NC, NASCAR country. He bought his first car from a friend of ours, a 1974 Maverick with 18,000 miles on it, and paid for it himself when he was fifteen. He was "chomping at the bit" to drive that car. He got his driver's license in October, and in early December he drove out of the parking lot at the high school and headed down M-36, and just before he reached the outskirts of town, which would only be about a half a mile, he was pulled over by the Police Chief of Pinckney for speeding and got his first ticket. Not more than three weeks later he got a ticket in Brighton for an illegal left turn. We could see the writing on the wall; this was just the beginning of a long list of tickets, mostly speeding tickets, that would plague him for years to come.

Steve had been in North Carolina maybe a year when he met Bonnie, Their friendship flourished, and eventually they married.

Steve and Bonnie's wedding, as only he can tell it:

So it was decided that after being together for over 5 years that Bonnie and I should probably get married. I had good health benefits with the city, and she could take advantage of those if need be. With all the kids staying with grandma, due to a court order, it was pretty good living for Bonnie and me.

The kids would stay with us during Thanksgiving, Christmas and Easter. Then a couple weeks during the summer, one of which was always spent at Sunset Beach. Even though things were going pretty good, we did not have enough money to have an extravagant wedding. In fact, we just wanted to get something done kind of quick.

We had driven past this so called wedding chapel several times on the way to the flea market, or Carowinds and we thought, what the heck, let's give it a try. We called the number and a lady answered. She was friendly enough, and said it would not be a problem. "How about the first week-end in November?" That would make it November 5th.

We talked it over and said, "Let's do it." Oh, and by the way, it was going to be $15.00, and if we wanted music, it would be $25.00, plus gratuity. We opted for music.

The day finally came. I was wearing a sport coat, and Bonnie wore a nice yellow dress. Our guest selection was limited, since everybody we knew lived out of state except for a few. Mike Wiles, my friend since middle school, lived near us in North Carolina, was best man. Our neighbors, Kip and Melanie, came. Melanie was the maid of honor.

Bonnie's family wasn't coming due to the short notice. We did have some neighbors, Tim and Sandy came by.

It's the big day, and we all arrive, but where is the lady that is supposed to marry us? Finally about thirty minutes later, we see this old, wood grain station wagon fly into the church parking lot with dust and smoke everywhere. Mike had to jump out of the way to avoid getting run over. As Mike walked behind the station wagon, all of a sudden a loud boom sounded. As we all turned around, we see that Mike had fallen. The car had backfired and shot out a plume of smoke and ash. When Mike stood up, his khaki, sport jacket was covered in black soot.

The lady apologized for being late, and told us to follow her into the church. Did I mention the "church" was a mobile home? Once we all gathered in the church it shifted and started leaning to the left. The power in the mobile home shut off and never came back on during the ceremony. Luckily it was a nice comfortable day. The minister told us not to worry, and to continue with the ceremony.

We were apprehensive, but we did start saying our vows. I interrupted momentarily and whispered to the minister "Where is the music?" She replied that she almost forgot, and went back to her car and grabbed, what was called, back in the day, a "ghetto blaster." She put in the cassette and boom, we had music.

As the vows were being read, the minister's glasses broke and fell off her head. I reached down to get them and handed them to her, but one part of the eyeglass frame had broken off. She had to hold the glasses to her head, and now, had to hold the book from which she was reading. So after all this, the "I do's" were said and we were married.

Note: Steve told me, when the lights went out, the minister lit candles. Surprisingly, it made the place look quite presentable.

Steve helped Bonnie raise her four children. Bucky, Rusty, Amanda and Brittney. They were quite young at this time. Each year in early spring, Steve took the family to Sunset Beach NC just north of Myrtle Beach. Jim and I would rent a house nearby.

The first time Jim and I did that we bought kites for the kids to fly on the beach. Many times Jim and I were able to bring Seth and Nathan. Usually Julie would come with us. Matt couldn't come until the next day because he played organ at his church. One Easter, Dave came down and we celebrated Easter Sunday at daybreak on the beach. It was beautiful.

It was a good marriage for the most part, but in 2011 Steve and Bonnie divorced. It was an amicable divorce. They parted friends. Steve attends all his step-children's and step-grandchildren's functions.

Bonnie managed the Starbucks coffee shops at Charlotte-Douglas International airport. Then started her own coffee shop.

Steve loves animals, as I've mentioned before. The following is a heartwarming story of his dog Boost, again, in his own words:

Steve & Boost

It was decided that our family needed another dog to keep Turbo company as he got older. The thought being that he would exercise more and be more motivated to play, move around and maybe lose a pound or two. That went for the owner as well. Bonnie and I felt a shelter dog was really all we needed. We did not see a good reason to pay hundreds of dollars for a pet when there were good looking dogs at the shelter. We were at the shelter and it came down to a beautiful shiny coat black lab or a mangy, dirty, kennel coughing chocolate lab that had been abused.

"I want this one." I said to Bonnie, as I pointed to the chocolate lab. She replied "Are you crazy? Look at that dog compared to the black lab." I said, "There is something about this dog that is attracting me to it, and I don't know what it is. Plus, that black lab will get adopted in a minute. Nobody will adopt this dog unless I do." Bonnie reluctantly agreed.

We were given the opportunity to get to know the dog before we adopted him. We sat in a glass cubicle and he was brought to us. He immediately ran to me, jumped on my lap and licked my face. Then he went to Bonnie and did the same. "This is our dog" I said to Bonnie and kennel attendant.

We commenced to fill out the paperwork and pay the $60. We took him home and it was a disaster at first. Turbo was not very thrilled at all about our new family member and Boost went and hid from him. We found out quickly that potty training was first on the to do list. Then after giving him kennel cough medicine, heartworm medicine, and several baths we started to see a thoroughbred evolve. Time went by and with help from Turbo, Boost was getting the hang of going outside when needed. They were becoming friends but you could tell that Boost was a "pain in the butt from time to time".

Boost was starting to get some confidence when it came to messing with Turbo. He would run up to him and try to nip at his ears. This was okay for a while until Turbo had enough. When this happened a return nip at the ears would take place and maybe even a takedown by Turbo letting Boost know who was boss. This was how the relationship would be from this point forward.

It was realized that Boost was becoming quite the athletic dog, extremely fast and strong. I would play tug-a-war with this relentless animal only to acquiesce the towel every time. Outside I would throw the Frisbee and he could catch it every now and then. My neighbor Ed said "If you knew how to throw the damn thing, he would catch it every time. Turbo by now was getting older and just wanted to watch. At least he was getting up and around and that meant our plan worked.

The day finally came when I had to put Turbo down. That was a tough decision. He was old and his health had been failing. I told the vet I would like to take the body home so Boost could see what happened to his buddy. I gently laid Turbo's body down in the yard.

Boost slowly walked up to the body and sniffed him and walked around him a then just laid down near him for awhile. Then I took the body back to the vet.

One thing that impressed me about Boost was the way he walked with me. With or without a leash he would stay within a 20 foot diameter of me all the time. If on a leash he would never tug. I decided to take him on a walk in one of our county parks nearby. I had been walking Latta Park for about a year, and decided to take Boost.

At first I would walk him with a leash but I noticed this wasn't necessary, so one day I just took the leash off and hoped for the best, knowing that if he wanted to run, I would never be able to catch him. Boost just stayed by my side. He ventured out about 20-25 feet but not much further. If I called him he would come back. When we came to a fork in the path I would point with my finger on which path to choose, and he would go that way. Who taught him this? When we came up to horses walking the same path or other people walking their dogs, Boost would just slow down wait for me and stand by my side until they passed. Again who taught him this? People would commend me on how well my dog was trained. I said thank you. If they only knew I did nothing to train him. This became our thing to do on weekends and sometimes during the weekday afternoons, if I snuck out of work early.

We would first stop at McDonalds and get an egg McMuffin

before we started. The walk was 6 miles but it went along the lake. We would stop so he could drink out of the lake and wade around for a while and cool off, then back to it. As more time passed, I noticed him not keeping up with me on our walk. In fact, I was the one leading. He kept up but stayed behind me. Boost was getting tired. Then one day I thought I was going to have to carry him the last mile. He barely made it. So I decided to shorten the walk, but he was becoming lethargic and was not doing well with the shorter walks either. One of the saddest days was when I got into my truck and went on my walk without him. Boost knew where I was going. Around our yard and down our little road was what our walk had been diminished to, but both of us looked forward to it. One other note; I was keeping our gate open so he could walk the perimeter of the yard. He never left the property.

An odd issue with Boost was his fear of thunderstorms. He was not afraid of anything. But as soon as the sky lit up with a bolt of lightning he was under a desk, in a bed, under the covers, or on the couch shaking on our laps. It was difficult to calm him down. I think he might have been left outside without any protection during thunderstorms from a previous owner. There were a couple instances that I could not get home in time to let him in the house while a storm was approaching. He did have the protection of a screened in back porch. One time I came home and he was outside lying in the middle of the yard while it was pouring rain and thunder. To this day I did not understand that. Another time during a storm I pulled in the driveway and could not find him. I became worried almost to a panic. Where is he? Did someone take him? Come to find out, he left the security of the back porch to lay on the front porch which was smaller and open to the elements. Why didn't he come to me when I pulled in the driveway? I had to open the front door and almost carry him into the house, he would hardly move. It just goes to show that storms created a bizarre and irrational behavior in him.

We consulted the vet who prescribed Xanax. We were to give him a pill before a looming thunderstorm arrived. Upon giving him a pill it was almost comical to see him go from extreme anxiety to a calm glassy eyed lazy dog in the middle of a storm. Needless to say we kept several "doggy Xanax" on hand during the summer months.

I started noticing after throwing the ball for him to fetch, or a game of tug a war, that he was having difficulty catching his breath. I knew he was getting old and I did remember that he had a rough bout with kennel cough during the time we were getting him from the shelter. Whether this had anything to do with it was merely speculation, but something was going on. So a trip to the vet was in store for Boost.

A couple days later, Boost was examined and x-rayed. The Vet came in to discuss what was going on with Boost. There was a big word for his diagnosis, but basically what was happening was his airway was closing up on him. This was not that unusual for aging Labs. What a terrible thing to have I thought. So from this point forward we had to be careful not to over exert him, which meant no more throwing the Frisbee or ball, real easy tug of war for a short time and no more long walks. He is not going to be happy. Those were the fun things in life for him. Then his hips started to bother him, and he could no longer jump on the bed, or couch. So he found he liked the thick throw rug in front of the fireplace. I went to Ikea, which is a European furniture store that had a king size bed that was very low to the ground. I bought it and set it up. Then after a little coasting, he was able to get up on the bed. It didn't look pretty, but he was able. I think he liked that a lot. This was slowly becoming the beginning of the end. Tammy my girlfriend, and I, were looking for anything that could make him more comfortable breathing. We looked for and tried homeopathic and prescription medicines thinking something will work. I even bought a nebulizer to help his breathing, but nothing seemed to help. Finally after several days of discussion and listening to Boost's very restricted breathing, it was decided that he was not happy and probably in pain all the time.

It got to the point that he could hardly move. What was holding me back from putting him down was his ability to eat everything in his bowl all the time, and go poop outside. Boost started pooping on the back deck instead of stepping down one stair from the deck to the grass and go on the grass.

I consulted again with the vet, as I was purchasing refills for Boost. I am reluctant to put him down because he ate so well. The vet told me that Labs eat 7 days after they're dead. I laughed but then realized that the point she was making is, eating is not necessarily the only guide to use when making this critical decision.

A couple weeks later on a Tuesday I left work early after setting up a time to put him down. I grabbed his leash and the keys to the truck. His head perked up, he was sure we were going to the park for a walk, even though he could barely get up. I reached down to lift his rear end up so he could move. We slowly walked to the truck his tail wagging all the way. I put three large blankets in the back for him to lie on.

Ten years prior he would have jumped in the back on his own, and barked with excitement that we were on the move. He knew that when I made a left on the main road, instead of a right, that we were not going for a walk. His head slowly lowered to the blanket and he no longer was interested in what was out the window.

When we arrived, I lifted him out from the back, and we slowly walked in to the vet. He had been here before, so he probably thought he was going to get weighed, and prodded a little, and maybe his nails clipped. Nothing he hasn't been through before. His breathing was very bad and in a strange way I was glad. Simply, that it helped assure me that I was doing the right thing. By now I was having a difficult time with my emotions. "This is really happening, just get this over with and go cry in the truck on the way home, but keep it together in the office." I said to myself.

I told the cashier that I wanted to pay now, so I could walk straight out of here without interruption. We were directed to room 3 and told to wait momentarily for the doctor. Boost sat on the floor and I sat on the floor with him. I took his collar and leash off. He wasn't going anywhere. I gave him some water from the sink to sooth his throat, and we sat there and looked at each other. I was looking into his eyes and wondering if he knew what was going to happen. I think that he did, because he always seemed to know when I was sad or troubled with something. I think he was ready as well. He couldn't do anything anymore, and could hardly breathe.

The doctor came in, she seemed friendly enough. She petted Boost and talked to him in her dog talking voice. "How's Boost?" and "Boost is a pretty dog." Boost seemed to like her. Two other young female assistants came into the room with a much somber look on their faces. They wanted to lift Boost onto the table. I told them I would lift him onto the table. He never minded me picking him up, ever.

The Vet concurred that this was the best for Boost. She gave Boost a sedative then left the room with her two assistants, to give me a few more minutes with him. The room became very quiet, his heavy breathing had subdued. He was just kind of dazed like the Xanax we gave him during thunderstorms. I petted him and petted him and told him he was a good dog over and over. Then the door opened and the three came back in. His head popped up and stayed up as he looked at all of us. Then the doctor gave him the final shot. His head tried to stay up but it could not. It gently fell over the vet's arm. She took out her stethoscope checked for a heartbeat and there wasn't one. He's gone she said and the young girl assistants started crying. Well that made me start crying, and I was sure I could keep it together till the truck. I told everybody thank you, and said "I really have to go now." and did.

I was having a hard time on the way home. Sat on the couch and called my girlfriend Tammy. I gave her the news that she was expecting. She assured me that we did the right thing. What a responsibility we take on, controlling the life of another living thing, and to choose when it dies. Boost cannot make that decision for himself. Most likely he would have remained in extreme pain just to make us happy.

After our conversation, it was clear we made the right decision, but it did not make us feel much better. As the night passed, it was obvious our routine had changed. No more letting Boost outside, and back in. No more holding the nebulizer up to his face as he tried to *breathe. No more trying to mask his pills in a piece of ham or peanut butter. Brand new bag of dog food just sitting there. No more snoring, that let us know he was at the foot of the bed.*

It was strange to realize how many things made him a part of our day. Then the next day I came home from work. Out of habit I started to look for Boost and quickly realized that my welcoming committee was gone. I thought to myself, "I have to get another dog. This house is so quiet." So to pass the time, I got onto the computer to see what was happening with the kids, and the nephews. How odd is it that Rusty, my stepson, has a Cane Corso Italian Mastiff, that just had 13 puppies. They were only planning on having 8. Tammy and I have a couple trips ahead of us in the next two months. After that, I believe one of those thirteen will be ours, and so it goes.

Tammy and Steve

On April 5, 2013, Steve and Tammy married. The following is a description of his wedding in his own words:

After almost two years of dating, and really having a lot of fun with each other, we decided that getting married would be a great *idea. Several reasons for this: Tammy was spending a great deal of time at the cabin already, and it was a lot closer to her job. Also, just for being married we would each get back about $80.00 a week in our paychecks. Oh…and we loved each other. If I didn't put that in there, Tammy would have a fit.*

Several discussions took place on how we should get married. Whether it was on our friend's boat, drive to the mountains for a weekend getaway or head to the beach. All of these choices sounded good, but first we had to get the marriage license.

On the first Friday in April, I was working in the same area that Tammy worked, which was also close to the courthouse. So I called her up and asked if this would be a good time to walk over to the courthouse and get our license, then have lunch afterwards. Tammy said, "Yes." So we met up at her work, and walked across the street to the courthouse. It took a minute to find where to go. We arrived and talked with a nice lady who asked us to sit at one of several computers and fill out our information, then print a copy and bring it to her. The license required a lot of family background questions that we had to ask the other for.

We took our copies to the lady who inquired why we had not filled in the specific date that we wanted to get married on. Tammy and I told her that we did not have a firm date. All we wanted was to get our license and then figure out what to do later. The lady smiled and said, "You know the judge is right down the hall and is getting ready to marry couples in ten minutes, and if you hurry you can get married within an hour." This information startled us a bit, but we decided that we can still do all the things we were talking about, and just get this technical stuff out of the way.

Since this whole thing was somewhat of a shock, we were unprepared. First, it would cost $20.00. Neither of us had hardly, any cash on us, and the cashier would not take a credit/debit card. So we dug into our wallets. I had $17.00 and Tammy had $3.00 on her. The first hurdle solved, but then who will be our witnesses? None of our friends could get there in the next 20 minute. We asked the couple in front of us, who we had been chatting with, if they *would do us the honor and be our witnesses. They happily agreed. Suddenly it was our turn, and the sheriff hurried us along to the front of the courtroom. The lady judge was waiting. She asked us how to pronounce our names, and then commenced with the vows. I said "I do" and so did Tammy, and boom we were married. We had to get out of there so the next couple could get married. We said thank you to our witnesses, who we will never see again. Then the first thing that came to our minds, after just getting married, was that we were way past our lunch hour, and both of us had to get back to work. We never did have lunch that day.*

Steve left out the part where Tammy was dressed in her office clothes, heels and all, while Steve was in his work clothes, work boots and all.

Every spring Steve drives me back home to Michigan. This gives him a chance to meet his buddies, Wally Baran, Matt Heath and others. Wally spends the night and they golf in the morning, weather permitting. Wally brings his tool box to help Steve fix things around my condo.

In October when Steve drives me back to Tennessee, Wally picks him up at the airport and they play golf, again, weather permitting and then Wally spends the night. He always brings his tool box and helps Steve fix things that need to be done around the condo.

Tammy is the Claims Manager for Charlotte/Mecklenberg, and the school system for that area. Steve is the Senior Planning Coordinator, Environmental Impact Consultant, Chatlotte/Mecklenberg Utilities, Field Operations Division.

21

David Michael

David

David Michael is our middle child, and as a typical middle child, is very out-going. We named him David which means beloved, and that's exactly what he is. He was born at 10:00 pm on August 7, 1965, a true Leo. David was a high maintenance baby, he thrived on attention, was very affectionate, and got into everything.

He was an adventurous little boy who liked to get into and/or involved in everything. A very affectionate child whom everyone just loved. Early on, he got into the habit of chewing on the bars of his crib until one day he had actually chewed right through them. He reminded me of a little prisoner breaking out of his little jail cell. He even tried to chew on the marble window sills.

When David was four I heard him singing at the top of his lungs. He was singing the Tom Jones song, "Delilah" as he walked down the street. The part of the song that I caught was, "*I saw the shadows of love on the blind.*" The neighbors thought it was hilarious, which only made him sing louder.

At five years old he took our little neighbor Mary Beth, also five, by the hand, and walked with her several blocks away. Her mother and I were frantic looking for them. When we finally found them four blocks from home, David said he was teaching Mary Beth how to cross the street. When I reminded him he wasn't suppose to cross the street alone, he said he wasn't alone he was with Mary Beth.

When kindergarten started, he would not let me walk him to school. He was adamant. "If you follow me, I won't go to school," he said. I asked the safety boy on the corner if he would make sure David got to school okay.

When he was seven he sub-contracted himself out to that same safety boy who now had a paper route, and he paid David to deliver the newspapers on one side of our block, while he did the other side. This was just the beginning of David's entrepreneurial skills. It was around this time that we moved to the lake.

As I mentioned before, Dave was a very active child. He wasn't what you would call hyper-active because he always channeled his energy in positive endeavors. For instance, he loved to build rockets, and the neighborhood kids loved it when word got out that Dave was about to launch another rocket. They all stood around, mostly young boys but some of the dads, too. Dave would send those rockets toward the sky with grasshoppers on board, and sometimes he would even put little cameras onboard. He worked hard for the money to pay for the rocket kits, and after awhile he didn't need the kits, he just built them on his own. They were beautiful rockets. It was always a big day in our neighborhood when he launched them. He became a member of NAR (National Association of Rocketry) and participated in many of their tournaments earning many ribbons.

One day we were taking the family to Farrell's in Ann Arbor, an ice cream parlor that was known for making a big deal out of kids' birthdays. We were trying to surprise Julie who was turning five. She figured it out on the way there and wanted no part of it. She made such a fuss, saying, "I won't get out of the car." Dave, who was eight at the time, said, "Can we pretend it's my birthday?" He always loved attention.

The year Dave received a train set for Christmas, he remembers to this day. He was so excited. He said it was his best Christmas ever. He built a table with cork bedding. Jim put a large piece of plywood on the table in the basement, and Dave just had a ball setting the trains up.

He was only eleven or twelve at the time. Jim told him, "If you need any help let me know," but Dave didn't. He had his manual, and he was all set. Jim would go down from time to time to check on him. Dave would save his money from mowing lawns and other odd jobs around the neighborhood to buy little buildings and other accessories. He built little towns and bridges for his model railroad. One day, when Jim went downstairs, he was surprised to see that Dave was just about ready to turn the switch on and start the train. He had studied that manual and figured out the wiring. Jim just couldn't believe Dave had wired it by himself. He called our neighbor Butch over. He was an electrician for the Hyatt Regency in Dearborn. Butch looked it over and said it was "good to go." He couldn't believe that an eleven year old set that train up by himself, but then he remembered Jim knew nothing about electricity, so what choice did Dave have.

We would take Dave to Ann Arbor to a hobby shop that had a wonderful selection of trains and accessories. He had his Christmas money with him, and it was eating a hole in his pocket. He asked the salesman for some items that he needed. The salesman got the items, and when he told David the price, Dave said to him, "Don't you think this is too much money? I can't afford these, I'm just a kid." The people waiting in line loved it.

Mrs. Marguare, an elderly lady who lived down on the lake, had a lot of trees on her property in back of her house. Dave, never one to miss an opportunity when he saw it, decided to build a tree house in one of her trees.

There were two new houses being built on our cul-d-sac (Tom and Krisanne Rae's and Butch and Cindy Briggs's) so Dave went over, introduced himself to the new neighbors, and asked if they had any extra lumber for his tree house? Of course they did.

Everybody loved Dave and thought he was a pretty neat kid. Some of the neighborhood boys helped Dave build the tree house. First they were satisfied with one story, and when they finished that, Dave put up a sign "*No Girls allowed. Any girls who enter will become dead.*" Then they decided to add another story to the tree house and then a third.

Mrs. Marquare, wondering through her woods one day spotted Dave in the tree house and told him, "If you make that house any bigger, they're going to raise my taxes." Dave figured that she was, in effect, trying to be polite but didn't want that tree house any bigger.

Jim, Steve, and Dave loved shooting pool in the basement, and to this day they are all excellent pool players. Dave played little league baseball, and in middle school he played basketball. Jim coached his team. In middle school he also played football, but his real love has always been golf. He'd golf everyday if he could. His older brother Steve and his dad are also excellent golfers, and they always enjoyed golfing with each other. In high school Dave lettered in golf and tennis.

One afternoon, as Jim and I were coming home, we caught a glimpse of our hose running up the side of the house and into Dave's second story bedroom window. We wondered what the heck was going on. Turned out, while we were gone, which must have been most of the day, Dave had built himself a king size waterbed, and was now filling up the mattress. We couldn't believe it. We asked him why he didn't get permission to do this, he said he knew what we'd say. . .

In ninth grade, Dave was inspired to build a Peugeot bike after watching the 1979 movie, *Breaking Away*. It is the story of a small-town teenager obsessed with the Italian cycling team. Dave bought all the parts himself, and built the bike. He has always been a take charge guy.

Our family would play volleyball regularly throughout the summer on our side lot with the neighbors and their kids. Dave, typically, would set the teams up telling everyone which side they were to play on. Our neighbor Gary Cook said in jest, "Why are we listening to Dave? He's just a kid!"

I believe it was Gary Ladd who answered, "Because he's a good player and knows the rules." They continued to let Dave set up the teams, because taking charge came so natural to him.

In Dave's sophomore year, at age fifteen, he formed a company that resurfaced driveways and parking lots, and Steve helped him out by driving him around because he couldn't drive yet.

Dave and Dad

While in college, Dave's business expanded into landscaping. He named it Huron Lawn Service, in Ann Arbor. He eventually took on a partner, Mike Kowalski. Just before he graduated, he sold his share to his partner. That business, now The Great Outdoors, is still going strong in Ann Arbor. It has turned into a large enterprise, and has expanded into several counties.

While at Eastern Michigan University, Dave pledged Lambda Chi Alpha International fraternity, Sigma Kappa Chapter, and belongs to the Alumni Association.

While he was still in college, Jim and I went to see him at the apartment he was renting with some of his fraternity brothers. Big mistake. First of all we could see a large pyramid of empty beer cans neatly filling up the large picture window in front of the apartment. Inside, we met some of his fraternity brothers. One of them showed us a live cobra he kept in his bedroom in a plexiglass table. The guys told us they fed him live mice. I don't know where they got the mice, and I didn't ask.

Dave and his fraternity brothers are still very active to this day.

They go on canoe trips, golf outings and such. Dave is very close to a lot of his fraternity brothers. He loves just about all sports, but his favorite leisure activity is golf, and he's very good at it. In 2014 to present, he has played in the Knoxville Open Pro-Am Tournament. The Knoxville Open is a stop on the web.com tour. He and Steve golf together whenever possible and both love to shoot pool.

After graduating from Eastern Michigan University, Dave took a job in Marion, Ohio. On Sunday May 25, 1986 Hands-Across-America was going to go right through Marion. It was a benefit event staged to raise money to fight hunger and homelessness. Dave had a lot of cajoling to do to get his dad to agree to participate; of course Jim relented. Dave and I were so excited to participate, Jim, not so much.

Dave met his wife Lisa in Tellico Village, Tennessee while visiting one of his fraternity brothers, Joe Hamilton at their parent's house. Turns out Lisa was living there. She's originally from Farmington Hills, Michigan. She was divorced at that time, and Dave had been divorced a couple years. They hit it off right away, and got married a year later.

They lived together in Lenoir City for three years with Courtney Pethers, Lisa's daughter. Courtney was born December 26 1993. Then they bought a house just north of Lenoir City. The three of them moved in. Dave loves his step-daughter, and to this day people who know Dave would never guess that one of his daughters is really his step-daughter.

Jim and I had bought a lot at Fairfield Glade in 1986 with the intention of building a house on it after we retired.

After marrying Lisa, Dave took us around Tellico Village and encouraged us to buy there, since he was living in Lenoir City. We bought our place in Tellico in 2004, and Dave found some workers to rent it for the first year because I wasn't going to retire until 2005. During the year before we moved in, Dave spent countless hours painting and redoing the floors. The place looked wonderful when he finished.

Lisa and David

The first week we moved into the townhouse the air conditioner quit working. Dave came over to see if he could fix it. He's handy with everything. When he couldn't fix it, and the temperature outside was upwards of 90 degrees, he got the phone number of our one year home owner's insurance from our real estate agent. Dave called and told them it was an emergency, since his dad was suffering from Parkinson's disease. After going back and forth with different people at the agency and getting names of people in charge so he could file a complaint, the agent finally relented and sent someone out. This was on a weekend. The repair man came out within an hour and fixed the air conditioner. He gave the bill to Dave. Turned out, it was the wrong insurance company...

Then little Carly Diane came along and proved once again that the "Mother's Curse" does work when we say, "I hope you have a child just like yourself, when you grow up," and he did. They are so much alike, and they have so much fun together. They turn the CDs up loud in the car and rap together. When fun music comes on in the house they'll dance together in the living room.

One of my favorite memories was when Carly was four. Dave built her a Playland with a swing set and a platform for a little table and chairs. Carly wanted daddy to have tea with her. So there they were,

Dave, 6'2" and approx. 250 lbs. sitting down to tea with Carly. His knees were almost touching his ears. It was hilarious.

Dave was the second grade lunch buddy in Carly's school room at Highland Park Elementary School. He would go one afternoon each month and the kids were crazy about him because he's just a kid himself. He'll never grow out of that, thank goodness.

Dave has always been involved in the sales profession. He has won numerous awards for top sales achievement from the various companies he's represented. He currently is an Account Manager for Airgas selling industrial and specialty gases in the manufacturing sector. Dave's wife Lisa is part owner in the family business, Apex Canvas in Loudon, Tennessee. They manufacture OEM marine canvas covers and bimini tops for the boating industry. The company has been in business since 1988 and has expanded almost every year since then. They currently employ over 40 people.

Dave and his family love to travel, having visited many states. They enjoy cruises and Disney World vacations as well.

Carly and Courtney

22

Julie Marie

This is the story of Julie, our only daughter who was born in 1968. Jim and I already had two sons, Steve and Dave, and really wanted to welcome a little girl into the family. This was before ultra sound, so the sex of the baby could not be identified until birth. The suspense was killing us. Of course it didn't really matter that much, because like all parents, what we really wanted was a healthy, happy baby. But a daughter would be a real bonus.

Julie

On the day before Julie was born it was raining quite heavily. I was struggling, trying to push little David in the stroller while trying to hold an umbrella over my head and Steve's. We called Steve "Tiger." I was taking the "Little Tiger" to St. Suzanne's school. It was his first day at first grade. It was also our eighth wedding anniversary. I was pushing little Dave, nicknamed "Charlie Brown" in the stroller.

Jim worked for the city of Detroit as a tree trimmer at that time, and just before I got to the school my water broke, and who should drive by but Jim and a truck load of city workers. I waved frantically, and Jim and the fellows, misreading my frantic signals, happily waved back and continued on their way. This was way before the advent of cell phones.

I quickly got "Tiger" to school, rushed "Charlie Brown" home, which was only a block and a half away and phoned Jim's work. He was home in no time.

The neighbors took over from there, and Jim drove me to Detroit Memorial Hospital downtown, which was about a 45 minute drive. We rushed through traffic like crazy, expecting the baby to arrive at any moment.

Julie was born the next morning at 8:00 right about the time our "Little Tiger" was on his way back to his second day of school. I kept thinking that Julie would be born on our wedding anniversary, instead she showed up a day late, September 4th. This was definitely an omen. She seemed to be late for everything. In high school, her principal told us that artistic people tend to be that way.

A strawberry blond with chocolate brown eyes, little eyes just like her dad's, and little freckles on her nose like Jim's mother.

Julie was a quiet little girl, very shy. She was so painfully shy that sometimes I had to hold back tears watching her interact with other children seeing how hard it was for her, unlike her brother Dave who was a real extravert. Our oldest son Steve was quiet and reserved but not shy. The interactions of the three could be quite amusing and between her and David sometimes volatile. Even though they were all three years apart they have always been close.

Julie didn't talk until the age of three. She just pointed at whatever she wanted,and the boys got it for her. I don't know to this day why it took us so long to figure it out, but when we did we made the boys just ignore her and in a week or two she was talking in full sentences.

The first summer we lived at the lake, the kids were all playing across the street. All except Julie.

She was sitting on the front porch step and watching the kids play. I kept asking her why she didn't go over there. She just shrugged and said she didn't want to. I asked her if she wanted me to walk over there with her. She just shook her head no. I went back in the house, almost in tears. She was so shy. Then I heard one of the girls from across the street, Barb Kapp, come over to invite Julie to play with them. That was so thoughtful. She had left playing with the other kids to persuade Julie to join the fun. Julie still would not go.

While in first grade she won what would be the beginning of many ribbons of assorted colors, awards and contests for art and creative writing. This carried through high school. She was a very talented artist, working in oils, acrylics, pen and ink, and pastels.

Her nickname was Juju. She liked to play baseball in Little League. She was not a tomboy. The boys were told not to roughhouse with her like they do with their friends.

She started wearing glasses in first grade because she was very near-sighted and had an astigmatism just like her Aunt Joanie. She hated wearing glasses and many times she either left them at home on purpose, or just forgot them. The teachers would place her in the front row so she could see the board.

Julie had never played the drums. We didn't even have drums at home but that didn't stop her from trying out for the high school orchestra and marching band. She beat out something like fifty other students, (no pun intended). I didn't even know she was trying out for band. Mr. Jones, the music teacher, and band director told me that every time he saw Julie squinting, because she didn't have her glasses on, worried him because he knew how near sighted she was, and couldn't see his directing. He finally realized that she could pick up the beat when to play the kettle drums, or the cymbals, or whatever was needed.

In high school, Julie was perpetually late and often missed her school bus. One particular day there was a kindergarten bus that went by shortly after the bus she just missed. She flagged it down and went to school on the kindergarten bus. She sat next to a cute little boy who looked up at her and said, "Whose mommy are you"? Julie was mortified and was on time the rest of the year.

Julie seemed to be allergic to manual labor. She never volunteered to do household chores, inside or outside. One afternoon, Steve came home for a visit and started washing his car in the driveway. As soon as he finished, he started washing our car. Trying to embarrass Julie, I had her look out the window and said to her, "Look, Steve just washed his car and without us asking, he went ahead and washed ours." To which she replied, "Do you think if I ask him, he'll wash mine?" No shame...

Julie blossomed into a lovely young lady who had a wonderful talent for humor. In fact, if there was one word that described Julie it would be "hilarious." She had the ability to imitate peoples' voices and mannerisms, and if they had an accent, she got that down pat as well. Her friends loved it when she imitated them. Her humor was always playful, never dark or hurtful. She simply was a delight and all her friends, family and coworkers got such a kick out of her quick wit and fun personality.

When Julie was a teenager, she and I were frequently at odds. However, she was very close to her dad. They shared the same sense of humor and were both loads of fun to be around.

The following is a copy of a typical letter or note that Julie would leave, usually for her dad:

10-30-87

Mom or Dad,
You know the old joke
about the sign in the cafeteria?

~~PROCRASTINATORS MEETING~~
CANCELLED

~~PROCRATINATORS MEETING~~
CANCELLED

Guess who needs to go to
Jo Ann fabrics to sew a
Costume on Halloween morning?

Yours truly

(Could you see that I'm up by noon)
THANK YOU! ☺

After Julie got married, her mother-in-law, Marilyn Petrill, described her as having a "cute as a button personality." She had a great sense of humor, and like her dad she had great comebacks. Steve and Dave have great senses of humor also, but different, for instance, Steve relates things that happen either to him or that he observes, and they turn out to be so funny. David on the other hand tells jokes, and he always gets the punch line correct. His timing is flawless.

Julie was somewhat rebellious in high school and began drinking beer at parties. More mother and daughter clashes. When anyone would ask me who is harder to raise, boys or girls,? I would always tell them, "From my experience, it's definitely girls."

After graduating from high school Julie got a job at the University of Michigan Medical Center. She enjoyed her job and her co-workers, and they enjoyed her as well.

Julie was twenty when Steve moved to Charlotte, NC. He gave her his mobile home if she was willing to take over the payments. It was just five miles from our home, so we could see each other often.

Dave was away at college and Julie and I had time to develop a much closer relationship. She met Mark, a very nice young man who was deaf since birth, and everyone was surprised at how fast Julie picked up sign language. They went together for about a year and a half, and Julie broke off the relationship for reasons known only to her.

A short time after that she met Matt Petrill, and they started going together. After a few months, Julie brought him home just before Thanksgiving and introduced him to us and also to let us know that she was pregnant... I felt sorry for Matt when she dropped that "bomb" because Matt had just met us and although Jim, at 6'2" is a much larger man than Matt, he is really a very gentle and kind person and he handled the news like the gentleman that he was, and made Matt feel comfortable in such an awkward situation. My jaw dropped and my mouth was still open, and for one of the few times in my life I remained speechless. Jim always mentioned how much he prized those moments because they were so few and far between. In fact the few times I had laryngitis Jim would look toward the heavens and say,

"There is a God." I realized, after talking to Julie, that they wanted to get married, and had been planning on it before they found out she was expecting. This sped up their decision.

While helping Julie plan her wedding, I asked her where she wanted to register for gifts. She said "Fifth Third Bank." She always was very practical?

Julie and I had lots of fun picking out flowers and planning this and that for the wedding. It took place at St. Paul's Lutheran Church in our little village of Hamburg, on the 31st of January 1993. It was a beautiful, sunny morning, blanketed in soft white snow, very cold, a typical January day in Michigan. Julie was 24 and Matt was 20. She was a cougar before her time. For such a short notice, Julie had a wonderful wedding with 125 guests to greet the newlyweds at the church's Fellowship Hall. She was a most beautiful young lady, the loveliest bride I had ever seen. Jim was so proud walking her down the aisle, and we sat in the front pew, alongside my mother who was 93. Steve and Dave were ushers along with Matt's brother Dave.

After twenty hours of hard labor the doctor finally decided to perform a caesarian section. Seth was born on July 12th at 8:00 am. He was our first grandchild. The joy of seeing and holding my grandchild for the first time was so wonderful all I could do was thank God over and over again for such a perfect and beautiful little boy. Jim was up north at our cottage. He could not stand to see Julie in pain and did not want to be at the birth, but came home as soon as he got word that he was a grandpa.

A year and a half later Nathan was born. Julie was having him caesarian and picked January 12th as his birth date. She wanted the boys to be exactly a year and a half apart. She wanted them to always be close, and they are.

Nate, Seth, and Julie

A very hands-on mom, she enjoyed playing with the boys. They bounced on the trampoline together, shot soaker guns at each other, and rode bikes together. She had such a sense of fun. She was the only person to this day who could make Seth giggle. She read books to the boys under the kitchen table because Seth liked to be cozy. Seth was a quiet child like Uncle Steve. Nathan was very out-going just like his Uncle Dave. Whenever Julie found the time, she liked to lie on the couch with little Nathan because he loved to cuddle with her.

Matt and Julie sold the mobile home and moved into a nice antebellum house in the village of Hamburg. We loved it because they were now within walking distance of our house, and Julie would come over frequently pulling the boys in their wagon. She took them in the wagon to the library where I took her when she was little. There are many bibliophiles in our family.

A couple of years passed, and they moved to Hartland, another little village about a half hour from us. Julie and Matt liked the Hartland school district. We felt bad because they were so close to us in Hamburg, but it wasn't the end of the world, and we visited often.

It was at this time that Jim, at age 58 was diagnosed with Parkinson's disease. Julie was devastated. She refused to believe it and talked to the top neurologists at U of M. They concurred that that was indeed what Jim had.

Matt played organ and piano at the Hartland Presbyterian Church and the boys went to Sunday school there. Nathan was just finishing up pre-school and Seth was through with kindergarten. They were looking forward to school in September when Seth would be starting first grade and little Nathan would be starting kindergarten.

We had lots of fun with the kids in summer, we took them to our cottage up north and to different side trips like the Mackinac bridge, Mackinaw City, and St. Ignace to name a few. Jim taught them to fish, and also let them steer the pontoon boat. They loved going to the cottage with us.

Towards the end of the summer of 2000 we took the boys to the cottage on the Thursday before Labor Day weekend. Everyone was excited. I invited Julie and Matt to come up with us, but Matt had to practice that Saturday with the choir at church. He is an accomplished pianist. He particularly loves jazz and classical music. Julie had things to do around the house, and with the kids up north she could get a lot more done. She was originally going to come up Friday but still had more chores to do, so decided to come up on Saturday morning to spend the day with us and then leave early Sunday, which was our 40th wedding anniversary. We were not planning any kind of celebration, instead we were going to Paris in the spring. Julie was planning on going to a Kenny Loggins concert that Sunday evening.

Friday afternoon we took the boys to town and bought paper and crayons so they could make birthday cards for their mom's 32nd birthday which would be Monday, Labor Day.

They were so excited, and as soon as we got back to the cottage, they started their cards. We put them on the kitchen counter next to the cake that we baked for Julie. Later on Friday, we went to the ice cream shop in town. Who doesn't love ice cream? Julie called us on our cell phone, and we talked for a bit. She wanted to know how the boys were doing. "Tell them I love them, and I'll see them tomorrow morning." The boys were anxious for their mom's visit and for her to see their cards. Jim talked to Julie for a little bit, and then we went back to the cottage.

Around 11:00 the next morning Julie called from a hotel in Midland to say that she would be at the cottage in an hour. Jim took the boys down to the dock to fish. Noon arrived. We continued to wait for Julie so we could have lunch and eat some of that birthday cake. One o'clock came and went, then two o'clock.

I started to get worried and called the Sheriff's Department in Clare and asked the dispatcher if there was anyone on the road needing assistance because my daughter was supposed to be at our cottage hours ago. I thought perhaps Julie was having car trouble, and she didn't have her cell phone with her. The dispatcher told me, rather abruptly, that they were all pretty busy because of accidents in the area. It was after all, Labor Day week-end, she told me, with a hint of annoyance in her voice. "Hold on" she said. When she came back to the phone, her tone had changed, and she actually wasn't talking to me so abruptly, although I didn't put it all together at that time. She asked, "What kind of car Julie was driving?"

"A '95 green Dodge Neon."

"Was she alone in the car?"

"Yes, if you find out where she is would you please call me."

She took my phone number and also wanted my address. Still nothing clicked in my mind. I still figured Julie either got lost or was having car trouble.

While waiting for the sheriff to call, I sat out on the screened porch and watched Jim fish with the boys. A little while later there was a knock at the side door. I saw two state troopers. I invited them in, thinking that they were going to tell me that Julie had been in an accident and which hospital we could go to see her at.

Jim told me later that when he looked up the driveway and saw the troopers, he knew immediately what had happened. I invited the troopers in and had them sit at the kitchen table, and that's when the trooper told me that Julie had been killed in a head-on collision with a pick-up truck, a larger type truck like an F-350 or something, just outside of Clare, Michigan. She was just 30 minutes from the cottage.

I remembered when I was twelve years old and had my tonsils out. They gave me ether, and I could hear the doctors voices like they were down in a tunnel and far away. That was what the trooper sounded like. His voice seemed off in the distance, and I had a hard time hearing him. I kept asking him to repeat what he had just said. I couldn't believe what I was hearing. I kept saying "what," and he kept repeating that Julie had been killed. He also told me that Julie's car caught fire, but assured me that she died instantly on impact and did not suffer. The driver of the truck was air lifted to the nearest hospital and died in route. His passenger, his future son-in-law, was taken to the hospital by ambulance with a severe, closed-head injury. He would survive his injuries.

A few minutes later I stood up and started to feel dizzy like I was going to faint, but in a minute or two it passed. I asked the female officer to go down to the dock and tell Jim what happened. I told her to please remember that he suffers from Parkinson's, and that the little boys with him were Julie's little boys. A while later, Jim came up the hill with his arms around the boys. I asked him if she told him, and he said "Yes" and never said another word the rest of the day.

No one was asked to identify the body; for that I was grateful.

The neighbors were wonderful. They helped us pack and even offered to drive us home, which was a 2 ½ hour drive. I declined. I tried to call the family. The only person I was able to get was my nephew Mike Kirby. He was able to leave an urgent message for Steve who was at work. When Steve received the message he notified Dave.

Everybody was busy helping us with the packing and putting things in the car. In the meantime, one of the officers, to distract the boys, started talking to them about their fishing gear and the type of fish in the lake. Seth remained quiet. Nathan, a cute little boy with big blue eyes and a cherubic face, was very outgoing. He was so excited about going to kindergarten that for the past several days all he talked about was how many days until school started. He looked up at the officer happily holding four little chubby fingers up and proudly told him, "In four more days my mom is going to take me to school." He stopped abruptly and came over to me, and we hugged, and he said to me crying, "Grandma, who is going to take me to school?" I could see that the officer was trying to hold back tears.

Small children have a hard time when the people or places that are familiar to them abruptly change. In their confusion they strive to seek continuity in their life. For Nate, all he had been talking about for days was going to school. He didn't understand what death meant or that his mother would not be coming back. I quickly assured him that one of his grandmas or Aunt Pam would be able to take him to school.

We arrived home late in the evening. I felt so sorry for Julie's little boys. They sat in the car very quiet. There was so much silence in the car it was deafening. It was a 2 ½ hour drive home. The boys were just 5 ½ and 7 years old. Every now and then the silence was broken by Seth. He wanted to know when we would be home, and would his dad be there. I told him that not only his dad, but his grandma and grandpa, Aunt Pam and all their relatives would be there. We arrived home and saw that our street was packed with cars, and Matt came out to meet us. He was inconsolable, and we just hugged each other and cried.

Steve and Bonnie arrived early Sunday morning. They decided it was quicker to just drive up from Charlotte instead of trying to get a flight out. Dave had arrived the night before. Steve spent his time looking after Jim who really was being very stoic but was having a hard time eating. He didn't have the type of Parkinson's that has tremors except when he was stressed. Eating was becoming difficult. He couldn't hold things and Steve, just by being there with Jim, had a calming affect on him.

In the meantime, Dave started making calls to let everyone know what had happened. He did quite well, but every now and then he would break down, gather his wits about him, and continued on. I don't know what I would have done without his help and Steve's. Matt had spent the night here with the little ones. My two sisters, Marguerite and Joanie, arrived to help in so many ways I couldn't count. There were so many friends and neighbors there to help that I couldn't name them all. Food overwhelmed our kitchen and dining room. In the afternoon while they were at the house, we went to the funeral home to make the arrangements.

As I stepped out the front door there was a beautiful basket of flowers from the neighbors down the road who had just moved in. We hadn't even met them yet.

It was our 40th wedding anniversary, and I was at the funeral home with Matt, Jim, Steve and Dave picking out a casket for our Julie. Matt insisted on a beautiful mother-of-pearl casket. I had never seen anything like it. Her casket was closed.

We had the funeral director put the birthday cards from the boys in her casket. I don't know to this day how we got through all this. Matt took it so hard. It was painful just to see him. A young widower at 28 with two little boys to raise. A beautiful young mother, 31, gone. We buried Julie on Wednesday, September 6, 2000, at Lakeview Cemetery in Howell, Michigan, in the family plot.

This was the first day of first grade for Seth. It brought to mind Steve's first day of first grade when Julie was about to be born, and now her little boy was starting his first day, the day of her funeral. It was also Nathan's first day at kindergarten.

Todd Borek, the funeral director, is a friend of ours and told us that Julie's was by far the largest funeral that year. The church was packed. We sat in the same pew we sat in seven years ago at Julies's wedding.

Matt's sister Lauren played the organ and sang my favorite hymn, "Amazing Grace." The only other hymn I remember the congregation singing was "On Eagles Wings" a beautiful hymn taken from the 91st Psalm. I tried to sing but nothing came out. I had such a lump in my throat from trying not to cry, that my throat actually hurt.

As I sat there in church I just wanted to scream at the top of my lungs, "WHY, WHY, WHY did this have to happen? What's going to become of Julie's little boys? What are they going to do without her? How is Matt going to deal with all this? Maybe by screaming, all the pain would go away, but I knew nothing was going to take that kind of pain away."

As we approached the cemetery, I realized how beautiful and

peaceful it was. We drove through the gates, and one of my earliest recollections as a little girl of five, came to mind. It was 1945, and we were going through those same gates to attend the funeral of my dad's Uncle Conrad Steinacker.

Julie was buried not far from my grandmother, in the family plot at Lakeview Cemetery. It is a beautiful cemetery on Thompson Lake. Jim was buried next to Julie six years later. His health failed rapidly after Julie's accident, and he died on September 16, 2006, at the age of 66. He was heart broken.

While Steve and Dave were still in Michigan, they went up to Clare to view the scene of the accident and tried to get some closure. There is no closure, ever. Be that as it may, they were able to talk to an eyewitness who told them that when Julie's car caught fire, passersby got out of their cars to help her, but they could see that she was gone

The state troopers from the Harrison Post were very accommodating and even blocked off one lane of US-10 where the accident occurred, to help explain to Steve and Dave what they believed happened. It had been a week since the accident, and they could still see the burnt tire marks of the collision, and the upheaval of grass by the highway.

Three years after the accident, Jim and I, Matt and a friend of his, and Seth went up to the cottage for the last time. It was a dismal day: gray overcast skies and drizzling rain. We sold the cottage earlier in the year. Matt, his friend, and Seth put up two large crosses by the highway. The crosses are still there today. More than just a memorial, they are there to warn drivers to drive safely.

I visit the cemetery often and always bring roses, Julie's favorite flower. She was holding a rose in her hand from one of her rose bushes by the front porch when we all waved good-by to her for the last time. In my last vision of Julie, she and Matt were standing next to each other as they waved good-bye to us. The boys were in the back seat of the van happily shouting their good-byes and waving back as we left for the cottage.

Tammy Ross and many of her other friends and relatives have left music tapes or trinkets that meant something to them, or her. Her friend Mary Ann left a tape of "Angels Among Us" by Alabama, she told me it was one of Julie's favorites. I always bring roses. Seth and Nate over the years have left handmade cards and drawings, Easter baskets, and balloons. Every year Matt lays a winter blanket of beautiful pines with a big purple bow. Julie loved the color purple.

On the second anniversary of her accident Seth made a very touching card for Julie. On it he drew happy faces of his family, it read "Happy Two Years In Heaven." Nate likes to draw animals on his cards. I continue to leave poems that I've written or that I have copied because their message is profound. Jim had a hard time going to the cemetery. He very seldom visited Julie's grave. He told me he had such a hard time going that he'd rather be in denial that she was even gone. Everyone grieves differently.

My neighbor Krisanne Rea said it best in a note she wrote on her sympathy card:

"'Special'" is a word that is used to describe everything one-of-a-kind like a hug or a sunset or a person who spreads love with a smile or kind gesture. 'Special' describes people who act from the heart and keeps in mind the hearts of others. 'Special' applies to something that is admired and precious and which can never be replaced. 'Special' is the word that best describes Julie."

Julie's boys have remained close just like Julie wanted. They attended the same high school Julie went to. Seth played guitar in the Jazz Band. Both boys were honor students. Nathan was "big man on campus," captain of the football team and their quarterback.

The boys and I remain close. We live near each other in Michigan. I see them regularly when I'm there, and we talk on the phone often when I'm in Tennessee.

Steve and Dave make sure they see their nephews at least once a year. They stay connected through Facebook and text each other frequently by phone. I can see Julie in Seth, and her brother Dave in Nathan. In fact we call Nathan, Dave Jr. I thank God everyday for giving us those boys. They are such a joy.

None of us could have survived this tragedy without our family, our faith, and our friends. It leaves an open wound that never heals. I never knew such pain was possible. On the days when I am particularly sad

I know I can call my sisters, and they listen. That helps me survive. I've always said, "Family is everything."

Dave's daughter Carly is 12 years old now. I talk to her often about her Aunt Julie. My biggest fear is that Julie will be forgotten. Everyone tells me that won't happen. I want everyone to know that she lived here among us and made a difference. She meant so much to so many people. I want to keep her memory alive.

Julie's legacy is her loving nature and wonderful sense of humor. She was always willing to forgive, and she never held a grudge. You couldn't ask for a more loving and fun mother. When you were around her, you were always laughing. Her children adored her. What a precious gift that is.

The family attended a memorial mass for Julie later that year at Our Lady of Loretta Church, in Redford.

We will always love and miss Julie.

23

Cub Scout Troop 488

Steve joined St. Suzanne's Cub Scout Troop in 1969. It was the largest Cub Scout Troop in Michigan. At one time it had over 120 Cub Scouts. At this particular time there were about 80 Cub Scouts. It was through this troop that we met Doug and Kathy Tadajewski. We've remained best friends ever since.

Doug was Cub Master. He is best described as a Rodney Dangerfield kind of guy. He's hilarious to be around, and the neat thing about Kathy, his wife, is even though she's heard his jokes and nonsense over and over again, she laughs harder each time she hears it. Like it's the first time she's hearing it, which only encourages him. You can't be around Doug without laughing.

Then there's Joe Claus, Jim Moco, George Barker, Jerry O'Malley, Walt Boesler, Bill Van Dyke and many others, who we met through the Scouts, all had a good sense of fun. We remained friends for many years. Mike Napolitan and Bob Hammond passed away early on. Mike from cancer and Bob from a heart attack. His wife Fran told us, at his funeral, that his dad had died at fifty from a heart attack. When Bob passed the fifty mark, he told Fran he'd made it, but he only lived to his 51st birthday and died shortly thereafter.

We had an annual Cub Scout Picnic at Rouge Park each year. They were a lot of fun. I remember one picnic, we were all playing baseball, Jerry O'Malley was pitching. I have always been able to hit the ball, unfortunately it would either be a pop up, so it was easy to catch, or it would be a foul, but at least I was able hit it.

Jerry pitched the ball knowing this. I saw it coming and I hit it hard, unfortunately it was a balloon full of water. Everyone got a chuckle out of that, especially Jim, who had tipped Jerry off about my batting record.

I found out, talking to Jerry O'Malley that his dad and my dad were policeman at Trumbull Station, Precinct 2, at the same time. I found some of the articles dad wrote in the Tuebor paper about Precinct 2, and sure enough, Dad joked about his fellow officers and Jerry's father was one of the guys my dad wrote about. Small world . . .

The first time I was ever on a school bus was when we went on our many adventures on the Cub Scout bus. This was the first time I'd ever been on a school bus. It was a 1952, GMC, school bus. However none of these adventures involved the Cub Scouts themselves.

The first of these adventures that I remember, was a Mystery Trip that would eventually lead to a dinner. Doug and some of the Scout leaders did all the planning. We were required to wear formal attire. I wore a floor length dress, as did the other gals, and the men looked gorgeous in their suits. Many of them I had never seen in a suit before. We all met at St. Suzanne's parking lot.

There, the Cub Scout bus was all warmed up and waiting for us. Our first stop was the horse barns at Rouge Park, because one of the Scouts's father was a mounted policeman. I couldn't believe it. I was wearing a lovely floor length dress and new high heels. Well, I wasn't going to get off the bus to see and smell the barns. Some of the gals actually lifted up their fancy dresses, high heels and all, and took the tour through the horse barns.

I waited with a few other gals in the bus. Eventually, the group came back to the bus laughing as usual, and enjoying themselves. Evidently they had hors d'oeuvres and drinks in the barn. With Everyone accounted for, off we went to our next destination.

Turned out to be Carl"'s Chop House on Grand River in downtown Detroit. Carl's Chop House was the oldest beloved steakhouse in Detroit. It was a city landmark for more the sixty years. I loved it because of its nationally renowned blue ribbon steaks. Yummm . . . As usual, we all had a great time.

Another time it was decided, by the powers that be, that we would have a wonderful dinner at an exclusive restaurant in downtown Mt. Clemens. Each couple was picked up by the bus, at each house, and Doug gave each babysitter an envelope with our itinerary. The destination was a German restaurant, but when we got there it was the wrong restaurant.

We ended up at the Heidelberg. The parking lot was in the rear and it had a wonderful long canopy for the patrons in case of rain. Walt Boesler was driving the bus that night when it started to rain. He drove the bus to the back parking lot and under the canopy. After we all got off at the door, Walt left to park the bus, and that wonderful canopy went with him. Again, we could not stop laughing.

After dinner we stopped at the Copper Kettle Bar for drinks. On the way there, Bob Hammond opened the back door of the bus and mooned the car following us.

After leaving the Copper Kettle, Walt decided to race the semi's on I-94. When we thought nothing else could go wrong, the lights went out in the bus. I don't remember what all happened, but we all did get home safely that night.

Then there was the time we were all dressed up to go to an upscale restaurant for dinner and dancing, but first we had to take a tour of George Barker's fire station. As George was giving us a tour of the station, one of the guys wanted to know if he could slide down the firemen's pole. Before you knew it, just about everyone wanted a chance to slide down the pole. Remember, we're all dressed in evening gowns and suits... I do remember that Jim and I and just one or two others chose not to go down the pole.

It was decided that the Cub Scouts were going to put on a circus. Steve was going to be part of several Scouts making three or four rather large elephants that could be used in their parade. Two scouts could fit in each one. The elephants were made out of baling wire, burlap, and wood, and then covered with papier maché. They also had several clowns including Jim Moco and Joe Claus.

St, Suzannes church and school were a block and a half away from our house. The circus was held on a Saturday night at St. Suzanne's gym. The next day, Sunday morning, after mass, cars from church drove down our street to get to Plymouth Rd. This was a weekly occurrence.

This particular Sunday, the morning after the circus, Jim and I noticed the people getting out of mass, were slowing down as they passed our house, and were looking up at our roof. We thought something had happened to some of our shingles. Jim called Mrs. Robak across the street, to ask her if she could see anything unusual on the roof. All she said was "Go out there and take a look, you won't believe it."

She was right, we couldn't believe what we saw. One of the big elephants from the Cub Scout circus was on our roof. These were big elephants that the scouts had made. Believe me, you couldn't miss it. It was as big or bigger than a large picnic table, and just about as heavy. We couldn't stop laughing, but wondered how the guys got the elephant up there without us noticing, and more importantly, how were we going to get the elephant down?

Our neighbor Joe Bomarito, came out and explained that two clowns asked to borrow a ladder and explained what they were going to do. Joe didn't know who they were, just two clowns. Jim said laughing, "They're clowns alright." We found out later that the two "clowns" were Jim Moco and Joe Claus.

Joe Bomarito helped Jim get the elephant off the roof and put it on the picnic table in the backyard for the time being.

It was the fall of '73 when all this took place, and we were in the process of moving to Hamburg Lake. Several of our friends, mostly from Cub Scouts would come out to Hamburg on week-ends to help us paint our new house. There must have been ten or twelve of us each week-end out in Hamburg painting the house. We would spend the day laughing and joking around, it was a wonder we ever got anything done.

Bev Ligget, the neighbor across the street, said her kids wanted to know if all those people were going to move into that house. We were quite noisy. While Gerry Bowser painted our living room, I asked him where his wife Sonia was. Doug said she was home painting their house. "That's so nice of him to come and help us." I said to Doug. "She won't let Gerry near a paint brush." He said. I thought, "Wow, and he's painting our living room . . ."

Two or three weeks later when we were ready to move in, our friends came over to help us. Bill Van Dyke, our neighbor across the street on Grandville, drove the truck. The guys from the Scouts, plus Dick and Lori and, Matt and Janie, all came out to help us move our belongings.

I said good-by to Mrs. Tosher the elderly neighbor down the block who was so good to the children on the street. She was a lovely lady and I knew I'd miss her. We hadn't got rid of the elephant yet so we just left it near the curb on the driveway. I was so excited to move into our beautiful new house, but sad to leave Grandville where we'd lived since 1964. I had the kids with me in our '69 Chevy Townsmen, station wagon.

When we arrived in Hamburg, Bill Van Dyke was backing the truck up the hill toward our front porch, but because of the incline, Jim and I were quite concerned that the truck would tip over with all our worldly possessions in it. I couldn't watch. All I heard were "whoas" and laughter, then "oh no!" more laughter, all of this to scare me, and it did. The guys loved teasing me, actually, they loved teasing, period. Finally, as it started to get dark, we said good-bye to all our dear friends who had helped us out so much.

Bill Van Dyke lived across the street from us on Grandville in a beautiful brick Tuedor house. He had a rather large dog, named Maggie. Every now and then Maggie would leave a rather large message on my front lawn. I never complained about it until one day when Janie Till and her little boy, Jeffrey and my three kids, were getting in the station wagon. Neither Janie nor I were quick enough to stop the kids when we saw what they were stepping in near the car door. Maggie had just left a large, message right on the lawn by our station wagon. The kids, of course, stepped in it and proceeded to get it all over the inside of the station wagon. It took quite a while to clean the inside of the car and the kids. I was so irritated. When Bill got home I let him have it. He took it well.

Several months passed, and now Bill was helping us move and unpack our belongings. There was a horse farm in back of our new house, across Strawberry Lake Road. One of the neighbors was riding her horse down Silver Lake Drive towards our house. Bill turned to me, and said, "After one of those horses leaves a message on your front lawn, you'll wish you had Maggie back." I got a kick out of that.

Early December of that year we invited Matt and Janie Till over for a nice, quiet evening. We were going to light the fire in our new fireplace. While we were entertaining in the family room, which is in the back of the house, we heard carolers. When we opened the drapes of the door wall, we were so surprised to see Santa Claus and all our friends. I knew Doug was Santa by his voice.

As I looked over the whole group, I recognized that damned elephant on my picnic table. They brought the elephant. I thought we had gotten rid of it when we moved. They asked us if we had heard the ruckus outside before they came. We had not. It appears that they all came on the Cub Scout bus with Santa (Doug) driving. Doug had a time maneuvering the bus onto Norene Ct. and finally parked it at the top of the hill.

In the meantime, Bev's husband Don, one of our new neighbors, saw a school bus that he thought had stalled on the hill and probably was lost, so he called the police. The police came and asked Santa to step out of the bus. Everybody on the bus was in a good mood, laughing and quite boisterous, having been drinking cocktails, and eating hors d'oeuvres for almost an hour. It took them that long to get here. After a long explanation by Doug, the police let Doug go. One policeman was overheard telling his partner, that he wouldn't know how he would explain to his kids, if he had to arrest Santa Claus.

Janie told us that Doug had planned the party and wanted Matt and her to go ahead of them to the house on the pretext of a friendly visit. They were to keep us in the back of the house so we wouldn't be able to see them arrive. Well, the plan sure worked.

We had so much fun that evening. They brought all the food and drinks and they had all gotten together and presented us with a wonderful housewarming gift, wrought iron hearth accessories for our new fireplace. Finally at about 3:00 a.m. the bus pulled out. Jim and I stood outside and waved good-bye as they drove up the hill and out of our new neighborhood. Jim and I had our arms around each other as we waved good-bye, and then I started crying. "Jim I don't know if this was such a good idea. There go all our friends." As it turned out most of them moved out our way within the next few years. It turned out to be the best idea, and we would soon find out what a wonderful neighborhood we had moved into.

Back to the hill and waving good-bye, Jim and I were so tired as we went back in the house. We decided we'd clean up in the morning. We went upstairs to our bedroom, turned the lights on, and there was that damned elephant in our bed. We had a king size bed and that elephant took up all of it. I slept on the living room couch and Jim slept on the family room couch, still wondering how they got that elephant up the stairs and thru the hallway to our bedroom, without being noticed.

It was explained to us days later that George Barker and a few of the other guys had a real hard time maneuvering it up the stairs and especially around the corner in the hallway, and all the while having look-outs making sure we didn't see what was happening.

The next day, I'm talking to Lori on the phone in the kitchen while the water softener man, having installed the softener, was writing up the bill. Lori was not at the party so I was telling her all about Santa almost getting arrested, and the elephant upstairs on the bed etc. When I hung up the phone, the salesman said to me "Next time you have a party would you invite me?" I couldn't stop laughing.

Eventually, some of our new neighbors helped Jim get the elephant in the truck and took it to the landfill. There was a lot of talk about the elephant at the landfill too.

24

Fertile Valley

Ever since I was a little girl I wanted to live on the lake. My wish came true when Jim and I moved our family to 7367 Norene Ct. on Hamburg Lake. We built our house on a hill overlooking the water. It was a dream come true. Right from the start I knew we had made the right decision. We had a side lot that served as the neighborhood volley ball court. The apron of the driveway was three parking spaces wide, and served as our basketball court. We shared the dock with our neighbors on Norene Ct. and Silver Lake Drive. Tom and Krisanne's house was next to our easement. Hamburg Lake is a private lake that does not allow motors. It's very clean and the fishing is great, although no one in our family cared much about fishing. Sailing and swimming is what our family liked.

Hamburg is a little village fifteen minutes north of Ann Arbor. We moved to Hamburg November 13, 1973. The kids liked their new schools. They had been attending St. Suzanne's school in Detroit, so the public school was a bit different to them, but they acclimated themselves quite well. Steve attended Pinckney Middle School, Dave was in Hamburg Elementary School, and poor, shy Julie wasn't able to start school on time because the Detroit Public Schools were in the middle of a teacher's strike. She started at Winan's Kindergarten School two months late. It was a small school with only two classrooms and Julie liked the school and the teachers very much.

There were seven houses on Norene Ct. and they were all inhabited by the best neighbors one could ever wish for. I refer to them as the "Magnificent Seven." We were like a little commune. Coffee pots, roasting pans, cake plates flew back and forth from one neighbor to another until we couldn't figure out what belonged to who, and didn't care.

Jim was not mechanically inclined, didn't know much about engines. When the neighbors wanted help building their decks, they would call on Jim. When Jim wanted our car worked on he called Don Ligget, and Butch was an electrician, Gary Ladd helped whenever he could, so we had a lot of things covered. Steve Linton and Jim loved golf and played often together with Gary Cook, our neighbor up the hill. Sometimes our Steve and also sometimes David would play golf with them. Jim also played golf with Steve's buddies Mike Wiles and Wally Baran. Those were some of Jim's fondest memories

The seven houses on Norene Ct, had a total of 15 kids and 4 dogs. On the hill in back of Cindy's house, there were 4 kids. Desmores lived on Silver Drive. Their backyard abutted the other side of our house, and the Reas, who were on the water, had between both families, 6 kids and 2 dogs. The Oestreich's also lived on the water and had 4 kids. So we had a total of 29 kids and 6 dogs. Remember, we didn't have fences. The people in the little town of Hamburg, which was just past the cemetery in back of our house, referred to Norene Court as Fertile Valley.

Louise and Denny lived next door, and every fall just before Halloween, they would arrange with Glenn Bennett, who owned the horse farm in back of us, to get a hay wagon and take us on a color tour. The only difference was that these color tours happened at night. We would all hop on the wagon and go down the back roads that were really beautiful that time of year, if only you could see them. We sang and laughed until we couldn't laugh anymore. Laura, our resident poet laureate, wrote a poem about Hamburg's color tour at night, in fact she wrote poems about lots of the happenings in the neighborhood.

We had only lived in Hamburg a couple of years when the big blizzard hit. We were all snowed in. Silver Lake Drive was our only way out and that was completely closed. The first day all the neighbors went to Gary and Vivian's house to play Michigan Rummy, and the kids all played outside or in the basement. The second day was at Gary and Connie's house, and the guys played poker, and on it went for four days. Every now and then when we were playing cards one of the neighbors would take their snowmobile into town to get groceries for anyone who needed them, or to make a beer run. . . They had to have one snowmobile at the ready because Nancy Bloomquist was due to deliver her baby at any moment. Finally on the fourth day the snow plow made it through.

Every once in a while one of the kids would miss the school bus. They'd go back home and see if any of the neighbors were available to take them to school. These were usually the high school kids. Cindy remembered taking Julie to school, but she wouldn't tell me how many times. Taking them to school was no small trek. Pinckney High School is eight miles from Hamburg. All of us looked out for each other.

Jim and I always had the Memorial Day picnics in our side lot. All the guys in the neighborhood would get everybody's picnic tables and bring them to our yard. The picnics were great fun. Volley ball, horseshoes, badminton, basketball, whatever we felt like. Usually it was volley ball.

Jim presided over the turtle races. Dave and his friend Ed Densmore got the turtles out of the lake. Then Jim formed the hose into a circle on the apron of the driveway. Everyone painted a number on their turtles with nail polish. One for each adult and one for each child. We put all the turtles in the center and off they went, or not. All the adults would put in a dollar for the winner. We had so much fun with those turtles. After the races, the kids had to put the turtles back in the lake. Louise's son Troy found his turtle the next year in the lake. He got a kick out of that.

The old adage "good fences make good neighbors" never held true in our neighborhood. It was amazing to me as I look back and remembered that most of the neighbors had dogs and no one had a fenced yard. I always knew where Julie was, because Ginger would sit on the front porch of the house where she was playing inside. The same with Tobie, Louise's daughter. We could see that big German Shepherd, Babe sitting on the porch where Tobie was.

The one adage that did hold true was "It takes a village." We never lacked babysitters, or for that matter neighbors that would look out for our kids when we didn't even know it. I found out years after the fact, that my son David, who always was an avid golfer, must have been eleven or twelve at the time, was hitting golf balls from Strawberry Lake Road in back of our house into our side lot and hit the siding on Louise's house. As David told me years later, "she wasn't very happy when I told her, and she told me, one more time and she'd tell dad." She never did tell him.

We were having Steve's graduation party in the side lot, and before the party started Louise brought over two or three dozen beautiful roses she picked from her garden and Phyllis Densmore, who lived on the other side of us, brought over either peonies or lilacs from her garden, I'm not sure which.

Whenever any of the neighbors were going to have a party or have company over, the rest of the street tried to make sure that their lawns were cut and clothes taken off the lines before said company arrived.

Bev, who lived across the street from us, and her sister Alice, who lived up on the hill, rented out Halloween costumes during October. Since we're on a court, there isn't much room to park, so we always let Bev know that her customers could park in our driveways.

Everyone in the neighborhood knew what a chocoholic Jim was, so when he took the kids trick-or-treating for Halloween, besides filling their bags, they filled Jim's bag with tons of chocolate and sometimes even a beer or two.

On week-ends the guys would all get together, fill their trucks with garbage bags and any other trash that needed to be discarded, and off to the landfill they went, not to be seen or heard from for hours. We finally realized why they seemed so enthusiastic about the landfill. They went for drinks at the Conservation Club after they emptied their trucks.

There are so many stories about my neighbors that I could go on and on. When word got out that Jim was suffering from Parkinson's Disease, Don Ligget plowed out our driveway in winter. That really helped us out. Tom Rae always came over to play cribbage with Jim, even after he could barely move the pegs. I was always so grateful to Tom for that. People with disabilities like to be treated as normal as possible.

Jim is Retiring
By
Laura Oestriche

Jim Wrobleski is retiring now, but from what we're not sure.
When he tries to explain what he does in
a day, to us it's all just a blur."
He says he climbs ladders, works on spouts and on gutters;
He rivets on straps to keep them from falling,
no wonder he's home in a flutter.

He's worked hard most of his life to provide for his family;
But his toughest job was to tell his daughter
about the "Birds and the Bees.
Julie asked him to explain about sex, her
enthusiasm came in a gush;
She knew the answers ahead of time, she
just wanted to see him blush.
She asked her dad if she could have some
money, and his answer left her shaken,
There's only two ways to make money said he,
Either find a job or marry me, and I'm already taken.
Jim's patience is known both near, and quite far
He just shakes his head . . . his kids have totaled another car.
His dedication to his family is legendary,
And so is his appetite for Ben and Jerry.
Does Jim love chocolate? Let's take a poll;
Yes to Lady Godiva, Hershey, and Tootie Roll,
Then there's Almond Joy, Milky Way and Chocolate Kisses,
Snickers, and Kit Kat he never misses.
Jim Bought the blue pick-up truck from Wayne
Williams, an electrician in our town,
People honked and waved, and Jim waved back, 'til
he realized it was Wayne who was renown.

He called his friends to go out to dinner, but
they soon caught on to his caper;
They knew he only ate at places where he
cut out coupons from the paper.
In Trivial Pursuit he is the best, all know that's not said in jest;
Just ask him yourself and he'll put you to the test.
Jim's always looking for his glasses, though
he claims he doesn't need 'em;
He's getting a guide dog for Christmas, just so it can lead him.
Now he has time to golf and to brag of his holes-in-one:
But let me tell you of a day on the course
when he nearly came undone.
A woman behind him teed off too soon,
and watched in horror and dread;
As Jim went down on his knees, she had hit him in the head.
Let's raise our glasses to his retirement and sing;
Cause tomorrow Jim won't remember a thing.

When my daughter Julie was killed, we were all devastated, but we knew the neighbors would be there for support. Cindy fixed my hair for the viewing and again for the funeral. They helped in many ways. Krisanne wrote such a beautiful letter I put it in the scrapbook I made of Julie's life. I plan on giving it to her boys when they're older. They were so little, 5 1/2 and 7 years old, that I wanted to make sure they would always remember what a wonderful person their mother was.

I lived on Norene Ct. from 1973 to 2007. I am still in touch with my neighbors when I'm in Michigan. Once a year we all meet for dinner except Gary and Vivian who live in Prescott, Arizona, but they come to town every now and then because their son Nate bought their house on Norene Ct. My neighbor Cindy bought a condo a block away from my condo in Brighton. Don and Bev live less then a mile from Norene Ct. Louise lives in Harrisville, Krisanne still lives in Hamburg and Lintons and Phyllis Densmore live in Howell.

My neighbors were, and still are unbelievable. We never had any fights or disagreements. I think it's because the common denominator was the fact that we all had similar backgrounds, and of course we all had children. Everybody got along. It was a wonderful time in my life, and in my family's life as well.

I am also proud of the fact that in 2013 Hamburg Twp. was named the safest municipality in Michigan with a population over 20,000 based on FBI crime statistics. The article read:

Hamburg gives residents and visitors the feel of a vacation, primarily due to the presence of the Brighton State Recreation Area, as well as Bishop Lake and the chain of lakes, thanks to the Huron River that meanders through its boundaries. The residents enjoy camping, swimming, boating, and hiking in one of the most beautiful settings this side of the Upper Peninsula.

The whole family loved Hamburg and enjoyed growing up on Hamburg Lake.

NOTE: My good friend and neighbor Bev Ligget passed away as I was putting this book together. Just a few things I personally remember about Bev I wrote in a letter I sent to her husband Don and family:

I was so sorry to hear of Bev's passing. What a shock. I have such wonderful memories of Bev. We walked together for awhile until I needed a foot operation and then I never did get back into it, but Bev continued on.

I remember when her and I walked to Dexter and had you and Jim meet us for breakfast and then drove us home. I always looked forward to our walks.

One time when we were walking down Hamburg Road towards Jennings Rd., it was the time when people kept spotting a black panther or some such thing, and we were walking one evening and I stopped Bev in her tracks. I whispered to her that there was something large and black in the tree several yards ahead of us. We kept trying to decide whether or not we should turn around or get closer and make sure what it was. What we were going to do if it was a panther, I don't think we thought that far ahead. We walked ever so slowly toward the tree, only to find out that it was a large, black garbage bag that someone had thrown up in the tree. We got a good laugh out of that.

I will always remember Bev as a good friend and neighbor. Always cheerful. Never said an unkind word about anyone. Bev was the first person Jim and I met when we were building our house. We knew we'd love our new neighborhood because Bev was so friendly and made us feel at home.

I'm so glad she came with us to Frankenmuth (2015) and then later in the summer to the Mexican restaurant in Brighton. What I cherish most is, I will remember her and I hugging each other before we parted after that last luncheon.

Bev died of a stroke. I felt so bad that I was unable to attend her funeral. I was in Tennessee.

25

Wintertime

Winter has its own beauty for those of us who grew up in the North. But as we age, that winter beauty belongs to those who can battle the blizzards, dig out the snow drifts, and experience the numbing hands, the frozen feet, and sometimes even a frost bit nose.

There are few visions as lovely as the splendor of the moonlight on the freshly fallen snow or the sunlight sparkling off the trees after an ice storm.

I will always miss my beautiful white Christmases in Michigan, but I must admit, there is a lot to be said for winters in the South. The sunny days and mild temperatures in Tennessee is what I look forward to now.

When Jim and I were dating, we had loads of fun in the winter going out after school and tobogganing down the hills on what is now the GM Tech Center on Van Dyke in Warren. I even talked him into a winter picnic, which by the way, we only did once.

When the kids were little we built our house on a hill overlooking the lake. They would toboggan down our front lawn. Since our house was close to the water, if it was icy enough, they were able to slide down the hill and clean across the street to the lake.

Another year we had a terrific ice storm and everyone stayed home because of the ice covered roads. Jim had to tie a rope to the fence in front of our house and throw it down the driveway to the street so that when the kids tobogganed, they would be able to get back up. They also had to carry the dog up to the house in their arms. They had a lot of fun that day.

We shared a dock with six of our neighbors. Tom and Krisanne's house was next to our easement. There were seven houses on Norene

Court and they were all inhabited by the best neighbors one could ever wish for.

Since Krisanne's house was closest to the dock, in winter everyone put their ice skates in the chest in Krisanne's garage. The skates were there for anyone who could fit into them. It worked very well, especially if any of the kids in the neighborhood had friends over and they didn't bring their skates, they could just go to Krisanne's and borrow a pair from the communal chest. There were always plenty of skates, because when the kids grew out of their skates they just left them there for the rest of the kids to use. The adults had skates in there too.

I didn't join the kids ice skating too often because I wasn't a very good skater. Jim didn't skate at all. David loved to play ice hockey, while Steve liked wind surfing, which could be a little tricky, because there were always ice fishing sheds out on the lake. Julie, on the other hand, would skate close to me, and I would sometimes go out on the ice pushing little Nate, our neighbor's boy in a stroller. That way I could skate without falling, and keep an eye on Julie. She was one of the younger kids in the neighborhood. She soon learned to skate but was never too crazy about it. Most of the neighbors had snowmobiles so Jim would ride with the guys through the woods, while the rest of us would be out on the lake skating. Everybody had a good time. But if memory serves me, as we got older, we spent less and less time outdoors in winter.

One winter, Jim decided it would be fun to try the Luge. What transpired is in Steve's own words (because he can tell it better than I can).

The Luge is something that not everybody can say they've done. What was startling to me is that my Dad came up with this idea and asked me if I would be game to do something like that. After talking about it we decided that Dad would bring his friend Doug Tadajewski and I would bring my friend Mike Wiles.

Dad read something about a Luge run in Muskegon, in southwestern Michigan. This was .near Lake Michigan. Mike surprisingly offered to acquisition a large conversion van from the Chrysler dealership he was working at. So it was a date. We all got together on a cold winter Saturday morning and headed to Muskegon. Mike drove, I had the passenger seat, Dad and Doug sat in the big captain's chairs in the back.

As we drove we talked about all kinds of stuff. I remember Doug being very funny and making us laugh the whole way there.

We arrived in Muskegon and stopped for breakfast. Afterwards, one of the customers told us how to get to the Luge run and we were on our way. We found it, and started having second thoughts immediately. This towering structure and the speeds at which we were watching people go down started making us a little nervous, although no one admitted that.

We went to the check-in place and had to sign waiver after waiver, which made us all a little more apprehensive. But upward an onward we went. I don't remember who went first, but we were shuffled into different lines. I remember getting on the luge and was given very little instruction before they pushed me down the run.

As I picked up speed I realized I had very little control of this thing. Hitting the sidewalls all the way down. All I could think of was ouch, ouch, and more ouch. My arms took the brunt of the run, but I was eager to go again. As I made my way up the hill I saw Dad, and he was holding his arm. "How the hell do you steer these damn things?" Dad asked. I said, "I'm not sure but I'm going to keep trying.". He was too.

Next time the attendant told us to use our ankles and feet to turn the sled. Once again I was flying down the run hitting the walls, but not as much. This happened time and time again. Finally we had enough. Having to climb the hill every time started to wear us out, so we agreed it was difficult but fun. All of us had bruised arms and other injuries that we bragged about as we left for a place to eat.

We stopped at an Italian restaurant and had a great meal. As we left for home, Mike and I talked all the way while Dad and Doug slept.

It's one of only three Luge Runs in the country. It was quite an adventure for them. They spent most of the day there, and when they finally got tired of climbing up the hill they took their bruised bodies and other injuries and headed for home to claim their bragging rights.

We lived in an area of many lakes, and every year without fail, someone would drive their snowmobile on one of those lakes when the lakes were just beginning to thaw. The police would have to come and rescue the driver, and try to rescue his snowmobile. Surprising though, I don't ever remember a snowmobiler drowning.

These are just a few of my memories of winters past. Winters up north are a lot of fun, but they are best enjoyed by the young.

26

The Kentucky Blizzard of 1993

We left Michigan early in the morning to visit Steve in Charlotte. .Driving through Kentucky we got caught up in the "Great Blizzard of 1993." We exited I-75 as directed by the police and soon found ourselves in the little town of Dry Ridge Kentucky, population less than 2,000. We were about 35 miles south of Cincinnati. Members of the National Guard directed us to Grant County High School where a shelter had been set up for this emergency. This was starting to look like the beginning of a real adventure . . .

In the school we were met by a couple of police officers and some National Guardsmen. They directed us to the gymnasium where at least a hundred or more people were already settling in. There were about eighty cots set up around the perimeter of the gym floor. All were taken. Jim and I staked a claim of about seven linear feet each on the third and fourth bleacher. As more people arrived, I watched as an elderly couple arrived and a young couple unselfishly gave up their cots to them.

It was announced over the P.A. system that dinner was being served in the cafeteria. This was looking good. I took my purse, like we were going on a date, and we were off to dinner. I don't remember what they served, all I know is, everything they served while we were hunkered down, was really good.

People with all kinds of pets were showing up. Several cats and dogs, a ferret, a bird in a cage, and two bunnies were all I remember. I'm sure there were more. None of them caused any problems and they all stayed in the gym near their owners. People quit arriving after dinner. We now had about four hundred people. I started talking to the people around me, asking them where they're from and where they were going.

It was pleasant watching the teenage boys, all of diverse

backgrounds, strangers to each other, play basketball. A couple little guys watched from the sidelines. Perhaps wanting a chance to play. The teenagers saw this and picked up the little guys every now and then to let them shoot hoops. Everybody got along fine.

It was announced over the P.A. that the basketball playing was to stop at 10:00 and lights would dim at 10:30. We tried to make the most of the sleeping arrangements on the bleachers. That was the worst part of the whole ordeal for me. Everything quieted down and four Mexican gentlemen from Chicago, who had settled down near us, started playing guitar softly and singing beautiful songs in Spanish. Their music was so beautiful and soothing.

Day One, March 12, came to a close.

In the night, not being able to sleep, I went down to the cafeteria and had coffee and chatted with the guardsmen and people that were up. We chatted, we ate doughnuts, we chatted some more, we ate more doughnuts. It was great. Of course I got very little sleep and after breakfast I slept on the couch in the teacher's lounge for a couple hours. I had a deck of cards with me and scared up another couple for Pinochle. We spend the day playing cards, reading, and chatting with each other.

I spent the next three days talking to all kinds of people from all over. Except for not sleeping that well on the bleachers I enjoyed myself. We were told we wouldn't be going anywhere for several days, so if we needed to call anyone, there were phones available. We called Steve, who had been waiting for us in Charlotte, and told him whenever we were able to leave, we would just go back home. He was glad we called. He had been worried, since he heard all the roads were closed in Kentucky.

After breakfast it was announced over the P.A. that there would be a school bus leaving for Walmart at 10:00. I declined because there was nothing that Jim or I needed. The Guard had provided us with everything. Toiletries of all kinds, even over the counter drugs. I noticed when the shoppers returned, most of them had pillows. Why hadn't I thought of that?

During the day we had an emergency, the only one we would have during our stay. A middle age man was either having a heart attack or a diabetes episode. A National Guard helicopter was flown in. It was big, really big, and the snow flew everywhere when it landed. We were told later that the man would be okay.

Each day in early afternoon we watched Jeopardy in the teachers's lounge. This was the day that we were all planning a Talent Show for after dinner. So far we had an amateur comedian who was on his way to entertain at Disney World. A very talented lady with a beautiful voice who was going to sing some popular songs, the four Mexicans, a country and western guitar player and others that have slipped my mind.

After dinner, everything was cleared, and chairs were arranged for the show. I was excited. Jim and I were really enjoying ourselves. All the contestants were very good, but the best by far was the comedian whose act consisted, mostly of a routine about Lorene Bobbit, who at that time, you will recall, had just been arrested for slicing off a particular part of her husband's anatomy while he slept, and threw it in a field. The police hunted for hours through the field trying to recover the evidence of her crime. It was hilarious. He, naturally, got a standing ovation, and won the contest. We wandered what kind of material he was going to use at Disney World. It certainly wasn't going to be that.

When word got back to the other high school in the area about our talent show, they wanted to borrow our comedian. Well, we'd have none of it, unless they had something to barter with.

Day two, March 13, came to a close.

We fell into a routine. We helped ourselves to any of the food in the cafeteria anytime. Ice cream, cake, cookies, potato chips, pop, whatever was there. One truck driver was hauling fruit in a semi. He called his boss and got the okay to unload all the fruit for us. Several young fellows helped unload the truck. What a treat. Fresh fruit in the middle of winter. No one went hungry. The school cafeteria workers were being brought in to cook for us and to clean up after us. We were really being treated royally. This particular evening we were going to play bingo. The people in town had generously donated prizes for us. I won a hand-held calculator. They were mostly inexpensive prizes, but everyone liked them. Address books, hand-held mirrors, decks of cards, you name it.

The little bakery in town got wind of the fact that an African American couple's Fiftieth Wedding Anniversary was today. They were on their way from Sault Ste. Marie, Michigan to Alabama to celebrate their anniversary with their family. The little bakery in town went ahead and baked a huge cake to surprise the couple. It was brought out as soon as the bingo game ended. The couple were really surprised and started to cry. I was a little teary eyed myself. They said it was the best anniversary they'd ever had. It was then that I fell in love with the kind and thoughtful people of Dry Ridge.

Day three, March 14, came to a close.

Jim and I were getting a little stir crazy. I hadn't had a shower since I'd been there. Remember school showers? No privacy. We asked a National Guardsmen if there was any chance we could go home today? He'd let us know, but only people heading north had a chance to leave. People going south would be staying for another day or two because the semis had blocked the highway at Jellico, Tennessee. After dinner we were told it would be okay to leave.

We had made so many friends here, that it was hard to say good-bye, but we had several addresses and phone numbers and promises to keep in touch, and for many years we did.

We headed north on the I-75 service drive because the highway was still closed. The roads were very icy and it seemed to take forever to get to Cincinnati. I-75 was open in Ohio, and the roads had been cleared. We pulled into a Holiday Inn Express just north of Cincinnati.

Day four, March 15, came to a close.

The blizzard of March 1993 was one of the largest winter storms in terms of snowfall and size in the history of Kentucky.

A year after the storm we were sent order forms from the high school to order t-shirts saying " I survived the blizzard of 1993" at Dry Ridge, Kentucky," we ordered two. Imprinted on it was the wrong year, 1994.

I wrote a letter to Gov. Steven Beshear on the 20th anniversary of the blizzard, and told him how wonderful our experience had been. He not only answered my letter but made me an official Kentucky Colonel, along with a beautiful embossed certificate, making it official.

27

The Cottage

Jack was the kind of man, that when you met him, you liked him instantly. A very interesting person. He loved to drink and he loved to smoke. He was a little rough around the edges. A WWII vet. He participated in the Invasion of Normandy. He was a bit older than Jim. I think he thought of Jim as a son. He was that wonderful type of guy who would do anything for you, but was insulted if you tried to reciprocate.

Jim met Jack Davis several years ago at the Livingston County Wildlife and Conservation Club. They were partners in archery and pool tournaments. That's really about all they had in common. Jack loved to hunt and fish. Jim didn't fish and didn't own a gun. In spite of that, they formed a wonderful friendship.

Jim found out that Jack was the owner of Jack's Body Shop where Steve took his car numerous times to get dents bumped out, and numerous other problems. Jim told Jack his business must have flourished after Steve got his license.

The kids were young adults now, so Jim spent a couple weekends in the fall hunting on Jack's property on Lake Lure, just outside of the little town of Evart, in Northern Michigan. Jim liked archery and thought it would be fun. Jack helped him build a tree stand in the woods in back of his property.

When we were first married, Jim went rabbit hunting with his buddies. He didn't really seem to care for it.

So now, all these years later, he decides to go up north with Jack, to hunt deer. The guys would always come back from their adventures with funny stories of the good times they were having, and the animals they shot. Jim had his supply of good stories too, but none of them included an animal, dead or alive.

One weekend Jack found Jim napping in his tree stand with a cross word puzzle on his lap, and deer tracks at the bottom of the tree stand.

I know what he really enjoyed was the camaraderie of his buddies. While they were up north, besides hunting, they would play cards, take turns cooking meals, occasionally go to the bar in Evart. It was just a good time for male bonding, and as Jim put it. "Once in awhile I'd go out to the woods and hunt."

Jim and I would go up to Jack and Marie's cottage for the week-end. It was very pleasant up there. Then Jack called Jim one week-end to tell him the cottage next door was for sale and wouldn't last long. Jim and I went up there that week-end and liked the deal they gave us, and bought the cottage. Our only regret was that we couldn't afford a cottage when the kids were little. Now both boys lived out of state, but Julie, Matt and their two little ones lived near us. So they could take advantage of the cottage.

Jack and Marie were good neighbors to have up there. We just had our sailboat. Jack let us use his row boat and paddle boat until we bought our pontoon boat. I never did sail, but I did love the pontoon boat. Occasionally, Jim would let Seth and Nathan steer the boat. They loved it.

We'd go up to the cottage on week-ends. Jim was putting a screened in porch on the front of the cottage. The cottage sat up on a steep hill and needed steps built. There was a large Amish community near us, so Jim hired a couple of their men to build steps, plus a deck midway down the steps to the water. It was wonderful to sit on that deck and watch the activity on the lake.

We were spending a quiet week-end at the cottage. Jim was on Jack's porch talking, when I called over to them in a panic.

"There's a duck drowning in the lake."

"What?" They said.

More agitated then before. "There's a duck drowning."

"What do mean?" they said laughing.

"This isn't funny, he dove in the water a few minutes ago and hasn't come up." In my defense, I thought he might have gotten stuck on sea weed.

They're still laughing. Then I saw it break the surface of the water. It was a loon. I forgot they can stay under water for several minutes. I couldn't tell a loon from a duck. I can now.

Lake Lure is a private lake and an exceptionally clean and quiet lake. That's the only kind of lake that loons live on. There's a small island at one end of the lake, and that's where the family of loons took up residence. They're an endangered species in this part of Michigan.

It's a small lake where the boats could not exceed 5 miles an hour. It'e also a spring fed lake with an earthen damn from the Muskegon River on the far side of the lake. That's the part of the lake where the large turtles lived. Some of the residents would catch the turtles and make turtle soup. The Muskegon River is the second largest river in Michigan. It is an amazing source of recreation all year round.

Jim and I would have our breakfast on the screen porch and watch the loons and ducks, or the occasional crane or heron. It was very peaceful. We also liked to play cards or Dominoes on the porch.

We brought our new dog Dusty, a 10 month old English Springer Spaniel to the cottage. He seemed afraid of the water. He stood at the edge of the dock trying to jump in, but kept pacing back and forth and looking at the water. Suddenly he slipped and fell in. He loved it so much you could hardly get him out. You couldn't take the boat out without him in it.

Carl's cottage was on the other side of Jack's. He was divorced and got his four little daughters every other week-end. When we came up they were crazy about Dusty and he just loved the attention. This particular week-end, one of the daughters yelled over to me, "Mrs., Mrs., Dusty's mother, Dusty caught a fish." Sure enough he had a large fish in his mouth. Julie's boys loved to walk with Grandpa down the dirt road in back of the cottage and pick apples from the apple trees They loved those walks. To this day, they still talk about their walks with Grandpa.

It was a Labor Day weekend when we waited with Seth and

Nathan for Julie to arrive and celebrate her birthday with us. The boys made beautiful Birthday cards for her. She never arrived.

We hardly went up to the cottage after the accident. We missed Jack and Marie, but we saw them frequently at the Conservation Club Fish Fries.

Carl, the father of the four little girls that loved playing with Dusty, never came by to talk to us after Julie's accident. People who have lost loved ones want to talk about them. They want their loved ones to be remembered. They would like to know you care. I understand that people feel uncomfortable with such sadness. I know, I used to feel that way myself. I felt bad that we never got a chance to say good-bye to Carl the day we packed up and left the cottage for the last time.

We sold our cottage four years after Julie died. We would have kept it for the sake of the boys, but Jim couldn't winterize it anymore. Doug always came over to help us with all sorts of things. We never had to ask him. Jim could see the writing on the wall, and so we decided that it was too much to take care of, even with Doug's help.

Matt and his friend Jim came up with Seth to help us move. Before we left, they put up two large crosses on US 10 just outside of Farwell. The crosses are still there. Jim and I only went there once to place flowers by the crosses. We never went back. It was too painful.

Jack died of cancer a few years later. I told Marie that I would like to eulogize Jack with the story of the bandages. She said that was okay. His funeral was held at the Livingston County Wildlife and Conservation Club in Hamburg. Jack had been a member of the club for over 25 years. He was well liked and had many friends.

I told the mourners about the time at the cottage when Jim and I were watching Jack pour gasoline on a tree stump he was trying to get rid of. The stump was in front of Jack's cottage down near the water. He'd had a few beers that day and decided to use gasoline, I suppose, as a last resort.

Jim and I were busy cleaning up the leaves in front of our cottage. As Jack started to pour gasoline on the stump, Jim hollered down to him not to light it. Jack wears a hearing aid. Of course Jack didn't hear a thing and proceeded to throw a match on the tree stump.

The fire immediately ran up the flow of gasoline and right up Jack's arm and the side of his face and ear. Jim ran down as fast as he could, to help him. Jack might be pushing 80, but he's pretty spry for his age. He was already near the water's edge so he just jumped in before Jim could get to him. Jim kept asking him if he was okay. Jack said yeah, and that he was going to the house to change clothes and he'd be right over.

He came over a few minutes later, and Jim offered him a beer. While he was talking to us his hands started to shake and the skin on his arm and side of his face, were turning red. Jim said, "Come on, we've got to get you to the hospital." Jack insisted on Marie taking him. She was in town grocery shopping, so Jim went and got her.

We took care of the groceries, and off they went to the hospital in Reed City which is about 20 minutes away.

They came back an hour or two later with Jack all bandaged up.

The next morning Marie came over really upset with Jack. Marie is a very pleasant and even tempered person but she was really upset.

"Marie, what's going on?" I asked.

"I'm so mad at Jack. I've got to take him back to the hospital. He was lighting up a cigarette this morning, and set his bandages on fire."

28

Politics in Hamburg

I was elected Hamburg Township Clerk in 1992 as the only Democrat on the Township Board, in what was a solidly Republican county. It was so unusual that a Democrat won, that it was written up in the Ann Arbor News. The vote tally was Republican, Martha Parrish 2,930 and Democrat, Diane Wrobleski 3,349. I served in that capacity until 1996. What an eye opener that was . . .

Hamburg Township, in 1992, had a population of over 20,000. A township that large should have either been a charter township, or at the very least should have had a township manager, someone with enough education and experience to handle the various issues that a township that size would present. We, however, were a general township. There were seven members who made up the Board. The township supervisor, the treasurer and the clerk. In our township these three positions were full time. The four trustees which made up the rest of the Board were part time. The supervisor, treasurer and clerk are equal in the eyes of the law and the supervisor is not over the clerk or the treasurer, although our supervisor tried to act like he was, on several occasions. The top three positions run the township and are responsible for the Police Department and, in some instances, the Fire Department as well. We had a Volunteer Fire Department with a very good reputation.

Hamburg Township, it seems has always had a long history of contentious politics. I always thought that it would be a real privilege to have the opportunity to serve in government at the grassroots level. My naive view of politics was that I could actually contribute something positive by being a member of the Board, specifically in the capacity of the township clerk, because I have an associates degrees in accounting and also in general business plus a bachelors degree in American history with a minor in General Business. I had not quite completed my masters program in Public Administration when I ran for office.

Running for public office offers citizens a unique and sometimes, satisfying experience. My first-time experience of vying for an elective office was a fulfilling witness to democracy in action. It was however short-lived.

I soon found that when you are involved in politics you can't trust too many people, and everyone seemed to have an ulterior motive.

I became fast friends with one of the four township trustees, Sally Bennett. We hit it off early on in our tenure. The reason, I figured, was because neither of us had a hidden agenda. We were just idealists who actually thought the same of the others. Well, we soon learned different. Some members of the Board worked in real estate. One of the members of the Planning Commission was a builder. Although none of these are illegal, they are unethical, because they are privy to so much inside information.

All we wanted to do was make a difference. Well, I soon found out how difficult it was to get motions passed, mostly because a lot of the board members didn't do their homework. You have to have three other members of the Board working with you, that you hope have studied the issues put forth on the agenda. They should be prepared to at least back up their decisions with facts. The key word is compromise. People always seem to want it their way, and no one seemed willing to compromise.

There was one member who was so focused on getting her own personal parking spot that she didn't seem to grasp the issues that were on the monthly agenda, or she didn't take the time to read the agenda. When we wanted to change township attorneys this same board member wanted her divorce attorney to represent the township.

Then there was the building of a wastewater treatment plant and sewers around some of the lakes. That was fodder for the newspapers the four years I was on the Board.

Four members of the Board including Sally and myself were being recalled by the anti-sewer people and the other three were being recalled by the pro-sewer folks. The judge threw both recalls out. That was how our first year went.

Sally and I took a trip around the lakes in the township that we, as a board, were talking about sewering. Lo and behold we saw porta-johns in the garages of some of the residents living on the lakes that were under consideration for sewering. We took pictures, and even then the board members couldn't agree what to do.

Dealing with the Police Department was a whole other ball game. We had one officer who was in charge of a traffic accident between a van and a car, with injuries involved. He coordinated the ambulances, getting the victims to the hospital, and then had the car and van towed, only to find out later that there was another victim in the van.

Then one of the police officers who filed a report of an arm injury and claimed they wouldn't be able to work until the injury healed. While collecting unemployment the officer showed up at the Township Hall carrying a young child in their injured arm.

Another police officer had two prison workers under his care. They were suppose to work at the police station washing cars and doing odd jobs, until we were informed that he had the workers helping him build an addition to his house.

After a couple of the board members, including myself, had a contentious disagreement with some of the members of the police department, I experienced an interesting incident. Sally and I were driving to Brighton, which is in a different township. We noticed a police car had been slowly following us for quite a while. Finally I couldn't take it any longer. I pulled over and flagged him down. I told him if he thought he was intimidating me or anyone else on the Board he was sadly mistaken. He could see I was upset. He apologized and said that wasn't his intent at all. It never happened again.

So not to give the wrong impression of the Police Department, I have to say that most of the men were wonderful.

Another strange thing some of the the Board members were working on, was to take over the fire department. This Fire Department had been written up years ago in the Readers Digest as an example of how volunteer Fire Departments should be run. They were efficient and they never went over budget. My question is, why would you want the township to take on that responsibility? I wasn't sure until after I left office. Then I found out why, but I can't print it.

Another time the Board went to the Renaissance Center in downtown Detroit for a Michigan Towns and Townships Association Convention. Sally and I were on our way to breakfast. As we stepped off the elevator on the main floor, we saw the supervisor. He was around 5'6" and very nondescript in appearance. Sally was about ten years his junior, 5'10" blond, and attractive. We'd been battling with him over so many issues the past couple years. Anyway, to get back to the story, we got off the elevator, saw the supervisor getting off another elevator. Sally proceeded to go right over to him, straighten out his tie, and pat him on the shoulder while telling him he looked pretty good. He was so flustered, his face turned red, he turned around and got right back on the same elevator he'd just gotten off of. We laughed all the way to breakfast.

29

Nobody's Perfect

You know how some days it just isn't worth getting up? Well this was one of those days.

Some time ago, my son Dave had mentioned to me that I could turn in metal, such as cans for money. He had taken a couple bags in, and was paid $30.00. Thinking, what a good idea, I could use $30, $40 or $50.00. I decided to save those cans instead of putting them in the recycle bin every week. So, today, I had quite a "To Do" list, including take books to Tellico Village Library for library sale, get stamps at the post office, get gas, and at the top of the list, the scrap yard.

As I mapped out my chores, post office first, then library, then head to the scrap yard. it is located down on US11, a short distance off US321 towards downtown Lenoir City. Ah, there it is, a run down little place with a worn, gravel driveway. Following the signs, straight ahead, go around back of building, turn left here. I drove along the back and then pulled up alongside the building. It was a bit of a tight squeeze. There was a car ahead of me with people taking lots of wire, tire rims and cable out of the trunk of their car.

A young fellow with yellow teeth, no doubt from chewing tobacco, wearing worn blue jeans and a torn shirt, came to the car and told me,

"Ma'am, you'll have to back up, 'cause they need to get a fork lift in here."

"I'm not backing up on this gravel. My car is new. I'm not sure I should have driven it in here in the first place."

"Okay ma'am, I'll talk to the boss" he smiled politely, left, then sauntered back a short time later.

"Boss says it's okay, we'll drive this car" he said, as he pointed to the car ahead of me with the trunk open, "and you pull up." I thanked him and apologized for the inconvenience.

"Oh, that's okay ma'am, I understand." he said in that slow southern drawl.

I pulled the car up, opened the trunk, and the fellow took out my two large bags of pop cans and tin cans.

Cars are beginning to line up behind me, including the fork lift. I got out of the car and went into the building to the cashier. In the meantime, the young fellow went off into the building with my two bags. The cashier asked for my drivers license. I looked at her in bewilderment, "It's the law" she said. It took me a little bit of time to get my drivers license out of my wallet. It's in a compartment in the front of my wallet and it's in tight. The cashier waited patiently as I finally was able to extricate it from it's small pocket. She continued to fill out the invoice while the young fellow was weighing or counting or sorting, whatever it was he had to do with the contents of my two bags.

When the cashier was finished, she asked me to sign the invoice.

"Here you are" she said, "70 cents. . ."

"70 cents, all this for 70 cents?" I said.

"Would you like a receipt?"

"No thank you, I'm too embarrassed to let anyone know I've been here."

I apologized profusely and left, only to find an even longer line of cars backing up behind the fork lift. They were kind enough not to honk their horns in frustration. I wouldn't have blamed them if they did.

On the way home I kept thinking, "why hadn't I flattened the cans? I would have been able to fit all that into one bag, but instead, I brought in two bags that weren't much heavier than air."

One thing is certain, I'm never going back there.

30

My Grandchildren

I have been blessed with three wonderful grandchildren. Julie's two boys, Seth Matthew born July 12 1993, and Nathan James born January 12, 1995. David has one daughter Carly Diane, born August 12, 2004. He also has helped raise his stepdaughter, Courtney Pethers, born December 26, 1995.

From the time my grandchildren were little I took notes of the everyday things they talked about and did.

Seth Matthew and Nathan James Petrill

Seth has always seemed to be like an old soul to me. Someone who has these wonderful thoughts similar to people of an earlier era. In the years right after his mother died, he spoke often of Heaven and had descriptions of a place with white houses, curtains in every window and flowers out front, and there was always a rainbow present. Drawing pictures of his family, even after Julie died, he always drew everyone smiling.

We were looking out the window one day and out of the blue he told me he'd been talking to God and told Him that he missed his mom and wanted her to come back home. He said to me "I'm praying real hard for her to come back." I told him through tears, "If prayers could bring her back she'd be with us already. Everyone wants her back." I had a hard time convincing him that wishing, and praying for her to come back, would not bring her back. I told him, "In cartoons they seem to come back, but in real life they don't." I talked to his dad about it and he said Seth had talked to him also.

Seth has his mother's freckles on his nose and cheeks, and the same light color hair. As he's growing older, his freckles seem to be fading. He walks like his Uncle Steve.

I bought some highly recommended books to read to Seth and Nathan concerning young children who have lost a loved one ."The Badger's Parting Gifts." It is a touching story that explains that grief can eventually give way to happy memories. I read that to them several times, then put it away. Seth was over one week-end, and the kids across the street were all playing. I heard one of the boys ask Seth to play. He kept saying no. Finally when one of the other boys came to persuade him, he told him in a louder than usual voice, 'I'm grounded." It reminded me of years before when Julie wouldn't play with the neighborhood kids, only Seth used a different approach, to get his point across.

Every year on Mother's Day, Matt and Julie bought me a hanging basket of beautiful flowers for the front porch. One year we noticed birds were building a nest in the basket. Jim picked Seth up so he could see the newly hatched baby wrens. He was puzzled about people having babies and birds laying eggs. I told him that elephants and bears and big animals like that have babies, but birds and alligators, and some other animals are hatched from eggs. We had a nice little conversation about it and finally Seth said, "God sure has a lot of directions."

The first Christmas after his Mom died, Seth insisted his Dad put her Christmas stocking up next to the rest of the family's stockings on the fireplace.

The second Christmas after Julie died, Seth said a prayer. "Dear God, I hope you love my Mom. She's the only angel in my family. Amen"

When Seth was in grade school he got a set of K-nex building blocks. He was so creative and built lots of things including a roller coaster. He didn't need the directions, he just built really neat things on his own. He told us, "The only thing better than K-nex is more K-nex."

When Seth was six he told his mom to call 911. "There's spiders in the basement." He said.

When Seth was seven he told me, "Good people go to Heaven and bad people go to Hell." "What kind of bad people ?" I asked. "People that don't believe in God or Santa Clause."

One day we were passing by Maxey Training School for Boys. Seth wanted to know more about the school. I told him it was a school for bad boys. Nate asked, "What did they do to have to be there?" Seth said, "They talked in church."

I asked him where he thought his mother was. "Above the clouds in a wooden house with a picture of me and Nate." "Is she happy?" I asked. He said 'Kinda." I took that to mean that since he's lonely, she's probably lonely too.

Two years after Julie died, we were coming home from the cottage, Seth was getting into the car (I don't remember if it was too hot, or what.) He exclaimed, "Holy Mother of God!"

One time just after Jim got a hair cut he sat down in his chair and bent down to tie his shoelace. This was an angle of Jim's head that, evidently up to now, Seth had never noticed. He looked at the top of Jim's head and said, "Grandpa, you've got a hole in you hair cut."

While we were watching the movie, Song of the South, Seth remarked that Uncle Remus looked like Eddie Murphy's grandpa.

Seth, talking to Nathan said, "You were really cute when you were a baby, now you're becoming a pill."

Nate was about six or seven years old when he came home from the barber shop and was so excited he wanted me to know that "I don't get the puppy cut anymore, I get the big dog cut."

I love my grandsons so much, and didn't want to talk about Julie's death unless they brought it up, and they did.

A couple years after Julie died, Nate asked me, "Why do people have to die?" I think the Lord helps us at this most vulnerable time. My reply was "Imagine if we never died, how many old people would be around. We wouldn't be able to go anywhere without falling over canes and wheel chairs. God knows what he's doing. He's got it all figured out. It's like getting on a city bus where there are people of all ages. Some have to get off at a stop and others get on. It doesn't matter their ages. That's what life is like." Nate seemed satisfied. I tried to make my answers somewhat upbeat, but appropriate to their age when I answered them. I wanted them to always be happy when they talked about their mom.

Seth, being older asked me if his mom was happy in heaven. I told him, "Your mom could never be completely happy without her little boys, so I think when we die, we enter a time warp, and your mom is stuck in a one second time warp, so that when you die she will see you right away. it will seem to her that just a second has passed and you and Nate will be with her." Seth loved that explanation because he has a deep interest in astronomy, especially black holes and time warps.

I couldn't tell how many times they would ask me, "Do you think my mom would be proud of me?" I would always tell them, "She's looking down at you and smiling all the time. She loves you so."

I didn't want to scare them, but I did want them to know their mother, and that she was in a wonderful place.

I always told them, "Anytime you want to go to the cemetery, just let me know and we'll go."

Nate was at our house one day, and the dog kept stealing his cookies. Finally Nate said, "Grandma, you should get a cat."

Nate, always tried to be helpful. He was shoveling the snow off the driveway with Grandpa. When they were finished he said "Did we do a great job, or what."

I was talking to Seth about being addicted to nail-biting, when Nate said "I think I'm addicted to myself."

Julie was trying to explain something complicated to Nate. She, evidently went on and on, finally Nate said, "Mama those sure are a lot of words."

Thanksgiving at Aunt Pam's house, their tradition was to have everyone say what they were thankful for. They started with Nate. He said "I'm thankful for my brother." (He was four.)

As Jim's Parkinson's progressed, I bought him an electric chair that could actually lift him into a standing position, because he could not get out of the chair by himself. Seth and Nathan loved that chair. Whenever the chair was empty, they'd both get in it and lift it to a standing position, all while trying to push the other one down to see who'd fall out of it first.

We had an English Springer Spaniel named Dusty. He was a wonderful dog. The boys just loved him. A couple years after Julie died we had to put him down. The boys wanted to go with us, so I called Matt and asked him. Matt said it would be okay.

At the vets, Seth, Jim and Dusty followed the vet into another room and Nate and I stayed in the reception area. We were looking at pictures of dogs on the wall. Nate started to cry and I could hear the receptionist, and another lady in the room begin to sniffle, then I teared up. Nate was so sad. He started to look at the pictures of the cats and kittens on the wall and changing the subject said through his tears, "Can we take home a cat?"

It was at this time that Seth and Grandpa came back into the office. Seth told us that the vet told him to count to ten and Dusty would be in heaven. "That's exactly what happened Grandma," he continued, "The vet gave Dusty a shot, he closed his eyes, and in a couple seconds he was gone." Seth took it stoically.

Nate was such a cute little guy growing up. A cherubic face with big dimples and the best smile ever. Nate has always loved sports. He loved football. He played it throughout grade school and high school. He was the quarterback at Pinckney High School.

I always knew which player he was because he walked just like his Dad.

Nate Patrill

Nate is all about sports, just like his Uncle Dave. He is glued to the ESPN channel on TV. Of course his favorite is football. He has a great memory, just like his Uncle Dave, and he can give you stats on any sport.

In High School, Nate went to the University of Michigan Football Camp and was named the MVP 2010 QB 10th grade champion.

Nate was in the locker room with his football buddies before one of his games. It was September 2nd. He told them it was the anniversary of his mother's death. He also told them that there was a memorial stone in Old St. Patrick's cemetery dedicated to his mom, because she went to that church when she was young. The football team didn't know that Nate's mom had died, so they dedicated their game to her. I could hardly contain my tears when Nate told me that. They went on to win the game.

I think he was in third grade when he could tell you all the presidents in order or randomly, and he knew most of the presidents wives as well. He could name all the states and their capitols. He told me his Grandma Marilyn would buy him flash cards with all kinds of things on them that he would memorize.

Julie was quite an artist and won first place at the Mid-Michigan Art Contest in 1984. Her art work was displayed at the Michigan Historical Center in Lansing. She won so many art contests, that I don't remember what the subject was.

In 2004, Seth won first place at the Michigan Art Extension Association. His work was also displayed at the Michigan Historical Center in Lansing. His was the Vanishing Point. A beautiful drawing looking down the Grand Strand at Myrtle Beach. He was 10.

Seth and Nate loved to go to the cottage with us, and grandpa would let them steer the pontoon boat. Both of them loved to go down the dirt road in back of the cottage and pick apples. Jim would cut out the little worms in the apples and give them nice clean slices. Whenever we mentioned the cottage, they both talk about their walks down the road to the wild apple trees with Grandpa.

Grandpa taught them both to fish. Jim and I also took them to the driving range. Jim loved golfing with Steve and Dave, and I know he was looking forward to the day when he would golf with Seth and Nate. Sadly, that was not to be.

In July 2006, Seth was 13, he had started to play guitar. We all knew that Jim probably would not make it to Thanksgiving. Seth wrote a piece of music, he titled it "Heaven's Lights." Jim died on September 16. Seth played "Heaven's Lights" at the dinner following Jim's funeral. We were all very impressed. He had only been playing guitar a couple months, and now he was writing music.

Seth Petrill

Carly Diane Wrobleski

I only see Carly six months each year when I go to Tennessee, November through April. We spend many weekends together. These are some of our conversations.

Jim passed away when Carly was two, but I still remember how cute she was with Jim.

We were over at Dave and Lisa's, and we brought over Jim's wheelchair. He only had it a few days. Carly was really intrigued by Grandpa being in the wheelchair. Next time I looked, she was trying to push him. Everyone thought how cute that was, but a little later, we just couldn't believe that little girl. She had grandpa pushing her in the wheelchair. That was really memorable.

Courtney and Carly had a little cat named Smoky that Courtney had named after the Smoky mountains. Carly and I were driving through Lenoir City one afternoon, I think Carly was four at the time, she pointed to a building and wanted to know what it was. I proceeded to explain that it was the Visitor's Center where people driving through the area want to know what's interesting to see in this part of Tennessee, like all the water around us and the Great Smoky Mountains. Carly said, "You know, those mountains were named after my cat."

Carly asked me one day if she could have my townhouse. "Why wouldn't you want your grandparents house? It's big, it's on the water, and so beautiful." "Oh, it's too much work." she said.

As I was combing my hair one morning, I remarked that I was losing a lot of hair. "Do you think I'm going bald?" I asked her. "Yes, you are, but don't worry Grandma, when you lose all your hair I'll loan you my hat." Mind you, she wasn't going to give me her hat, she was only going to lend it to me . . .

Carly drew me a pretty card for my 74th birthday. On the outside she wrote "Happy Birthday Grandma" and drew several, cute, little hearts. Inside she wrote "Happy Birthday Grandma. I can't believe you're going to be 74. You look more like 59 to 61."

On one of her Mother's Day cards to me she drew a picture of a lady with beautiful, long, eye lashes. I called to thank her and told her I especially loved the eye lashes, to which she replied, "Those aren't eye lashes Grandma, those are wrinkles."

Carly is quite a swimmer. She's been swimming since 1st grade. Her name is in the Lenoir City newspaper quite often. She also is an all A student.

Carly, at eleven was already showing her talents. She was definitely following in Courtney's footsteps. Both their bedrooms are filled with ribbons and trophies. Both of the girls still own the records on the Tellico Village swim team and Lenoir City Schools swim team.

In 2014, Carly won an audition to sing the National Anthem at the

Greater Knoxville Interscholastic Swim Meet held at the University of Tennessee pool. There was over 4,000 people in attendance. She knocked it "out of the park." People were clapping and whistling, and some, had tears in their eyes. I told her "I can't believe you can sing like that and you're only ten." She looked at me a little surprised, and said "Grandma, I am almost eleven." When she finished the National Anthem she had to quickly run back downstairs.. She had to compete in the relays just a couple minutes after singing. She won all the relays she participated in.

She has been asked to sing the National Anthem at several of their schools sporting events. She attends North Middle School in Lenoir City.

Carly has been involved in dance since the age of 5. Among her disciplines are Tap, Ballet, Hip-Hop, Modern and Jazz. She performs annually in the dance recital which takes place at the Lenoir City High School Auditorium.

Carly had just bought a very interesting book at Barnes and Noble. Her and I both love biographies. In the car on the way home she began to read, to herself, the story of Sacagawea. We had about a half hour drive ahead of us. As she started reading I asked her where she wanted to have lunch? "Grandma," she said, while she put her fingers to her lips, in a zip the lip, motion, "I'm reading." "Oops! sorry" I said. Five, ten minutes later I remarked about something else. "Grandma!" again, I said "Sorry!" We finally stopped to have lunch.

The following week we were back at Barnes and Noble. She was buying another book and proceeded, with a smile out of the corner of her mouth, that reminded me of Julie, to tell the cashier, while looking at me, "Do you believe that my Grandma talks to me while I'm trying to read?" All I could say was "Guilty." She won't let me get away with anything. She loves to tease. She's my "Book Buddy."

Carly and I stopped at a red light, and we had our arms going in unison to the music on the radio. Swaying this way and that way and snapping our fingers. We looked over at the car next to us, and the man was smiling at us. He was waving his arms around just like us. He rolled down his window. He had the same music on. We got a laugh out of that.

After showing Carly how to scrapbook, she did a complete book of twenty pages. They were really good. It demonstrated her artistic talent. I think Carly was either eight or nine at the time. She was so proud of herself, she told me, "I want to put this scrapbook in my coffin when I die." (she motioned having it on her chest with her arms crisscrossed over it.) I think her and Courtney have watched too many scary movies. She proceeded to say, "I'm going to tell my children that their great-grandmother taught me how to scrapbook. My parents are going to be so proud of me."

31

A Love Story

(Told in Vignettes)

I had just turned seventeen and from the first day I saw Jim, I wanted to marry him. I don't know what I ever did in my life to deserve him, but whatever it was, I was very grateful.

Not only was Jim tall, dark, and handsome, but he had a wonderful sense of humor, and exquisite manners. He was intelligent, thoughtful, I could just go on and on.

My first Valentine card from Jim had a caricature of different animals in two's, and the two giraffes had there necks entwined. On the inside it said "Everyone's "twoing" it, why don't we?" Then Jim gave me a small gold band to signify that we were going steady.

People would tell us how much Jim looked like Burt Reynolds, or Jim Garner, and later in life, some would say John Forsythe. He reminded me most of Jim Garner. Same build, same personality.

I said to myself, "I've got to take this slow, and see where all this is going. After all, we are both only 17."

I hadn't dated very much before I met Jim. I had gone to all girl Catholic schools for the last three years. Two years at the Ursuline Academy and one year at Girl's Catholic Central High School. Before that, six years at St. Francis de Sales Catholic school.

I was really naive. I had two sisters, but no brothers growing up. My dad died when I was 16. I think that's a crucial time, when daughters really need their dads. So you can see that I really didn't know very much about guys or dating.

I tried not to be too nervous when we first started dating, but right from the start he made me feel comfortable. What I loved most about him was his sense of humor. Even in later years, when he was ill with Parkinsons disease, that humor was still there. A little slower, but still there.

He had a very pleasant personality, very genuine. Everyone liked him, especially Mama. A very easy going person. After we got married, I realized he was also a low maintenance guy.

I usually referred to Jim as "My Jim" because Marguerite's husband was also a "Jim." He was older than my Jim, tall and thin. I couldn't refer to him as "Big Jim" or "Old Jim" so I just referred to my Jim as "My Jim." Eventually I asked Jim Kirby if it would be okay if I just called him Kirby. He agreed. So we solved that problem, but out of habit I still referred to him as "My Jim."

I learned a lot from Jim. He, like his mother, was never afraid to admit when he was wrong, and was not afraid to apologize, when necessary. I remember Jim apologizing to our little son Steve, admitting that he was wrong. Steve was five at the time. I don't remember the circumstances, but I was very impressed with that. It became easier for me to apologize or admit when I was wrong.

Jim embodied the word gentleman. But what shines out the most about Jim was that wonderful, quick wit of his.

One day when Julie was 16, she went out on the deck to talk to her dad. I heard Jim laughing and saying to her, "You're not going to tell your mom are you?" She came into the kitchen and said,

"You know how dad laughs when he thinks he's said something funny?"

"Now what," I said.

"I asked dad if I could borrow some money, and he said, 'There's only two ways in this world to get money. One is to get a job and the other is to marry Jim Wrobleski. Second one's taken."

We had good friends Dick and Lori Guinan. We spent a lot of time together. We all liked to play Trivia Pursuit, among other things. Lori came from a large Irish Family and they liked to tease Jim. They would banter back and forth all the time. One year, in doing genealogy, I found out that Jim's mother was part Swiss and part Scotch-Irish. It was around that time that Cathy Guinan, Lori's sister, called Jim about a Trivia Pursuit question. Jim and Cathy were the best at Trivia Pursuit. When they would be at Trivia Pursuit parties that we weren't attending, they'd call Jim for the answers that they didn't know, or weren't sure of. This particular evening, Cathy called Jim and asked him a question, and he didn't know the answer. Cathy said, "I can't believe it. All these years, this is the first time you didn't know the answer." Jim said, "Ever since I found out I'm part Irish, I'm not worth a damn." Jim could hear them all laughing in the background.

Jim used to tell people, "I've got the Wrobleski curse." "What's the Wrobleski curse?" they'd ask. "Mrs. Wrobleski." I would just shake my head, and roll my eyes.

I was in the kitchen one day, and started yelling at Jim about something. (I was the one that yelled. He never did.) Steve came in from the garage and asked who I was yelling at. I said, "Your father." Steve said, "He's in the garage."

"How long has he been in the garage?" I asked. "Probably since you started yelling at him."

A short time later Jim came in the house. He came over and hugged me. I thought, here comes the apology. Jim said to me, while giving me a nice big hug, "Anytime you want to apologize, I'll accept." You can't stay mad at someone like that.

We were at a wedding reception and were seated across from Quinto, Joanie's husband. The waitress came to our table, dressed in an outfit that exposed her cleavage. Just as she started to bend down to pour water for Quinto, Jim Kirby asked "Is everybody happy?" Jim said, "Well I know I am."

When we first moved into our house on the lake, we couldn't afford air conditioning, so we had screens. It was a summer night. Our bedroom window faced the lake. I could hear the frogs croaking in the lake, and I could also hear wasps hitting the screen.

I was in my thirties at the time, I think I looked pretty good. I went to bed with a nice negligee on, and Jim turned out the lights. Suddenly I felt something on my leg, and then a terrific sting. It was one of those wasps. I jumped up and started screaming. "There's something on my leg that just bit me. I think it's a wasp." I said through tears.

Jim turned the lights back on. I pulled off my negligee while jumping up and down naked on the bed. trying to get rid of the wasp. I kept thinking there were more wasps in the room.

All while I'm screaming and crying Jim is laughing.so hard at the sight before him. I kept saying, "Quit laughing it's not funny. "I'm trying not to, really I am" He kept saying, while still laughing.

The next day, Jim and the guys in the neighborhood were talking out on the deck. I could hear them laughing, as Jim related the story of the wasp and me. Then I heard Jim tell them "I hadn't seen action like that in the bedroom in ten years." More laughing.

Jim and I were walking around the lake one evening after work. On an impulse, I reached over and pinched his behind. He was a little startled, and jumped a little, but immediately said "You're the third one today, what's with you women?" He was quick.

Julie wrote Jim a letter on his birthday, telling him how much she appreciated him, and especially his sense of humor. She said, when her friends would come over, they would remark about it also. She told of the time her friend, Theresa Marhoff was over and Jim was on the couch in the family room, and Bruce Springstein came on and started singing. Jim put a bandana on his head and started imitating the "Boss." Julie said it was hilarious and Theresa kept telling all her friends about it.

Julie was shopping with Jim and me at the Brighton Mall. I went into a little jewelry store. They sat on a bench in from of the store. I found this really cute pair of earrings and took them over to Julie and her dad, asking what they thought of them. They both started laughing. "What?" I said.. Julie said, "They're marijuana leaves." More laughing. I said to Julie. "How come you know so much about marijuana at 13" "Oops!" she said with her cute smile.

Julie and her dad were always close, and always loved to laugh at my expense. Every time a song came on by either Phoebe Snow or Roberta Flack, I always got them mixed up. I'd say, "I just love Phoebe Snow" and they would both look at each other and say at the same time, while laughing. "It's Roberta Flack."

One evening, Jim and I went to Ann Arbor with Butch and Cindy, our neighbors, to a very nice restaurant downtown. Its name escapes me. While they were parking the car, Jim spotted a bookstore across the street. Knowing how much I love books, he suggested Cindy and I go over there and we'd meet up with them as soon as they had parked the car.

We were only in the bookstore a few minutes when we realized it was a porn store. We got out of there in a hurry, and there Butch and Jim were, across the street, laughing. I could've killed them both. Jim wanted to know what took us so long. . .

Another time, we went up north to Mackinac Island with Doug and Kathy. Doug is a good friend of ours. He is so funny. He reminds me of Rodney Dangerfield. Kathy laughs at all his nonsense. She really enjoys him. We all do.

I kept reminding them that I wanted to buy the book, "The Loon Feather" by Iola Fuller. It's the story of an Indian girl destined to grow up in conflict with the traditions of her people, and the French on Mackinac island.

I couldn't find it in any of the stores around town. It was an old book. If I could find it anyplace I was hoping it would be up north.

I looked in the bookstore in Mackinaw City. Nothing there. I realized I wasn't going to get that book. By this time everyone was sick of me talking about that book.

We got a motel for the night, right by the Mackinac Bridge. The motel had vibrating beds and Doug couldn't wait for Kathy and him to test it. Their room was a few doors from ours.

They left to unpack, and came back 15, 20 minutes later. Jim asked Doug how the bed was. "It was great." He said, and started making a big show of gyrating all over the place, and wiggling all over. We're all laughing at his antics, and Doug said. "Then I put the quarter in."

We took the ferry to Mackinac island, and right after we got off the boat, Jim took me by the shoulders and turned me around towards town, and there amongst these quaint little shops was a bookstore named "The Loon Feather." I was happy.

We were in the bedroom one night getting ready for bed when

Dusty came in the room. Jim said. "How many times do I have to tell you to stay out of this room."

"Don't talk to the dog that way." I said.

"I wasn't talking to the dog." Jim quipped..

In doing genealogy, I had been searching for my great-great-grandmother Anna Schindehette's death certificate. I finally had to write to Lansing. I was so excited when I received my long awaited answer. Jim said "Do you realize you're the only person I know that gets excited over death certificates?"

I opened the envelope, and to my surprise, great-great-grandma Schindehette died at the Eastern Michigan Asylum for the Insane, in Pontiac, Michigan.

When I told Jim that she died at the insane asylum, he said, "That answers all my questions."

While delving a bit more into her background, it appears she most likely had Alzheimer's, plus the fact that she came from Germany, and spoke very little english.

Jim and I went to New England on our 25th wedding anniversary. In Boston we each went our way to shop, and agreed to meet by this lovely fountain.

When I was through shopping, I went back to the fountain. I saw Jim standing their throwing some coins in, so I snuck up on him and pinched his behind. He turned around so startled, but not as startled as I was. It wasn't Jim... I was so embarrassed. I told the fellow I thought he was my husband and apologized profusely.

25th wedding anniversary

I turned to see if Jim was anywhere in sight, and saw that he was not too far in back of me, laughing, as usual. I kept saying to him,

"Why did you let me do that? Why didn't you stop me?"

"I was just curious to see how you would react." He said.

Throughout our marriage, I always had a passion for books. Jim built me beautiful, dark wood bookshelves in our family room. The wood matched the mantel on the fireplace. The bookshelves covered two walls, floor to ceiling and on the other two walls, one of which was a brick fireplace wall, and hearth. Jim extended the mantel on the fireplace across the remaining wall.

I placed my collection of tea pots across the top of the bookshelves. I loved that room. It was my favorite. I miss it to this day.

Just before he became bedridden, while he was still able to stand, we hugged each other for a long time. As we slowly swayed in each others arms, I started to cry. I said to Jim, "Why did this have to happen to us?" I miss those hugs so much.

Jim passed away two weeks later on September 16, 2006

Now, I always picture the family room with Jim sitting in his favorite chair, and Dusty at his feet, as Jim did the crossword puzzles that he enjoyed so much. He also loved word games, and word puzzles.

Jim made all my dreams come true.

32

Tears

When I was growing up we had a heat register in the living room. It was at the base of the wall down by the floor. It measured about a foot high and a foot wide. It was on the wall between the dining room and living room, near the archway dividing those two rooms. I liked to warm up by that register. In winter when my sisters and I came home from school, we'd take turns standing by the register to warm up before dinner. When we washed our hair we would sit on the floor in front of the register and let the heat blow our long hair dry.

It was early fall of 1956 when I came home from school and was standing by the register to warm myself from the chilly autumn air. I was sixteen at the time, and Mama was on the couch. She looked at me with a somber expression. I knew something was bothering her. She looked tired. She was usually cheerful, but had been taking care of Dad since mid-summer. That's when Dr. Margrave told Dad he might have to have a kidney operation. I asked Mama what was bothering her. She just looked at me with a kind of sad look, and told me that Dad was dying of cancer. As I look back, I wished I would have gone over to Mama and hugged her, but all I could think of, as my whole world was crumbling, was to just go upstairs to my bedroom and be alone with my thoughts. I couldn't quit crying and I didn't want Mama to see me this way. I don't remember what else happened that day.

Dad had been in a lot of pain for a long time, and I had started to pray that if Dad couldn't get better, hopefully God would look mercifully on him and end his suffering. Both Dad and Mama suffered through this terrible ordeal and tried to shield us from it as best they could. The whole family prayed and prayed. Mama prayed to Father Solanus, who as I write this, is in the first of three stages, "venerable" to sainthood in the Catholic church. I prayed to Saint Jude, the patron saint of lost or hopeless causes.

Finally, one day late in January, an ambulance came and took Dad to the hospital. He never came home. Mama was trying to be cheerful and told Dad, as they were carrying him to the ambulance, that he would be better in no time. Back then people tried to shield patients with cancer from the inevitable. Although Mama did not want us to tell Dad, I think he knew.

Dad mercifully passed away on February 20, 1957 after spending four weeks at Mt. Carmel Mercy Hospital in Detroit. I couldn't believe that God had taken my Dad when he was such a good father to us all. I was angry that God would take my Dad when I wanted him so badly, and needed him in my life to see me graduate, to walk me down the aisle on my wedding day and dance with me on that special day. I wanted him to bounce my children on his knee. It's odd that you pray for your loved one to die, to end their suffering, but when they do die you have tremendous guilt for those thoughts. The finality of it all is overwhelming, especially to a girl of sixteen. We need both our parents, but I think daughters especially need their fathers.

In the weeks following the funeral, my grief was all consuming, it was hard for me to think of the future. Everyone seemed to be telling me that wounds heal in time, or words to that effect. What I found very odd at that time was that I didn't seek comfort from Mama or my sisters, nor did I give it. Probably because they were in their own world trying to come to grips with it all. I hardly ever saw Grandma. She seemed to just stay in her bedroom. Dad was her only child.

I wanted things to return to normal, to be the way they were before. Eventually things slowly returned to a different kind of normalcy. After awhile I began to date again. I remember thinking that I could never possibly be happy again, ever. Then, because Dad had been sick and I had to go to summer school, that's where I met Jim. So the worst year of my life ended up being the best year of my life. God had taken a wonderful man away from me, but then he gave me another wonderful man. I loved both of them so much. "The Lord giveth and the Lord taketh away."

Mama died in 1995 I was heartbroken as I realized I would never see her again. I knew I would miss her words of wisdom. She always gave my sisters and me good advice. She loved us unconditionally. She had been healthy all her life and died in her sleep at 95 years of age. I was at peace with that.

At the funeral home as I looked down at her, she still had that regal look of hers. Mama was very approachable. She commanded respect just by her demeanor, and wonderful command of the English language, and at age 95 she still was a remarkably good looking woman. She was a woman at peace.

There were many people at her funeral including two Capuchin Franciscan monks, from Fr. Solanus's soup kitchen in Detroit. Marguerite went over to talk to them and was told that they came because whenever they see donations made to their soup kitchens in the obituaries, they would go to meet the family and pray for the deceased. I found that very comforting.

Then in 1998 Jim was diagnosed with Parkinson's at age 58. The same week as his Father's funeral. That was quite a blow. We were devastated, but we dealt with it.

Parkinson's disease is a relentless foe that dispenses the challenges one by one. Slowly over time, the aches and pains, the frustration, wore Jim down. Through all the pain, and heartache he remained resolute. He never complained, never wavered from his attitude that he could deal with this devastating disease. Eight years from the time he was diagnosed he succumbed to this terrible malady.

In 2006, at the age of 66, Jim fell into a coma and one week later, died. The family was expecting it, but I wanted so much for us to do the things we had planned for, in our retirement. The sadness and pain of living without him is difficult to get use to. Everyday living with Jim was so much fun, even in his illness. He was such a kind, thoughtful, funny guy. I loved him so much and I missed him even more.

In the fall of 2006, after Jim died, the hospice nurses told me Jim was the most pleasant patient they'd ever had. You have no idea what that meant to me.

Grief for your child is unbearable. When Julie was killed in 2000, she was a young mother 31 years old. She was taken from us in a sudden and untimely death. Several things began to happen to me.

First, I began to have health issues.
Second, I began what I call, inner reflection.
Third, a healing of some sort began to take hold.

First: Health Issues

The day Julie died my heart went into arrhythmia. I saw doctors for three years trying to get my heart back to normal. I had the paddles twice and two heart cauterizations and eventually had a stroke. Even after my stroke, my heart would still not pump correctly. There is a term for it called tachycardia when the heart beats too fast but also irregularly. All this time I'm trying to care of Jim. Finally, as all else failed in 2010 it was decided that I needed a pacemaker. That seemed to be working pretty good. It really is true when they say people die of a broken heart, because I almost did.

Christmas of 2000 was the first Christmas without Julie. Jim and I looked upon it with much trepidation, not so much for our loss, which was indescribable, but for the loss Julie's two boys age 7 and 5 would feel. We wanted to make it special for them. The boys were distracted by all the wonderful gifts and the big dinner the Petrill family put on.

The following is a letter I sent in lieu of Christmas cards, the first Christmas without Julie:

December 2000

Dear Friends:

This is the first year we have not sent out Christmas cards. The family has spent this Christmas with much reflection. Julie's little ones are doing fine. Seth began first grade and Nathan began kindergarten at the time of Julie's accident. They have grief counselors at school that are available on an as needed basis.

We love and miss Julie very much. This loss is so profound we're still in disbelief. We feel her love around, between and within us. Our family, our neighbors, our co-workers, and many other friends have been a tremendous unfaltering support for us. Just being around people has been uplifting well beyond anything we ever could have imagined

The following is an excerpt from a "Holiday Memorial," author unknown. It is so comforting. As you read this, think of Julie, and anyone else special whom you have lost:

As we light these four candles in honor of you, we light one for our grief, one for our courage, one for our memories, and one for our love.

This candle represents our grief. The pain of losing you is intense. It reminds us of the depth of our love for you..

This candle represents our courage, to confront our sorrow, to comfort each other, and to change our lives.

This light is in your memory. The times we laughed, the times we cried, the times we were angry with each other, the silly things we did, the caring and joy you gave us.

This light is the light of love. As we enter this holiday season, day by day, we cherish the special place in our hearts that will always be reserved for you. We thank you for the gift your life brought to each of us. We love you.

We will always love and miss Julie.

We wish you all a happy, healthy, uplifting, loving, fun, 2001. Cherish each day.

Love, Jim and Diane

On January 12th, the Petrills, celebrated Nate's 6th Birthday. His first Birthday without his Mother. I stayed at the party as long as I could tolerate, and made our excuses, then Jim and I went home. There are no words in the English language to express such pain and agony. No little boy should have to experience what Julie's boys went through. In the midst of all this is Jim, trying to hold it all together. So stoic. He never complained about his Parkinson's, but it definitely got worse after Julie's accident.

Seth said to me a couple days after the party. "Grandma, you never said good-bye to me."

All of this was so sad on so many levels that as I look back I don't know how we made it. How we survived. Here's our beautiful Julie, our youngest child and only daughter, at 31, gone. Here's our two lovely grandsons, so young, having to put up with such sadness. Their dad, Matt, devastated, a widow at 28 with two small boys to raise, and of course, Jim suffering with Parkinson's in silence. I still can't believe we made it through in one piece.

Second: Inner Reflection

Everyone admired Mama. I just wish I would have visited her more the last year of her life, but I was working late almost every night at the Hamburg Township offices. I know Mama would have understood, but I still felt guilty. She was always there for me whenever I needed her. So, I thank God for giving me such a wonderful Mother. She was always willing to help out. God blessed her with good health. She was only in the hospital a few times and that was when each of us were born. To die peacefully in your sleep at 95 is truly a wonderful blessing from God.

There are things I regret. Things I wish I'd have done differently. Even where there had been time to say all the appropriate things, images would flash in my mind that I'd give a lot to be able to change. I know that Julie has forgiven me, but can I forgive myself? I missed several of her baseball games, when she was little, I didn't always read to her at night when she wanted me to. Maybe I chastised her too much, maybe not enough. That scenario plays over and over in my mind.

A few months after Julie's death, I saw a young woman who looked just like her driving the same type car, a 1995 green Dodge Neon. Same color hair, same profile. I had such an urge to follow that car and talk to that woman. Maybe it is Julie and I am just in a dream. I'll wake up and everything will be okay. I've seen someone looking or walking just like Julie several times since her death. I'm shaken a bit afterwords but the feeling eventually goes away. I still kept hoping I was living in a nightmare and I would wake up and everything would be back to normal and Julie would be back with her family like before. Other times I would wake up in the morning and still feel as if I was in a nightmare. I just couldn't believe it.

Third: Healing

How do people face adversity? I started a journal and that morphed into stories of her little boys. Since Nate was only five I wanted to make sure he'd know what a wonderful and fun-loving person his mother was. Seth drew pictures of Julie and we'd talk about her anytime they felt like talking.

I took the boys to the cemetery any time they wanted to go. The boys drew cute pictures that we left by her headstone, and I wrote several poems. The following is a poem I wrote a year after she died:

Lakeview Cemetery

Your stone stands stoic in this park like setting.
It gives your death its year.
You once lived like us all,
Now we just want you near,

Where are you now?
Where are you?
How sad we all feel without you.
These words would have made you laugh.
You found humor in everything.

The tulips planted in the fall,
Now blossom so beautiful and tall.
We bring the boys, they miss you so.
They talk to you. They laugh, they sing,
They pray, and then we go.

Nestled here among our ancestors,
Who helped make us who we are.
Grandma Elizabeth lies close to you.
Seth puts a rose on her stone.
It helps to make us feel,
You'll never be alone.

Oh God if we could turn back time,
What would we say or do.
We'd put our arms around you,
We'd couldn't love you more.
We feel so helpless,
We didn't know what was in store.

God be with you always.
'Til we meet again.
Love Mom
2001

Sadly we left most, but not all of these items at the cemetery. I remember one day I went back to the cemetery because Seth had left a card for Julie that he made. On it he had drawn a nice house with his dad, Nate and himself standing in front of the house looking up to heaven. He wrote "Dear Mom, Happy two years in Heaven. I miss you. Love, Seth." He was nine years old. Nate's drawings always had happy faces on them. A nice house with the family in front of the house, and always flowers, lots of flowers. He usually ended it with "I love you Mom and I miss you."

As I said before, I'm not writing this chapter for sympathy. What I do want, is your prayers, your friendship, your understanding. I want people, especially my family, to think of me as a strong person who got through Jim's illness, and that I am still surviving Julie's death, but it's a day at a time. When asked, I tell them, "I'm just fine, thank you."

When my Dad died, Mama was very stoic. I never saw her cry in public, but I could hear her crying behind closed doors in her bedroom. It broke my heart. So I've tried very hard not to let the family see me crying, but Seth, he was only seven or eight, did see me crying one day, and he came over and hugged me and said, "It's okay Grandma, we're going to be fine."

I'm expressing my thoughts and feelings. I'm trying to make people aware that they too can survive life's terrible moments. We all have them. Some are worse than others, indescribably worse. But we can survive. We have to survive.

I thank God that it wasn't any worse than it was. Julie was alone that day. She could have had her family with her. I also thank God that she didn't suffer. The police told me that she died instantly.

I cry, crying is cathartic. You are so busy trying to survive that you don't have too much time for reflection. Jim was ill with Parkinson's, Matt was devastated, and Julie's two little boys were scared and bewildered.

Then, as the years went by, I began to wonder how I survived all this and am still surviving. The whole family is surviving, The saying is true, "Just take it one day at a time."

I began to thank God for everyday he allowed me to have, Julie and her precious boys. I thought if the Lord would have said to me, "I'll give you Julie for 31 years and then I'll take her back." I would have said "Yes" in a heart beat. The same for my wonderful grandsons.

After Julie's accident I thought I'd never be able to laugh again. But eventually I did start to laugh. At first I felt so guilty about laughing, when a big part of my heart was not there, but you adjust. You get use to a new kind of living. One of the things I've learned about grief is that, it's exhausting.

I have a good life now. It's not the same life. I use to laugh all the time with Jim. I loved his sense of humor. Every day was fun and exciting living with him.

Now I have my sisters, my grandchildren, my son-in-law, two of the best sons and daughters-in-law a mother could ask for. Life is good, just different.

33

My French Ancestry

Brault dit Pominville Family

Two heads of families brought the name BRAULT to America.

Vincent Breau born in France, came to Acadia and married Marie Bourg in 1629. The descendants of Vincent and Marie are the Acadian line.

Sieur Henri Brault dit Pominville was born circa 1635 in LaRochelle, Annis France. His occupation was listed as pioneer. The son of Jean Brault dit Pominville of France, and Suzanne Jonseaume born in de Ballon, Annis, France. Henri married his first wife Claude de Cheurenville, 12 August 1665. She was from an upper class family. She also was a filles du roi(1), who was born in St. Nicolas-des-Champs of Paris, daughter of Jacques de Cheurenville, "Sieur de La Fontaine"(2), who was écuyer (3) in the court of Louis XIV, "The Sun King", and Lady Marguerite-Leonarde Baudon. Henri and Claude settled on the coast of Lauzon in Quebec. Their descendants are our line, the Quebec line.

Henri and Claude had twelve children, eight sons and four daughters. Three sons were licensed voyageurs, that interesting class of frontiersmen, many of whom, though uneducated, had a dignity about them.

These were Canadian boatman in the fur trade. These voyageurs were men of tremendous strength, when realizing that few were taller than 5 ft. 6 in. They paddled canoes 15 to 18 hours a day, often carrying from 200 to 450 pounds of merchandise on their backs over rocky portages. Among the many services rendered by the voyageur, was that of soldier. One of the most interesting traits of the voyageur was his extreme courtesy. His French background was most evident in the social ease with which he addressed his superiors, the Indians, the ladies, or men of his class. The French language came to his aid here, for though many were illiterate, theirs by birthright were the graceful French phrases and expressions which are so effective in establishing cordial relations. They were a fun-loving group of men, always singing and laughing. Many of the voyageurs stayed in the interior and some took Indian wives. However, this was not the case with our Braults.

Voyageurs were licensed by the government, and should not be confused with the coureur-des-bois who were unlicensed entrepreneurs who independently trapped and traded beaver pelts. They were considered renegades.

According to the Montreal District Notarial Records, Georges and Jean Bro (sic) signed an agreement 2 April 1707 with Sir Antoine de le Monthe Cadillac, founder of Detroit, to leave their parish at Lachine and carry in canoe with 300 pounds of merchandise to Fort Ponchartrain (Detroit) and exchange it for 300 pounds of furs in "good condition".

From 1707 to 1818 the Brault family handed down the license of voyageur from father to son, uncle to nephew.

The last item found in the Montreal District Notarial Records concerning the Braults is dated 31 March 1818.

The hiring of the brothers Gendron and Joachim Breau, Amable Lefevre dit Ducote, all from Chateaugay, Solomon Chapeau living at L'Assumption, by Mr. W.W. Mattheu, negotiator, to spend three years at Michilimacinac.

Note: Those hired will have to tour the lakes if required.

Henri Brault, resident of the coast of Lauzon, made a deal with Antoine Dionne. Brau (sic) would cede a piece of land 6 arpents by 40 with fishing rights, in exchange for the place that Antoine had in Quebec. Antoine used these fishing rights by marketing eels to Lucien Boutteville.(4)

On 22 September 1689, Henri Breau de Pominville, inhabitant of Lauzon, signed a three-year lease with Laurent Levasseur for a piece of land bordered on one side by the property of Noel Penaut and on the other by that of Jean Bourassa. The land was leased complete with house and domestic servant, fishing rights, 2 cows, 2 bulls, and 25 minots of grain in the field, which was harvested and returned. There were some fruit trees in good condition to be looked after as well. All this for the price of 200 livres (a unit of currency) per year. Both Jean Huard and Mattieu Amyot, witnesses to the transaction, signed with a flourish, but Laurent timidly affirmed that he could not write. Breau had the fore-thought to reserve 8 square along a brook for his own use.

Four years later, on 10 September 1673, we note that Laurent owed 180 livres to Henri. Evidently he was having trouble making his payments, however, all must have ended well, because we know that this land, leased in 1669, later became the family home for generations of Lauvasseurs. The homestead was located in Saint-David de Lauberiviere. The house later numbered 6999 Commerciale, became the focal point of family life and was kept in the Levasseur name until 1925.

By 1727 many of the Brault family were living in the Chateaugay area. After the death of Claude, Henri married M-Ursule Buldoc. They had three children.

There are many variations of the Brault name: Berea, Bereault, Brau, Breau, Breault, Breaux, Bro, Brod, and Brough. Some of the descendants have adopted the name Pominville omitting Brault entirely.

Appendix:

1. Filles du roi or King's daughters, were part of King Louis XIV's program to help settle his colony in New France (Canada). Under his financial sponsorship, these courageous young women came to Canada for the purpose of marriage to the many unmarried male colonists. They were given a dowry by the king and had letters of reference form their parish priests.
2. Sieur is what you would call a gentleman in the court of King Louis XIV.
3. écuyer means "shield bearer," The lowest specific rank of nobility to which the vast majority of untitled noblemen were entitled; also, called valet or noble homme in certain regions.
4. Thomas J. Laforest "Our French-Canadian Ancestors" Vol 1 (The Lisi Press, Palm Harbor, Florida) page 56-57.

Note: Information on the voyageurs from Grace Lee Nute's "The Voyageur".

Jean Brault dit Pominville

We first find Jean Brault *dit Pominville born, in Balon, Annis, France. Suzette Jonseaume was also born in Balon Annis France, date unknown. They were married in Rochefort, France.

Jean's son Henri Brault is the progenitor of the Brault dit Pominville's in North America.

In the charts that follow, are the direct ancestors of our Brault dit Pominville line.

11th Generation:

11th Generation:
Jean Brault dit Pominville married Suzanne Jonseaume in Rochefort, France some time in the seventeenth century.

10th Generation:

Henri Brault dit Pominville (Sieur de Pominville) was born in 1635 in LaRochelle, Annis, France. He married Claude de Cheurenville 12 August 1665 in Quebec. She was a *"fille du roi". She was born in Paris in 1646. They had twelve children. Her father Jacques de Cheurenville was a court écuyer to King Louis XIV.

9th Generation:

Georges Brault dit Pominville (voyageur with Cadillac), married Barbe Brunet, 26 November 1696 in Lachine, Quebec. It was a second marriage for both.

8th Generation:

Jean-Baptiste Brault dit Pominville married Marie Caron, 14 December 1721 in Lachine, Quebec

7th Generation:

Vital Brault dit Pominville (Vital Bro) married Marie-Anne Prejean, 18 February 1754 in Lachine, Quebec.

6th Generation:

Vital Brault dit Pominville (Vital Bro) married Marie Primeau, 14 November, 1785 in Chateaugay, Quebec.

5th Generation:

Viral Braulit dit Pominville (Bro-Pominville) married Charlotte Chevrefils 22 January 1818 in Chateaugay, Quebec. it was a second marriage for Charlotte.

4th Generation:

Vital Brault married Celina Philomene Roi (Roy) 24 October, 1854. Probably in Chateaugay, Quebec. Celina's second marriage was to Mr. Leon Forget

3rd Generation:

Philias Michael Brault married Rose Velina Fisette 25 February 1889. Either in St. Boniface or Winnipeg, Manitoba.

2nd Generation:

Dewey Archibald Sautter (name legally changed to Archie D. Stuhlfaut) married Elissa Madeleine Brault 28 May 1936 in Toledo, Ohio. Both had been married previously.

1st Generation:

James Frank Wrobleski married Diane Genevieve Stuhlfaut, 3 September, 1960. in Detroit, Michigan

Notes: *dit in French means either from the area of, or from the family of.

Abraham Fiset/Fisette Family

We first find the Fisets in Dieppe, France in the seventeenth century.

The children of Abraham Fiset and Catherine Labrecque were born in Dieppe between 1630 to 1645, and were all baptized at the church of Ste. Jacques in Dieppe. The names of the four children known to us are:

Catherine, François-Abraham, François and Michel.

François-Abraham Fiset is the progenitor of the Fisets of North America.

François-Abraham was born on August 21, 1635 in Dieppe, France and was baptized also at Ste. Jacques in Dieppe. His godparents were Jacques Lebreque and Catherine DeCaux.

He became a carpenter, and married Denise Savard, who was born in 1661 or 1664 in Vincennes near Paris. They married in Chateau-Riche, Quebec. She was the daughter of Simon Savard and Marie Hourdouil, of Montreuil-sous-Bois, Seine

They settled in L'Ange-Gardien, Quebec. This couple died rather young. Their estate was handled by Mr. Jacob Sr. the notary, on January 26, 1701.

On July 7, 1704, François and Louis (children of François-Abraham and Denise Savard) obtained from the Supreme Counsel (Court) letters of emancipation so they could obtain a share of their parent's estate. (Judgements and Deliberations IV, 1032-1033.)

François-Abraham left descendants up to sixteen children. We are sure that eight of them were married.

These children settled first on the estate of the Beauprés, between Chateau-Richer and L'Ange-Gardien. They had very large families.

The Fisets were more or less farmers, but over the years there were many scientists, politicians, and teachers among them.

In 1661, François-Abraham Fiset settled on land that was just west of Jean Trudel's land, and to the east, his neighbor was Etienne Jacob, the notary.

*Louis, after a first marriage in Chateau-Richer to M-Anne Voyer, remarried *Louise-Angelique Sylvester, in Pte.-aux Trembles in 1720. Louis had sixteen children who settled all over Quebec.

* Denotes direct ancestor.

Fiset is masculine, and Fisette in feminine

The following are the direct ancestors of our Fiset/Fisette line.

10th Generation:
Abraham Fiset married Catherine Lebrecque in France, date unknown.

9th Generation:
François-Abraham married Denise Savard in Chateau-Riche, Quebec, February 5, 1664.

8th Generation:
Louis Fiset married (we descended from his second wife) Louise-Angelique Sylestre on April 1, 1720 in Pte.- aux Tremble, Quebec.

7th Generation:

François Fiset married Charlotte Bourdon, January 16, 1758 in Lavaltrie, Quebec.

6th Generation:

François Fiset married Marie-Genevieve Bonin on October 27, 1794 in Lavaltrie, Quebec.

5th Generation:

Pierre Fiset married Françoise Hétu October 26, 1830 in Lavaltrie, Quebec (Dispensation from 3rd to 4th degree consanguinity). Note: They were either second or third cousins.

4th Generation:

Desiré Fiset married Philomene Brisset de Beaupré October 7, 1862 in Joliette, Quebec.

3rd Generation:

Philias Michael Brault married Rose Velina Fisette on February 25, 1889 (either in St. Boniface or Winnipeg, Manitoba.)

2nd Generation:

Archie D. Stuhlfaut (name legally changed from Dewey Archibald Sautter in the early 1940s) married Elissa Madeleine Brault on May 28, 1936, in Toledo, Ohio.

1st Generation:

James Frank Wrobleski married Diane Genevieve Stuhlfaut on September 3, 1960 in Detroit, Michigan.

34

My German Ancestry

Sautter Family

Johann George Sautter was born in Wurttemberg, Germany 6 September 1800, He married Katherine Eiberle. She was born 18 October 1806 in Wurtemberg, Germany. They came to America with their son, after an ocean voyage of three months and landed at Montreal. They lived in Ontario for a number of years, then travelled to Michigan over waterways and on foot with Indian guides to a settlement in Sebewaing, Michigan, on a tract of land he homesteaded to gain title. The above information comes from Helen Dubay, Henry Sautter's daughter.

The following was taken from the Minutes of Immanuel Lutheran Church in Sebewaing:

> Johann George Sautter, born 6. Sept.1800 and died on Oct. 4, 1865 and so was 65 years and 27 days old. He lived in great impertinence, though in hypocrisy he continually promised improvement until shortly before his end, his whole wicked and impertinent life became evident. As he lived so he died. He was buried without Christian honors. J.J.L. Auch Pastor

> Katherine Sauter nee Eiberle, widow of the late Johann Georg Sauter was born Oct. 18, 1806 in Gertrumgen, Oberamt Nagold, Kingdom of Wurtemberg, died on Sept. 17, 1872 at 6 a.m. She reached the age of 65 years, 11 months and 7 days. The burial took place on Sept. 18, at 3 p.m. The funeral text: Isaiah: 57:2.

Gottlieb Frederich, son of Johann George, was born 1840 in

Wurttemberg, Germany. He married Maria Ziegler, 24 December 1864 in Waterloo, Ontario, Canada. He became a shoemaker in the village of Sebewaing. Maria Ziegler was born in Baden-Baden, Germany in 1843. (1880 Census, Huron County, MI pp. 6 & 7). They made there home at 235 S. Center Street, Sebewaing, Michigan. They had nine children. Their eighth child, Henry Johann Sautter was born 1878 in Sebewaing.

Henry Johann Sautter married Elizabeth Martha Schindehette on February 6, 1898. They had one child Dewey Archibald Sautter. Henry and Elizabeth divorced on 2 February 1900. Dewey had his name legally changed to Archie D. Stuhlfaut.

Henry married Martha Lange 21 April 1908. They had five children. Henry bought the Lull farm, located four miles outside of Saginaw on S. Washington Road. In 1910 he sold the farm, and became a bartender in Saginaw, then later bought a saloon and then a grocery store. The Great Depression hurt them badly, but Henry was able to buy a rundown hotel in Lincoln called the Twin Lakes Hotel.

Henry died in Lincoln on 13 August 1938 of a stroke, cancer and other complications. He was laid to rest in Forest Lawn Cemetery 15 August 1938.

Several variations of the Sautter name: Sutter, Suter, Sauter

The following are the direct ancestors on our Sautter line:

5th Generation:
Johann George Sautter married Fredericke Katherine Eiberle in Wurtemberg, Germany.

4th Generation:
Gottlieb Frederich Sautter married Maria Ziegler on 21 March 1865 in Waterloo, Ontario Canada.

3rd Generation:

Henry Johann Sautter married Elizabeth Martha Schindehette 6 February 1898 at the German Methodist Church, Sebewaing, Michigan. Divorced, 2 February 1900.

2nd Generation:
Dewey Archibald Sautter, name legally changed. (Wayne County Probate Records 1952.) to Archie Dewey Stuhlfaut (though he had used that name for most of his adult life) married Elissa Madeleine Brault, 28 May 1936 in Toledo, Ohio. (Both had been married previously.)

1st Generation:
James Frank Wrobleski married Diane Genevieve Stuhlfaut, at St. Francis de Sales Church, 3 September 1960 in Detroit, Michigan.

Schindehette Family

Anna E. Karkel was born in Germany in April of 1824 or 1827. She came to America around 1857. I don't have any information on her husband or husbands.

We first find Henry, son of Anna E. Karkel Schindehette, in the manifests of the ship Meta. He sailed out of Bremerhaven, Germany. His arrival date is listed as 8 September 1857. Place of origin is Hesse. Destination Prince Edward Island. Port of arrival is New York. His birth date is listed as, about 1840. According to his military records he was born, 2 August 1840 in Kassel, Germany.

Henry lived in Detroit until 11 August 1862 when he enlisted in the army. The 24th Michigan Infantry, the famous Iron Brigade. He was engaged in battle at Gettysburg where he was wounded in the left hip. He was sent to recuperate at the army hospital in Philadelphia, and later was transferred to Harper Hospital in Detroit. It is thought that it was here that he met Samantha Diamon. She belonged to the Women's Relief Corp. She delivered and read the mail to the wounded.

They married 16 April, 1865 in Howell, and moved to Hampton,

Michigan, just outside of Bay City. He was an entrepreneur. According to the Bay City Directory of 1873-74, Henry owned the Hampton House (Dutch Gardens) on Center Street. His brothers George H. and Martin built the Republic Hotel. At one time Henry was a wholesaler and retail dealer in wines & liquors, cigars and tobacco and smokers articles at 404 Center St.

One brother owned the Johnson Bottling Works. Henry and his brothers owned many businesses in and around Bay City over the years. They were all well known and respected business men in the Saginaw and Bay City area.

Samantha and Henry

In the list that follows are the direct ancestors on our Schindehette Line.

5th Generation:
Anna E. Karkel born in Germany.

4th Generation:
Henry Schindehette born in Kassel, Germany, married Samantha Diamon 16 April, 1865 in Howell, Michigan.

3rd Generation:

Elizabeth Martha Schindehette married Henry Sautter 6 February 1898 in Sebewaing, Michigan.

2nd Generation:

Dewey A. Sautter (name legally changed to Archie D. Stuhlfaut.) married Elissa Madeleine Muller Brault, 28 May 1936, in Toledo, Ohio. Both had been married previously.

1st Generation:

James F. Wrobleski married Diane Genevieve Stuhlfaut, 3 September 1960 in Detroit, Michigan

35

My English Ancestry

Diamon Family

John Diamon was born in western New York state, probably Ontario County in 1778. He died in Bloomfield Center (later Bloomfield Hills) Michigan, 26 May 1857. He married Sarah (last name unknown). She was born 13 December 1779 in New York state. She died in Bloomfield Center 6 July 1862, at age 82 years, 6 months, 24 days, according to the inscription on her tombstone. She was buried next to her husband.

John Diamon was a farmer, and sometime between 1810 and 1820 (before the Erie Canal) he moved his family from western New York to Michigan, thus becoming one of the original landowners of Oakland County, settling in Bloomfield Center in the early 1820s. The first settler was Judge Amos Bagley in late 1819.

John and Sarah Diamon bought their 80 acres of land from the government 11 June 1823. Their land was situated near the Saginaw Trail (Woodward Avenue). More precisely Section #15 E1/2 SE1/4. Today that property is located at Vaughan Road between Country Club Road and West Long Lake Road in the city of Bloomfield Hills. The Bloomfield Hills Country Club.

Just think of it. In the year before the Erie Canal was opened, fewer than 62,000 acres of Michigan land had been sold, all of it in the Detroit area, and John and Sarah were among those who bought some of that land.

John is mentioned in Miss Fanny Fish's recollections of early pioneer life in Bloomfield and Birmingham, Michigan as told to her by the Oakland County Pioneer and Historical Society 1888 (Michigan Pioneer and Historical Society. Volume 14, pages 603-609). John is also mentioned, although inaccurately, in the History of Oakland County (1877) Everts page 320.

According to the Bloomfield Township Board Minutes 1827 to the present, John Diamond was overseer of the Highways #35 in 1833 and #12 in 1836, 1837 and 1843. His son Henry H. (presently, no documentation is available to prove relationship.) was overseer of Highway #12 in 1840.

John is mentioned in the book Bloomfield Blossoms, as one of the first ten settlers in Bloomfield Center.

John and Sarah moved to Pewaukee, Wisconsin sometime after 1843. The property of John and Sarah was valued at $1,200.00(1). They lived in Pewaukee with their son William and his wife Frances. John died in Bloomfield Center in 1857.

Their son John H. was born in New York state probably Lima Twp. Oakland County, 1811. He married Mehittable Turner, daughter of a native American or an alleged part native American from New York state that had lived in upper Canada (Ontario), and John W. Turner. This is the only information I was able to find on Mehittable. She was born 23 February 1818 in New York state, They married 3 April 1840 at Bloomfield, Michigan. In 1841 a daughter Sylvia was born in Oakland County Michigan. By 1843 they had moved to Pewaukee, Waukesha County, Wisconsin. where Samatha was born.

In 1850-1851 George H. was born in Pewaukee. When John H. wife Mehittable died in 10 June 1851 they may have all moved back to Michigan. John H. then married Martha Jane Turner, who may have been related to Mehittable. Martha Jane was born in 1825 in west Canada (probably Ontario). John H. remarried on 27 December 1851 in Oakland County.

The family then moved to Livingston County, just north of the present city of Howell. In 1855 they purchased 80 acres of land in Howell Township located in section #15, E1/2 SE1/4. They had a son John C. Diamon in Howell in 1857.

On 17 December 1869, John H. petitioned the Circuit Court of Livingston County to obtain a pension to provide for his grandchildren,

George D. Carl and John Carl, since he was their legal guardian. They were the children of his daughter Sylvia and Henry Carl, who died at the Battle of the Wilderness, Virginia, during the Civil War. Sylvia's second husband was an older man, James Edmond. His daughter Alida married George H. Diamon, Sylvia's brother.

In 1873, John H. had personal and real property valued at $6,100.00 according to the tax assessment rolls of Howell Township for that year. He owned 160 acres. 80 in Section #15 and 80 in section #10. John H. paid $31.86 in taxes for that year on this property.

John H. eventually became deaf. He died from a fall in Howell, Michigan 4 August 1887. He was 76 years old.

Martha Jane Diamon died two years later 22 December 1889 at 64 years old. According to the Probate Court Records, (order to determine heirs), Howell, Michigan, 79 1/2 acres were left to John C. Diamond, son and sole heir of Martha Jane Diamon. (Liber 91 p.40, 1890).

John C. was 32 years old in 1890 when he was deeded the land left by his mother. Five years later he lost it all. Sold at public auction to pay debts. (Register of Deeds, Volume 7, Liber 98, Page 31, 1895).

John C. Diamon married Emma Randall. They are buried in our family plot at Lakeview Cemetery, Howell, Michigan.

1. According to the 1850 Wisconsin Census.
2. Bloomfield Center Cemetery is no longer in existence. It is now the Bloomfield Hills Golf and Country Club. Bodies were disinterred around 1923 and removed to Oak Hill Cemetery in Pontiac.

In the charts that follow are the direct ancestors on our Diamon line:

6th Generation:
John Diamon and Sarah (last name unknown) married in New York state.

5th Generation:
John H. Diamon married Mehittable Turner 3 April 1840 in Bloomfield Center, Michigan.

4th Generation:

Samantha Diamon married Henry Schindehette 16 April 1865 in Howell, Michigan.

3rd Generation:

Elizabeth Martha Schindehette married Henry Johann Sautter 6 February 1898 in Sebewaing, Michigan.

2nd Generation:

Dewey Archibald Sautter (name legally changed to Archie D. Stuhlfaut) married Elissa Madeleine Brault 28 May 1836 in Toledo, Ohio.

1st Generation:

James Frank Wrobleski married Diane Genevieve Stuhlfaut 3 September 1960 in Detroit, Michigan.

There are several variations of the Diamon name: Dimon, Dymond, Dymon, Damon, Diamond, Dimond.

Turner Family

I have not been able to find anything on Samantha's grandmother, (Mehittable Turner's mother) except that she was listed on a census roll as part Indian from Upper Canada. (Southern Ontario, including areas surrounding Hudson Bay.)

Note: Results from Ancestry DNA Ethnicity dated 12/19/16 states that I have only Western European ethnicity.

36

Jim's Polish Ancestry

Rozmarynowski Family

Not much is known about the Rozmarynowski family except that they were born in Poland. Michal Rozmarynowski was born in 1852 and his wife Helen Dych was born in 1850. Michal died in Detroit in 1902, and Helen died in Detroit in 1932, (probably Hamtramck.) They are both buried in Detroit at Sweetest Heart of Mary Cemetery on Mound Road and Six Mile Road. This cemetery was formerly called Greenwood Cemetery. These people are Jim's great-grandparents. Their daughter Margaret was Frank's mother. She was born in Poland. She is buried next to her parents and her sister Antonia.

The following are the direct ancestors of the Rozmarynowski line:

4th Generation:
Michal Rozmarynowski married Helen Dych (probably in Poland.)

3rd Generation:
Boleslaw Wroblewski married Margaret Rozmarynowski in Detroit, Michigan

2nd Generation:
Frank Aloysious Wrobleski married Louise Mae Wingier 16 May 1933 in Toledo, Ohio.

1st Generation:
James Frank Wrobleski married Diane Genevieve Stuhlfaut 3 September 1960 in Detroit, Michigan.

Researched by Diane Wrobleski 26 April, 1988

Anthony Wroblewski/Wrobleski Family

Little is known of Anthony Wroblewski except that he was born 1850 in Poland, and came to America with his wife and children in 1888? William Wrobleski is buried in Mount Olivet Cemetery, located at 17100 Van Dyke in Detroit. His son Frank is buried in Starville, Michigan and Jim Wrobleski is buried in Lakeview Cemetery in Howell, Michigan.

The following are the direct ancestors on the Wroblewski line:

4th Generation:
Anthony Wroblewski married Mary Szawadkowski in Poland.

3rd Generation:
William (Boleslaus) Wroblewski, married Margaret Rozmarynowski in Hamtramck, Michigan, 5 September 1898.

2nd Generation:
Frank Aloysius Wrobleski married Louise Mae Wingier 16 May 1933 in Toledo, Lucas County, Ohio.

1st Generation:
James Frank Wrobleski married Diane Genevieve Stuhlfaut 3 September 1960 in Detroit, Michigan.

Researched by Diane Wrobleski 26 April, 1988

37

Jim's Scotch/Irish Ancestry

Crosky/Croskey Family

My research on this family is incomplete.

Henrietta Croskey was born 12 December 1881 Clark Twp. Coshocton, Ohio. Her parents are James Croskey and Hannah Randles. She married Gottlieb Wingier 1 August 1898 in Coshocton, Ohio. They had two children:
Charles and Louise.

Louise used August 26, 1900 as her birth date. She was never sure, because it was never recorded.
Louise Wingier first marriage was to Harold Koch in Lucas County (probably Toledo) Ohio. Her estimated birth is listed as 1901. States she is 19 on date of marriage.
Louise married Frank A. Wrobleski 16 May 1933 in Toledo, Ohio.

James Frank Wrobleski, born 13 February 1940 in Detroit, Michigan.married Diane Genevieve Stuhlfaut 3 September, 1960 in Detroit, Michigan

Note: Scotch/Irish ethnicity has not been proven as of January 2017.

38

Jim's Swiss Ancestry

Wingier/Winiger

The research on this family is very limited.

This genealogy is incomplete. Louise knew almost nothing about her family except that her mother died when she was so little she doesn't remember anything about her except her name, Etta. She probably died in childbirth, since Louise was born at home, and was the youngest.

Nicklaus Wingeyer married Anna Nikles 30 July 1847 in Bern Langnau, Swtzerland.

Gottfried was born 10 Nov. 1848 in Bern, Langnau, Switzerland

(At this point in time, I'm not sure if Gottfried and Gottlieb are not the same person.)

His son? Gottlieb (Golly) Wingier was born in Switzerland.

Married Henrietta Crosky (no date available)

They had a son Charles D. married Althea (last name unknown)

A daughter, Louise est. birth date August 26, 1900.

Louise married Frank A. Wrobleski 16 May 1933 in Toledo, Ohio.

Son, James F. Wrobleski married Diane G. Stuhlfaut, September 3, 1960 in Detroit, Michigan.

About the Author

Diane Wrobleski was born and raised in Detroit, Michigan. She earned her bachelors degree at Eastern Michigan University, and is a member of Phi Alpha Theta National Honors Society. Diane retired from the Environmental Protection Agency in Ann Arbor, Michigan, in 2005. She spends her summers in Brighton, Michigan and her winters in Tellico Village near the foothills of the Great Smoky Mountains of Tennessee. This is Diane's debut book.